T0305255

Principles of Housing Finance Reform

THE CITY IN THE TWENTY-FIRST CENTURY

Eugenie L. Birch and Susan M. Wachter, *Series Editors*

A complete list of books in the series
is available from the publisher.

PRINCIPLES
OF HOUSING
FINANCE
REFORM

Edited by

Susan M. Wachter

and

Joseph Tracy

PENN

UNIVERSITY OF PENNSYLVANIA PRESS

PHILADELPHIA

Published by
University of Pennsylvania Press
Philadelphia, Pennsylvania 19104-4112
www.upenn.edu/pennpress

Printed in the United States of America
on acid-free paper
10 9 8 7 6 5 4 3 2 1

A Cataloging-in-Publication record is available from
the Library of Congress
ISBN 978-0-8122-4862-3

CONTENTS

PART III. HOUSING FINANCE INFRASTRUCTURE

Introduction

Susan M. Wachter and Joseph Tracy

In the fall of 2008, the world watched in horror as the U.S. housing finance system shattered, triggering a global financial panic and ultimately the Great Recession. Now, nearly a decade later, the long and slow recovery has reached a critical moment. Though the housing finance system has stabilized, it remains in the hands of the federal government, leaving taxpayers, rather than private capital, largely exposed to the credit risk. Fannie Mae and Freddie Mac—the government-sponsored enterprises (GSEs) responsible for most of the country's residential mortgage securitization—continue to be held in conservatorship by the Federal Housing Finance Agency (FHFA). Meanwhile, private funding remains mostly on the sidelines, with the source of ongoing financing necessary for sustainable, affordable homeownership still unknown. An eager young generation is unable to access the credit or afford the down payments necessary to successfully transition from renting to owning. This lingering inertia is a critical weakness in the American economy. The system must be rebuilt.

This volume identifies changes necessary to modernize the housing finance system. The chapters lay out a road map for reforms to achieve the goals of access, liquidity, stability, and sustainability. They represent some of the best thinking of policy researchers and economic experts to the challenges that lie ahead for the rebuilding of this key sector of our nation's economy.

Housing finance reformers have not been short of options. In the wake of the Great Recession, proposals have arisen across the political spectrum, spanning the range from immediate privatization to complete government takeover. The chapters in this book center around four points of consensus that have formed among the major stakeholders.

First, the thirty-year fixed-rate mortgage should remain available as a source of funding for households, correctly priced for risk. This mortgage allows households to own and hedge rent increase risk while also hedging interest rate risk. The mortgage product shifts that risk to capital markets, which are better equipped to manage rate risk than households. This mortgage is also simple to understand and to evaluate in terms of the household's ability to pay.

To ensure this, the to-be-announced (TBA) market, as presented in the chapter by Akash Kanojia and Meghan Grant, is necessary to ensure a liquid secondary outlet, without which originators would be far less willing to issue this type of loan. This liquid secondary outlet helps to keep this mortgage affordable.

Second, borrowers followed by private capital must take the first losses when mortgages default. Market discipline is necessary to prevent borrowers, originators, and MBS investors from taking excessive risks. Equally important, however, is government support for *catastrophic* losses that the private market cannot sustain without total collapse. In contrast to the past, this support should be made explicit and priced going forward.

Third, securitization must operate in daylight with some form of standardization—on a common, transparent platform where investors and regulators can obtain information for pricing. All participants must understand the risks involved in securitization, unlike the information asymmetries that allowed underpriced credit to fuel the latest housing bubble.

Fourth, the government should not abandon its policy of encouraging affordable housing by simply leaving the free market to its own devices. Across the country, rapidly rising rents and tightened underwriting standards have combined to make the cost of housing a significant strain on the budgets of an American middle class that is already suffering from decades of income stagnation and is still struggling to deleverage. However, government efforts to support affordable mortgages must also ensure that they are sustainable as well.

These principles must be implemented through a newly structured system that is sustainable with fundamental restructuring for stability. To this end, the authors in this book present proposals for long-term structural reforms. Though they are varied in their aims and their strategies, they demonstrate the bounty of innovation that is possible within these guiding principles. Each chapter suggests reforms that would infuse new life into our housing finance system as well as provide long-term stability.

The first three chapters show how multiple approaches can achieve these goals through GSE reform. In Chapter 1, David Scharfstein and Phillip Swagel compare four legislative proposals, with particular attention to the Johnson-Crapo bill. In Chapter 2, Patricia C. Mosser, Joseph Tracy, and Joshua Wright offer a public utility alternative, addressing the public–private tension via a cooperative structure that internalizes risk for all parties. In Chapter 3, Diana Hancock and Wayne Passmore propose the mandatory usage of private-sector mortgage insurance to encourage investment without putting taxpayers at undue risk.

The second three chapters acknowledge that these reforms require attention to affordability, highlighting the role of the Federal Housing Administration (FHA), Federal Home Loan Bank (FHLB) system, and affordable multifamily housing. In Chapter 4, Mark A. Willis and John Griffith show how these same challenges face the rental market—and therefore this approach is equally necessary to strengthen multifamily properties. In Chapter 5, Kevin A. Park and Roberto G. Quercia highlight a similar tension in the FHA's mandate to promote affordable housing while maintaining a strong balance sheet—and reiterate how affordability will continue to be a widespread need in years to come. In Chapter 6, W. Scott Frame tells the story of the FHLB system (the "other" housing GSE), how they weathered the financial crisis and how they too can better balance public lending with measured risk taking.

Finally, the last three chapters describe the basic requisites for reform—a twenty-first-century infrastructure to ensure widespread dissemination of real-time information and access to liquidity for all market participants. In Chapter 7, Akash Kanojia and Meghan Grant underscore the necessity of a TBA market and how such a market can continue to exist even after the GSEs have been replaced by one of the aforementioned reforms. In Chapter 8, Stephanie Heller and Dale A. Whitman complete the supply chain by proposing a national residential mortgage note registry to track the multiple ownership changes that occur as part of the securitization process. They also advocate a break from a paper-based to a digital-based document inventory. Chapter 9 identifies the information requisites for more stable securitization.

Together, these chapters provide us with the full scope of reform efforts that are likely to enter into discussion. In truth, we are unlikely to see another moment so full of opportunities to improve the housing finance system. We have waited long enough to begin the great task of rebuilding the foundation that cracked beneath our feet in 2007. The conservatorship of the GSEs has lasted too long and needs to be replaced with a new vision. Housing finance is the final piece of a puzzle that deserves to be finished. The path of its reform will determine the future of the American dream. We believe that the research in this volume can inform the important policy choices that will help determine that future.

PART I

Structural Reform Options

CHAPTER 1

Legislative Approaches to Housing Finance Reform

David Scharfstein and Phillip Swagel

I. Introduction and Background

By the standards of the contemporary American political system, proposals to reform the U.S. housing finance system moved relatively far through the legislative process in 2013 and 2014. Two of the four bills introduced in Congress received positive votes in their respective congressional committees—the bill sponsored by Representative Jeb Hensarling (R-Texas) in the House Financial Services Committee and the bill sponsored by Senators Tim Johnson (D-South Dakota) and Mike Crapo (R-Idaho) in the Senate Banking Committee. Although the Senate bill, which itself had built on a bipartisan proposal from Senators Bob Corker (R-Tennessee) and Mark Warner (D-Virginia), had bipartisan support and the backing of the Obama administration, it never received a vote on the floor of the Senate. Nor did the Hensarling bill receive a vote in the full House of Representatives, and neither became law. Prospects for housing finance reform faded in 2015, with Fannie Mae and Freddie Mac—the two firms that purchase mortgages and bundle them into securities with a guarantee—now likely to remain in government control with an explicit government backstop into the foreseeable future.

While it is difficult to say when (or even whether) the U.S. political system will again focus on housing finance reform, the debate over the proposals considered in 2013 and 2014 will inform future efforts. This chapter reviews the legislative proposals for housing finance reform, highlighting the common and different features of these proposals and analyzing their economic implications. The chapter concludes by looking at the political obstacles facing legislative efforts and discussing the ways in which housing finance is evolving in the absence of legislation.

The impetus for reform came from the remarkable failure of the housing finance system leading up to and during the financial crisis. The period of 2000 to 2007 saw extraordinary growth of housing credit, particularly to nonprime borrowers but also to prime borrowers (Mian and Sufi 2015; Adelino, Schoar, and Severino 2015). This growth resulted in high default rates, a rash of foreclosures, dramatic declines in house prices from 2007 to 2010, and a near unraveling of the financial system, which was kept together only by extraordinary government interventions. One such intervention was the decision by the Federal Housing Finance Agency (FHFA) to put Fannie and Freddie into conservatorship in September 2008, and the commitment by the U.S. Treasury to explicitly guarantee that the two firms would have the ability to make good on their obligations. While there is considerable debate about whether Fannie and Freddie played a central role in the growth of subprime mortgages, there is widespread agreement that the implicit government support of Fannie and Freddie in the decades leading up to the crisis, combined with lax regulation, led them to take excessive risks—risks that paid off for their shareholders and management in normal times but that had disastrous outcomes during the crisis.

The concern about excessive risk taking by the government-sponsored enterprises (GSEs) was not new, as evidenced by the 1990 General Accounting Office, now the Government Accountability Office (GAO), study of risk at the GSEs and the quality of their regulatory oversight. At the heart of the concern throughout was the implicit government guarantee of the obligations of Fannie and Freddie. These obligations included both debt issued to fund the firms' investment portfolios and the payment guarantees they provided to mortgage-backed securities (MBS) holders. Given their low levels of capital, this implicit guarantee allowed Fannie and Freddie to raise financing at below-market rates and earn a spread between their portfolio yields and their debt financing costs, encouraging them to expand their portfolio dramatically to take advantage of what was effectively government-sponsored arbitrage. In 2008, the combined investment portfolios were more than $1.6 trillion. The implicit government subsidy also allowed them to issue guarantees on MBS, which traded as if they were free of any credit risk even though Fannie and Freddie were required to fund with only 40 basis points of capital for each $100 of guarantees (Goodman 2014). By 2008, the implicit government guarantee and lax capital requirements had allowed Fannie and Freddie to expand their MBS guarantees to almost $5 trillion, approximately half of all residential mortgages in the United States. With such a thin capital cushion, Fannie and Freddie were well positioned to fail when the housing bubble burst, defaults grew, and mortgage-related losses soared.[1]

Indeed, in September 2008, amid growing concern in financial markets about whether Fannie and Freddie could meet their obligations, the two GSEs were put into government conservatorship.[2] Given that securities guaranteed by the GSEs were held widely among U.S. financial institutions, a default by the two firms would have had significant systemic consequences, requiring many banks to recapitalize, whether through costly equity issues or "deleveraging" via the sale of assets (perhaps at fire-sale prices) or a contraction in lending. Moreover, the expectation among foreign lenders of U.S. government backing meant that a GSE failure could put at risk the availability of capital inflows more broadly, resulting in funding difficulties for all borrowers, including the federal government itself. The U.S. Department of the Treasury made explicit the previously implicit guarantee that the government would stand behind the two GSEs, ultimately injecting nearly $200 billion into the two firms. Long-standing concerns over the moral hazards induced by the implicit government guarantee and lax regulation turned out even worse than had been anticipated.

In light of this failure, there were widespread calls for reform. A key dimension on which reform proposals differed was whether to include a government guarantee on housing finance in the first place. One set of proposals called for the end of implicit or explicit government guarantees for housing finance.[3] Under this view, private-market participants rather than the government would provide the capital for housing, taking on the risks and rewards of their decisions just as with any other type of investment. A second approach would allow private entities to guarantee MBS and purchase "reinsurance" from the government so that the private market would bear losses ahead of the government, but MBS would continue to trade without credit risk to the investor. Advocates of this approach believed that well-capitalized private entities would limit moral hazard and protect taxpayers from the risk of loss. Another motivating factor for this type of proposal was the belief that policy makers would intervene in the event that a future crisis made it difficult for U.S. households to obtain mortgage financing. The concern, then, was that a proposal that claimed to abolish government support for housing would instead inadvertently re-create the implicit guarantee. As discussed below, a key question is which liabilities would receive such an ex post bailout in the event of a future crisis.

This latter set of proposals formed the basis of bipartisan reform efforts in Congress. In essence, these proposals sought to preserve a relatively liquid market for default-free MBS such as those issued by Fannie and Freddie by maintaining the government guarantee but with better protection for taxpayers. Many advocates of this approach saw the government guarantee as necessary to ensure that mortgages were available on reasonable terms. They argued that a government guarantee against catastrophic loss would lower mortgage costs both because the government can absorb credit risk more efficiently than the market can and because MBS are more liquid when holders do not have to evaluate credit risk along with interest rate risk and mortgage prepayment risk. Advocates of this reform approach also argued that the guarantee was critical to maintaining the prepayable thirty-year fixed-rate mortgage (FRM), which had become the most popular form of mortgage and which they viewed as desirable from the perspective of consumer protection. A further motivation for providing a government guarantee at all times was the belief that this was necessary to maintain the to-be-announced (TBA) market for MBS, which was seen as important both for enhancing the liquidity of the MBS market and for providing homebuyers with the ability to lock in an interest rate on a mortgage ahead of buying a home (for discussion, see Kanojia and Grant, Chapter 7, this volume; Vickery and Wright 2013).

With this background in mind, in Section II we first describe the policy proposal that elicited the most bipartisan support and got the furthest in the legislative process, the Johnson-Crapo bill, formally known as Senate bill 1217 (S.1217), the Housing Finance Reform and Taxpayer Protection Act of 2014. Key elements of the legislation centered on the amount and form of private capital required, the structure of the housing finance market (whether one, two, or many firms would undertake securitization with a guaranty and government backing), and the conditions under which the government backstop could expand in times of significant stress to the financial system.

In Section III, we analyze the main design elements of Johnson-Crapo after first considering the basic premise on which the bill and similar proposals are based—the idea that a government guarantee is critical to ensuring the availability of mortgage credit on reasonable terms and the existence of the prepayable thirty-year FRM. In Section IV, we describe the other proposals that were under consideration by highlighting their differences with the Johnson-Crapo approach. Section V describes the political challenges that ultimately stalled legislation and will likely recur in any future legislative efforts, and concludes by discussing the evolution of the housing finance system absent legislation.

II. Features of the Johnson-Crapo Bill

The Johnson-Crapo bill would have established a government insurance program on MBS composed of qualified mortgages, with a "hybrid" capital model under which the taxpayer backstop kicked in after private investors had taken a specified amount of losses. The existing entities of Fannie and Freddie would be wound down, and the secondary government insurance on MBS sold on equal terms to new private firms that would undertake mortgage securitization by bundling together mortgages—this emphasis on competition and entry was a distinguishing characteristic of the approach taken by both the Johnson-Crapo bill and its predecessor proposal by Senators Corker and Warner. The government would not guarantee the operation of entities involved in securitization, only the repayment of their MBS. Guaranteed MBS from all firms would be standardized and issued together using a common securitization platform. The FHFA would be transformed into the Federal Mortgage Insurance Corporation (FMIC) and become both insurer and regulator of the housing finance system—akin to the role of the Federal Deposit Insurance Corporation (with the name chosen intentionally to mimic that of the FDIC). The Treasury backstop on existing GSE bonds and MBS (so-called legacy securities) would be turned into a full-faith-and-credit obligation; investors would have the option to pay a fee to have their legacy MBS reissued on the common securitization platform if they wanted the liquidity of the new system. A fee levied on guaranteed MBS would subsidize affordable housing activities. Seidman et al. (2013) discuss a proposal similar in many respects to the Johnson-Crapo proposal and to the predecessor Corker-Warner bill.

The first-loss capital ahead of the government backstop would be organized by private firms acting as MBS guarantors, with each guarantor required to maintain a capital level equal to 10 percent of the value of mortgages in guaranteed MBS—a private guarantor putting together an MBS with $100 million in mortgages would have to fund itself with at least $10 million in capital. The secondary government insurance would kick in once the private guarantor for an MBS extinguished its entire capital (the capital required across all its MBS), after which the FMIC would ensure the timely payment of cash flows from all the guaranteed MBS from the defunct guarantor.

The focus on competition and entry in the Johnson-Crapo bill would have entailed important changes to the market structure for the housing finance system. Rather than the previous duopoly, the bill envisioned five or more firms undertaking securitization and purchasing the backstop government insurance. Components of Fannie and Freddie would be sold to new entrants and the two firms wound down. Competition among securitizers was intended to push the benefits of an unintended government subsidy resulting from underpriced secondary insurance to homeowners in the form of lower interest rates, rather than being captured by the firms as in the past (although see below for a discussion of an innovative proposal by Representative John Delaney [D-Maryland], by which the pricing of the government insurance would be set through a market-based framework). Expanding the number of firms was further intended to guard against a situation in which any one entity was too important to be allowed to fail. A key challenge for the Johnson-Crapo approach was that it involved a switch from two firms that exist and operate to a system in which unknown new firms enter and carry out the business of securitization and guaranty. The legislation would set up a cooperative guarantor to ensure that smaller originators could sell mortgage loans into guaranteed MBS without going through a large bank. All guaranteed MBS would be issued on a common securitization platform to ensure that these securities traded in a common pool rather than in separate markets, such as for the current Fannie and Freddie MBS. This would have increased liquidity in the mortgage markets (with the hope of resulting in lower mortgage interest rates), while also allowing new firms to enter into the business of guaranteed securitization without facing a liquidity disadvantage.

Part of the premium for the secondary government insurance would have been earmarked to subsidize activities related to affordable housing, providing several billion dollars each year—a sizable increase from the several hundred million devoted to affordable housing under a law enacted in 2008. The affordable housing fee would average 10 basis points across all guaranteed MBS, but would be set so that guarantors serving relatively large numbers of low- and moderate-income households paid less than guarantors serving relatively large numbers of higher-income households did. This "flex-fee" arrangement was meant to provide a financial incentive for firms to serve diverse populations of borrowers. These funds would have replaced the housing goals in the old GSE system, under which Fannie and Freddie were required to purchase or guarantee certain numbers of mortgages for low- and moderate-income households.

III. Analysis of the Johnson-Crapo Bill

Although the main focus of our chapter is an evaluation of the various features of bipartisan reform proposals that would make government guarantees explicit, we start by considering the premise on which the bipartisan proposals are based: that the government guarantee is critical to ensuring the wide availability of mortgage credit and, in particular, the prepayable thirty-year FRM. In short, there are reasons to doubt the economic basis for claims that a guarantee is needed in normal times (even while recognizing the political reality that a guarantee has strong support among industry and housing advocates). In particular, a number of studies show that the "jumbo-conforming spread"—the difference between the interest rates on jumbo mortgages, which do not qualify for a government guarantee, and conforming mortgages, which do qualify for the guarantee—is less than 30 basis points, often much less.[4] This casts some doubt on the value of the guarantee. Admittedly, this spread may underestimate the true value of the government guarantee because jumbo mortgage lenders may have had more risk-taking capacity given that so much credit risk was absorbed by the government. Thus, jumbo rates may have been lower than they otherwise would have been absent a guarantee of conforming mortgages. That said, under a new regime in which the government charges for taking on credit risk rather than providing the implicit guarantee without compensation, the difference in rates between conforming and nonconforming mortgages should be even smaller.[5]

Moreover, there is also limited theoretical support and empirical evidence for the view that the government guarantee increases the availability of the thirty-year prepayable FRM. On a theoretical level, it is difficult to see how the government guarantee could affect the supply of FRMs, as it protects MBS investors from credit risk, but not from interest rate or prepayment risk. The empirical evidence also sheds doubt on the importance of the guarantee. Although Fuster and Vickery (2014) show that prime conforming mortgages are more likely to be FRMs than prime jumbo mortgages are—which at first glance suggests that the guarantee is important in increasing the supply of FRMs—it is also true that households that take out prime jumbo mortgages are different on a number of other important dimensions, such as FICO score, that could affect their demand for FRMs. Indeed, Fuster and Vickery show that when these demand differences are taken into account through more advanced statistical techniques (including regression discontinuity), there is no meaningful difference between the share of jumbo and conforming mortgages that are fixed rate. This is contrary to the idea that the guarantee increases the supply of FRMs on average.

The evidence does point, however, to a potentially important role of government guarantees during periods of significant stress to the financial system. First, although the jumbo-conforming spread is small in normal times, in 2007 in the early stages of the financial crisis, the spread widened substantially. This suggests that a government guarantee could be beneficial in maintaining the supply of mortgage credit in stressed periods. Moreover, although Fuster and Vickery (2014) show that on average there was no meaningful difference between the FRM share of jumbo and conforming mortgages, this difference became substantial in 2007 as private-label MBS markets broke down and it became more difficult to securitize jumbo mortgages without the guarantee. With banks having limited appetite to take on the interest rate and prepayment risk associated with the thirty-year FRM, they were likely reluctant to hold an increased volume of jumbo mortgages in their portfolios. Thus, one could argue that securitization is helpful in promoting the availability of the FRM, but the government guarantee per se is not the driving force in normal times when securitization is readily available.[6]

Although the benefits of the government guarantee accrue when financial markets are in crisis, the backstop under Johnson-Crapo and similar proposals exists in all periods. An alternative approach, put forward as an option in the Obama administration white paper on housing finance reform released in February 2011, would be to target the guarantee to periods of significant stress and limit the scope of the guarantee in normal times.[7]

We now turn to a discussion of the key design components of the Johnson-Crapo legislation. The most contentious set of issues centered on the design of the first-loss capital provided by the private sector—the quantity (10 percent or less), the type (mix of equity and debt), and the source (monoline insurer or capital market securities). Another set of issues that had to be worked out was how the government guarantee would be structured and priced. Yet a third consideration was the extent and form of private-market competition that would be allowed. A fourth major issue had to do with the government's role during a crisis—not just with respect to guarantees on legacy MBS but also the policy around first-loss capital and government reinsurance of newly issued mortgages during a crisis.

A. Capital

As has been noted, the financial crisis revealed that Fannie Mae and Freddie Mac were inadequately capitalized relative to the risk they were bearing. Indeed, they funded themselves with just 40 basis points of capital for each dollar of mortgage they guaranteed (Goodman 2014). With losses during the crisis well exceeding 40 basis points, there was widespread acceptance of the view that mortgage guarantors should fund themselves with considerably more capital than they had previously, even while the precise amount of additional capital remained a matter of considerable debate.

Johnson-Crapo required private capital of 10 percent of guaranteed MBS available to bear first loss ahead of coverage by the FMIC. The government's Mortgage Insurance Fund (MIF) was itself required to maintain 2.5 percent capital against losses that exceeded the private capital. This capital would be accumulated over ten years through fees on government reinsurance. This setup was meant to avoid another tap into general revenues that occurred when the GSEs were put into conservatorship.

In light of this significant increase in capital requirements, there was pushback from industry and housing advocates who argued that the heightened capital requirements could lead to a large increase in mortgage rates. With these concerns in mind, the housing finance reform bill sponsored by Maxine Waters (D-California), ranking member of the House Financial Services Committee, required 5 percent first-loss private capital.

The magnitude of the effect of enhanced capital requirements on the cost of mortgage credit is an unresolved issue. It parallels in important ways the debate about the effect of bank capital requirements on the cost of credit. On one side are those who argue that the effect is large because guarantors (or banks) require a high rate of return to put their capital at risk. In this view, the more such private capital is at risk, the more investors will require in return and thus the more an insurer will charge to guarantee mortgages (or provide credit). On the other side are those who argue that additional layers of capital are not as costly as initial layers of capital because incremental amounts of capital are less likely to bear losses. This is essentially the famous "Modigliani-Miller Theorem," which has been used by Hanson, Kashyap, and Stein (2011) and Admati and Hellwig (2013) to argue that enhanced bank capital requirements should have a limited impact on the cost of bank credit.

To understand the Modigliani-Miller logic in the context of mortgage guarantees, consider a world in which investors just invested directly in a $100 billion portfolio of prime thirty-year FRMs. Ignoring for simplicity the typical prepayable feature of such mortgages, these investors would need to earn a spread over Treasuries to compensate them for the losses from mortgage defaults. This spread would include a component for expected losses as well as a "credit risk premium" to compensate investors for bearing losses when the economy is doing poorly and asset returns are low (i.e., "beta risk"). Suppose that expected losses are 40 basis points of the principal balance ($400 million per annum), and the credit risk premium is 20 basis points ($200 million per annum). This implies that investors would need to be promised 60 basis points more than Treasuries to compensate them for the credit risk they bear.

Now suppose that these investors buy insurance from a mortgage guarantor who promises to bear the losses and insure that the investors are paid in full on their mortgage holdings. To provide this service, the guarantor is required to put up $5 billion to cover potential losses; that is, there is a capital requirement of 5 percent. This sum is invested in Treasuries, which are available to pay any losses on the mortgages. In exchange for this insurance, the guarantor receives guarantee fees. The guarantee fees needed to cover expected losses of $400 million per annum and the credit risk premium of $200 million per annum equal 60 basis points of the principal balance. Ignoring administrative costs, the net profit to the guarantor would be $200 million plus the yield on Treasuries. The excess return over Treasuries would be 4 percent, that is, $200 million/$5 billion.

Consider what would happen if the capital requirement for the guarantor is increased to 10 percent in the form of $10 billion in Treasuries. Expected losses on the mortgages ($400 million) have not changed, nor has the credit risk premium ($200 million). The same 60 basis points in guarantee fees cover the default costs. Now the required excess return over Treasuries is 2 percent, that is, $200 million/$10 billion, rather than the 4 percent required excess return when there was only 5 percent capital. Why has the required return gone down? Because the likelihood that the second $5 billion of Treasuries ever has to be turned over to cover losses is much lower than the likelihood that some of the first $5 billion is turned over. In both cases, guarantors collect $600 million of guarantee fees and are compensated fairly for the losses they expect to incur. By the Modigliani-Miller logic outlined above, raising the capital requirements is not costly at all.

By contrast, those who see higher capital requirements as costly often assume that the required return for guarantors does not depend at all on the amount of capital, which is inconsistent with the Modigliani-Miller logic. For example, if the required excess return is 4 percent regardless of the amount of capital, then going from 5 to 10 percent capital on $100 billion of guarantees increases the guarantee fee from 60 basis points to 80 basis points. To see this, note that in both cases, guarantors need to cover the $400 million of expected losses (40 basis points). But with 10 percent capital, guarantors also need $400 million to cover the credit risk premium (4 percent × $10 billion of capital at risk). This adds another 40 basis points to the guarantee fee. With 5 percent capital guarantors need only $200 million to cover the credit risk premium (4 percent × $5 billion of capital at risk), adding just 20 basis points to the guarantee fee. Note that in the limit, by this logic, where capital is 100 percent, the guarantor would need to earn a credit risk premium of $4 billion (400 basis points), and the guarantee fee would be 440 basis points. This is obviously unrealistic as it implies that investors in these mortgages (with low expected losses of just 40 basis points) need to earn returns similar to those of junk bonds (which tend to have considerably higher expected losses). Thus, although the application of the Modigliani-Miller logic to capital requirements may have its limitations,[8] the effect of capital requirements on mortgage costs is often overstated because it takes no account of the effect of capital on required returns.

Those who believe that higher capital requirements would raise mortgage costs are focused on having enough capital to cover losses in another crisis, but not an excessive amount. Goodman and Zhu (2014b) estimate that Freddie Mac had a loss rate of about 4 percent on the mortgages they guaranteed in 2007, the worst-performing vintage, whereas Fannie Mae had losses of more than 5 percent. Thus, if capital requirements are based on this loss experience, a 5 percent capital requirement is probably not enough for at least two reasons. First, these losses were incurred despite extraordinary government actions to support house prices, financial markets, and the overall economy, and could have been much higher absent this costly support. Second, when bank regulators set capital requirements, they seek to ensure that there is a significant buffer to withstand adverse shocks so that a bank can continue operations despite the shock. Likewise, the capital requirement for MBS insurers should be high enough so that guarantors have enough capital to continue providing guarantees even with an adverse shock.

Of course, one could argue that the 2007 vintage included mortgages that were riskier than those that would be allowed under the new legislation and with the oversight of the new regulator, the FMIC. Indeed, Goodman and Zhu (2014b) estimate that mortgages guaranteed by the GSEs in 2010 would have generated losses of 2.4–3 percent if they went through the same shocks experienced by the 2007 vintage. This lower loss rate relative to the 4–5 percent loss rate of the 2007 vintage reflects the higher average quality of mortgages guaranteed in 2010. Thus, the appropriate size of the capital requirement will depend in no small measure on the quality of mortgages that the regulator will allow and the protections put in place for lower-quality mortgages (such as mortgage insurance). If quality of mortgages is uncertain, as it likely would be, it suggests that some risk weighting of mortgages would be necessary, with riskier mortgages having higher risk weights and thus effectively more capital behind them.[9] A further question is whether 10 percent makes sense in light of current bank capital requirements. Basel III currently requires a Tier 1 common equity ratio approaching 10 percent for large, systemically important financial institutions. In one version of the capital requirements, mortgages have a risk weight of 50 percent, meaning that banks need to fund themselves with 5 percent capital on the mortgages they hold in their portfolios. This would seem to suggest that banks undertaking balance sheet lending rather than selling mortgages off for securitization would face lower capital requirements than mortgage guarantors, leading mortgages to migrate to the banking sector rather than to be put into guaranteed MBS. This migration could be desirable if institutions holding loans on balance sheet have a heightened incentive for prudence in origination. However, it is not clear that this migration would happen. Banks hold diversified portfolios of assets that include securities, commercial and industrial loans, commercial real estate loans, and credit card loans. Indeed, for the U.S. banking sector as a whole, residential mortgages (including home equity lines of credit) account for just 22 percent of assets. Thus, when a bank holds a mortgage portfolio, it is supported not just by the 5 percent equity capital for mortgages but also by the equity required to fund the other assets on its balance sheet. Put differently, part of the reason overall bank capital requirements are 10 percent and not higher—and thus why they have to fund themselves with only 5 percent capital against mortgages—is that they are diversified entities.

Nevertheless, whether a 10 percent capital requirement for mortgage guarantors is consistent with bank capital requirements remains an open question. Before the next round of legislation, it is critical that a serious calibration of capital requirements be undertaken, one that seeks to reconcile capital requirements of the mortgage guarantors with bank capital requirements.

Although the Johnson-Crapo legislation specified a 10 percent capital requirement, it left the regulator to determine what counted as "capital." A lesson of the crisis is that the quality of capital matters immensely. A considerable part of the capital of Fannie and Freddie before the crisis, for example, was in the form of tax-deferred assets that provided the firms with a tax benefit on future profits to offset past losses. But the possibility of losses for years to come implied that these assets did not actually provide resources with which to absorb losses. A pliable regulator—a natural concern given the history of the GSEs—could define *capital* to include debt or preferred securities in addition to equity capital. For the most part, support of financial institutions during the crisis was structured to ensure that the debt securities of financial institutions were not impaired, likely out of concern that such impairment would trigger creditor runs. Moreover, the existence of subordinated debt and preferred stock reduced the incentive of banks to raise common equity during the financial crisis because the benefits of such an equity issue would have accrued first to these more senior claimants. This is the so-called debt overhang problem that led to inadequate private-sector recapitalizations and was one of the rationales for equity injections in the Troubled Asset Relief Program (TARP). As a result of this experience, Basel III not only raised capital requirements but also improved the "quality" of capital, substantially increasing *common equity* requirements and downplaying the importance of preferred equity and subordinated debt. Allowing mortgage guarantors to count subordinated debt and preferred stock as capital would lead to similar problems as those experienced by banks during the crisis. Policy makers might hesitate to allow these more senior securities to bear losses, and their existence would make it more difficult for guarantors to recapitalize during periods of significant stress.

B. Pricing the Government Guarantee

Another key aspect of the legislation was the establishment of a mechanism by which to set the fee for the government guarantee. The fee would be paid to FMIC, which would hold in reserve capital accumulated from these fees, eventually equal to 2.5 percent of the outstanding MBS it guaranteed.

In one view, the fee would be set to cover the expected losses that the government would incur. These are, of course, difficult to estimate given that the first-loss capital is supposed to protect the government from loss in all but the most catastrophic scenarios. Zandi and deRitis (2011) estimate that the government guarantee with a reinsurance fee would lead to significantly lower mortgage rates than if the private market had to self-insure against catastrophic losses. This conclusion relies on the assumption that the government can better withstand catastrophic losses because it can borrow at the risk-free rate to fund losses while the private market faces higher funding costs.

Scharfstein and Sunderam (2011) question this conclusion, arguing that the government should factor in a risk premium on top of expected losses to compensate it for bearing risk in bad states of the world. Although it may be true that the U.S. Treasury has been able to borrow at the risk-free rate in periods of significant financial stress, this borrowing comes at a cost—either higher future taxes or reduced government spending on other programs. If these taxes are distortionary or if other government programs have value, the cost is greater than the risk-free rate (see Lucas 2011 for a related discussion). Moreover, if there are other constraints on spending, losses arising from the guarantee could come at the expense of countercyclical fiscal expenditures, such as expanding unemployment benefits during a significant negative shock to the economy associated with high rates of mortgage defaults. Thus, the optimal fee could well be greater than the fee that covers actuarial losses, and there should be no presumption that the government should charge significantly less than private markets for bearing catastrophic losses.[10]

Thus, if the government charges a reinsurance fee at or near what the market would charge to compensate for the fiscal risk it bears, the potential benefit of the government guarantee would be reduced relative to pricing based on expected losses. However, there might still be a benefit of the government guarantee to the extent that eliminating credit risk of MBS promotes a more liquid market for MBS. This greater liquidity should lower required yields on MBS and thus reduce mortgage rates. Nonetheless, these benefits are likely to be small given that more liquid securities tend to trade at yields only 10 basis points (bps) below similar securities that are less liquid. With imperfect pass-through of MBS yields into mortgage rates because of market power in mortgage origination and securitization, the effect on mortgage rates is likely to be even lower than this 10 bps estimate.

A legislative proposal by Representatives John Carney (D-Delaware), John Delaney (D-Maryland), and Jim Himes (D-Connecticut) provides an innovative approach to pricing the government guarantee. Five percent private capital would be required in the first-loss position, along the lines of the Waters proposal. Of the remaining 95 percent, 10 percent of the mortgage credit risk would be required to be sold off to private investors pari passu to the government exposure. The pricing of this 9.5 percentage points of capital would then be used to set the price of the secondary government insurance.

C. Countercyclical Capital Requirements

The empirical evidence points to a modest effect of a government guarantee on mortgage rates in normal times. This effect would likely be even smaller with enhanced capital requirements and with a reinsurance fee rather than an uncompensated implicit guarantee. There is evidence, however, that a government guarantee could facilitate the availability of new mortgage credit during periods of significant financial stress. Indeed, Fannie and Freddie gained considerable market share during the financial crisis because the government guaranteed the GSE mortgage pools without private capital required at the MBS level (just homeowner down payments and private mortgage insurance [PMI] on individual loans). Thus, if 10 percent capital is required in all states of the world, it is likely that in a crisis the guarantors would have insufficient capital to guarantee new mortgages even if they have government reinsurance. If so, then the secondary government guarantee has limited value: it has little effect on the supply of credit in normal times and is insufficient to ensure the availability of credit in bad times.

Recognizing that low levels of guarantor capital during periods of significant financial stress could reduce the supply of mortgages, Johnson-Crapo includes a mechanism for the first-loss capital requirements to be reduced in the face of credit market strains. If the director of the FMIC, in conjunction with the chair of the Federal Reserve Board and the treasury secretary, and in consultation with the secretary of the Department of Housing and Urban Development, "determine that unusual and exigent circumstances threaten mortgage credit availability," they can authorize private guarantors to obtain the government insurance for a limited period with less than 10 percent first-loss capital. Thus, a countercyclical capital requirement can be used to stabilize the supply of housing credit.

If indeed the value of a government guarantee mainly accrues during periods of significant stress to the financial system, a natural alternative to having a guarantee widely available at all times would be to focus reform on ensuring that the government guarantee is available on newly issued mortgages during times of stress. Scharfstein and Sunderam (2011) propose that the government have a limited footprint in normal times when the private market is willing to bear risk, but expand the government's role when it is needed most, that is, when the markets are under significant stress. The countercyclical capital requirement embodied in Johnson-Crapo is one way to achieve this goal. A key difference is that the guarantee is available to most mortgages under Johnson-Crapo, with the extent of the government exposure depending on the size of the required first-loss private capital. This contrasts with the Scharfstein-Sunderam approach in which few mortgages receive a government guarantee in normal times. The guarantee is made widely available in a crisis, but the insurance is not extended retroactively to nonguaranteed mortgages. This focuses the government involvement on ensuring the flow of mortgage credit going forward in a crisis while avoiding an ex post bailout to market participants who have already invested in mortgages.

Which of these two approaches is more desirable depends on whether there is a robust and durable capital requirement in the Johnson-Crapo approach. If the capital required in normal times remains of high quality, then both proposals protect taxpayers, with the Johnson-Crapo approach having the advantage of maintaining a liquid market for MBS, including a well-functioning TBA market. This liquidity confers some benefits to mortgage markets and likely to the broader financial system, which is made safer by the existence of liquid, safe securities.[11] The possibility that a hybrid capital model such as in Johnson-Crapo will eventually result in a watered-down capital requirement—including in the face of future lobbying efforts to try to weaken it—is a significant drawback of that approach.

D. Competition

In an effort to promote competition, Johnson-Crapo allowed the entry of multiple guarantors with the approval of the FMIC. Greater competition may reduce the economic rents that could accrue to the guarantors so that more of the benefit of the government reinsurance would pass through to borrowers—in the event that the price on the government reinsurance is set too low (as might happen under political duress), competition was meant to direct the resulting subsidy to homeowners rather than allowing it to be captured by the intermediary guarantors. Moreover, although there is an important systemic component of housing risk that could lead to the failure of multiple guarantors, the failure of any one guarantor in response to an idiosyncratic shock would be less likely to have systemic implications if there are many guarantors.

A difficulty with having too many guarantors—and a high level of competition with rents competed away—is that it could induce a race to the bottom in credit standards as guarantors seek to increase current earnings. Thus, a more competitive market means that the FMIC would need to be more vigilant regarding capital standards and mortgage quality given the heightened incentive of the guarantors to increase risk.

IV. Alternative Approaches

This section discusses several other proposals that received attention during the housing finance policy debate of 2013 and 2014, focusing on key differences from the Johnson-Crapo approach.

A. Corker-Warner

The proposal by Senators Bob Corker (R-Tennessee) and Mark Warner (D-Virginia) introduced in June 2013 was the starting point for the Johnson-Crapo bill, with the common features of private capital in a first-loss position ahead of a government guarantee on MBS, entry and competition among firms that would supplant Fannie and Freddie, a common securitization platform and thus a unified pool for guaranteed MBS, and funding for affordable housing activities. A key difference between the two proposals was that the predecessor Corker-Warner bill would have allowed private capital to attach to one or more MBS, as an alternative arrangement in addition to the system of a private guarantor firm that aggregates capital for a portfolio of MBS. That is, a guaranteed MBS could have 10 percent private capital directly connected to that one MBS—perhaps as a junior tranche in the securitization—or could instead be covered by a private guarantor required to maintain capital equal to 10 percent of all MBS covered by that guarantor.

The Corker-Warner "capital markets" approach could have been implemented through securities in which the cash flows paid to loss-absorbing investors decreased in the event of credit losses, with the FMIC guarantee kicking in after investors had taken losses corresponding to the required 10 percent capital level. An advantage of this approach is that investors hand over cash up front, leaving no risk that the 10 percent capital will not turn out to be present when the loss actually occurs, as might happen if a bond guarantor is unable to honor its obligations.

This capital markets approach was omitted from the Johnson-Crapo bill in response to critics who argued that such capital markets transactions would dry up in a future housing crisis as the firms engaged in this activity turned away from housing as an asset class. They asserted that, in contrast, bond guarantors would ensure that private capital was available even in housing downturns because this would be these firms' only line of business. The idea that guarantors would be a more stable source of capital is difficult to square with the fact that monoline private mortgage insurers retrenched during the crisis in the face of losses and found it difficult to raise new capital, with some requiring waivers on their capital standards from Fannie and Freddie to continue to write policies for new mortgages. Allowing for a second channel for private capital to enter the housing finance system would instead seem to have potential benefits in making the system more resilient and not less.

As discussed below, the GSEs in conservatorship have been employing similar capital markets transactions to sell off part of the credit risk in their guaranty portfolio to private investors—and these transactions are widely seen as having been successful in reducing the risk to taxpayers of the now-explicit guarantee on GSE activities. Again, it seems useful for future reform efforts to allow multiple channels by which private capital can take on risk ahead of the government guarantee, including through capital markets transactions.

B. Hensarling PATH Act

The distinguishing feature of the proposal from House Financial Services Committee Chairman Jeb Hensarling (R-Texas) was a narrow scope for government guarantees on MBS. The Protecting American Taxpayers and Homeowners Act of 2013 (known as the PATH Act) would have eliminated Fannie and Freddie, with the combination of FHA and Ginnie Mae (as insurer and securitizer, respectively) rather than GSEs or private guarantors providing the taxpayer backstop. Eligibility for FHA-backed mortgages would be restricted to low- and moderate-income families and first-time homebuyers of any income, rather than all families as in the current system (and as in the other proposals discussed here). Other provisions of the PATH Act likewise would require a greater share of housing credit risk to be borne by private investors, including through lower limits on the size of FHA-backed loans (meaning that a larger share of mortgages would not qualify for a government guarantee) and a requirement for risk-sharing transactions to cover 10 percent of new FHA business (which now includes no private capital at the MBS level). In the public debate, it was common for critics to claim that the Hensarling approach eliminated the government guarantee (and thus would lead to dire consequences for the housing market), even though a guarantee remained available at all times in this proposal, though to a narrower set of borrowers than in other proposals. In a period of "significant credit contraction," the PATH Act specified that FHA loans would be available to all borrowers regardless of income.

The PATH Act faced considerable opposition from both industry and housing advocates worried about the consequences of the narrow guarantee for mortgage interest rates and the availability of mortgage credit. The bill received a positive vote in the House Financial Services Committee, but the Republican leadership in the House declined to take up the bill on the floor of the House of Representatives, presumably because representatives would not want to vote in favor of a proposal fiercely opposed by home builders, real estate agents, and other influential groups—especially when the proposal had no chance to garner sixty votes in the Senate (let alone the sixty-seven votes to override a veto by President Obama).

C. Waters Proposal

The proposal from House Financial Services Committee ranking member Maxine Waters (D-California) focused on broadening access to credit. The bill shared the hybrid capital approach of Johnson-Crapo and Corker-Warner but required 5 percent capital in a first-loss position rather than 10 percent.

This reflected concerns that the additional 5 percentage points of capital would lead to undesirably higher mortgage interest rates and reduced access to credit for lower-income families, while 5 percent was seen as sufficient when compared against the losses of Fannie and Freddie in the crisis. As discussed above, 5 percent capital seems low if requirements are based on the 4–5 percentage points of loss on the 2007 vintage of GSE-guaranteed mortgages, which was the worst-performing vintage. This requirement would not take account of the need for a capital buffer in periods of stress, the extraordinary support of house prices that limited losses, the concentrated nature of guarantor risk, and the need for consistency with bank capital requirements. Ultimately, the capital requirement should depend on these factors as well as the quality of mortgages that are allowed under the new system, which will affect the expected losses incurred by the guarantors. It is also worth noting that with 5 percent capital at the MBS level, the appropriate premium for the secondary government insurance should naturally be higher than with 10 percent capital. Thus, even if one believes that 5 percent capital would be less expensive, the higher reinsurance fees—properly calculated to reflect the fiscal risk to the government as discussed in Section III.B above—should dampen this cost advantage and be reflected in mortgage interest rates. The Waters proposal specified that the insurance premiums were to be calculated using the Credit Reform Act accounting methodology, which, as Lucas (2011) explains, provides for smaller insurance premiums and thus lower costs for borrowers, but incomplete compensation for the risks taken on by taxpayers as compared with the insurance premiums calculated under the fair market value approach used in the Corker-Warner legislation.

The Waters bill would have established a single firm eligible to obtain the secondary government guarantee, organized as a cooperative made up of originators; this followed along the lines of a proposal from the New York Fed (see Dechario et al. 2010; Mosser, Tracy, and Wright 2013). To ensure that this cooperative would not be controlled by large originators, governance would have been shared equally across members—one vote for each institution, regardless of size. The idea was to retain the private incentives for innovation through a profit motive. However, a drawback of this approach is that it concentrates risk in one too-big-to-fail institution and exposes the members to the credit risk associated with mortgage guarantees. If one of the benefits of having a guarantee on MBS in the first place is to reduce credit risk in the leveraged banking sector, this structure seems to reduce this benefit.

D. Recapitalization of Fannie and Freddie

A final proposal is to simply end the conservatorships of Fannie and Freddie and restore the two firms as ongoing entities. As argued by Krimminger and Calabria (2015), this option does not require new legislation because the FHFA has the authority to end the conservatorship. The bilateral agreements between the two firms and the Treasury would provide an explicit taxpayer backstop (in this case, on the two firms rather than merely on their MBS), in exchange for which the firms would be required to fund themselves with considerably more private capital than in the past and would not be allowed to rebuild their retained investment portfolios. This would leave essentially an improved version of the old system: Fannie and Freddie would be a duopoly with market power and too-big-to-fail status—and presumably designated as systemically important financial institutions under Dodd-Frank—but with more capital, a more powerful regulator, and an explicit and compensated guarantee rather than an implicit and unpriced one. Compared to having the firms in government control, some would argue that this arrangement would restore private incentives for innovation, although whether such innovation is always desirable remains an open question given that it sometimes takes the form of products or activities that could be excessively risky. But presumably this approach would involve less competition than with multiple firms competing in securitization with a backstop government guarantee, as in the Johnson-Crapo or Corker-Warner approach. This would be a familiar system that already works—in contrast to the uncertainties inherent in replacing Fannie and Freddie with new entrants. However, it would give rise to the same dangers as the old system, with two firms that are likely too important to the economy to be allowed to fail and that have considerable market power—and a history of exercising this power. The government's ownership stakes in Fannie and Freddie (79.9 percent of the firms' common stock plus $189.5 billion in preferred shares) could be sold over time, following the approach used with AIG. The two firms would then pay an annual fee to the Treasury for the taxpayer commitment to back them with public capital.

None of the approaches discussed above succeeded in moving forward. The Johnson-Crapo bill received a positive vote in the Senate Banking Committee on May 15, 2014, with seven Republicans and six Democrats in support and three Republicans and six Democrats opposed—an unusual outcome in that the proposal came from the Democratic chair of the committee. With progressive Democrats voting against the bill in the banking committee, Senate Leader Harry Reid (D-Nevada) declined to bring it forward for consideration by the full Senate. Senator Johnson retired following the November 2014 election, the results of which brought a Republican majority in the Senate, giving Senator Richard Shelby (R-Alabama) the chair of the Banking Committee in 2015. Senator Shelby has introduced financial regulatory reform legislation that includes some GSE-related provisions, but a complete housing finance reform bill has not received further congressional consideration since May 2014.

With the Obama administration and the FHFA as regulator both opposed to restoring the firms to private control, the failure of the legislative proposals means that the GSEs are likely to remain in conservatorship until the next president takes office. The next section thus assesses political prospects for reform and several developments that are changing the U.S. housing finance system in the absence of legislation.

V. Changes to the U.S. Housing Finance System

The failure of legislation to advance to enactment in 2014 reflected opposition to the compromises in the Johnson-Crapo bill. A central concern on the left was over access to credit for diverse populations, in particular that the flex fee was not an adequate replacement for the affordable housing goals that were repealed by Johnson-Crapo and under which Fannie and Freddie had affirmative duties to support mortgages for low-income families and in areas with low incomes. Housing advocates worried that private guarantors would "cream" the market by focusing on serving higher-income borrowers, and they wanted the bill to include a "duty to serve" provision to ensure that lower-income groups would have access to affordable mortgages. On the right, conservatives balked at the idea of formalizing a new government guarantee on housing, even with substantial private capital in a first-loss position. The obstacles faced by the Johnson-Crapo bill thus illustrate the difficulty of enacting housing finance reform legislation.

Even with legislation stalled, changes are taking place in the U.S. housing finance system. In conservatorship, Fannie and Freddie operate under the direction of their regulator, the FHFA, which has instructed the two firms to carry out initiatives that, taken together, achieve some of the aims of housing finance reform. This includes putting private capital at risk ahead of the government guarantee in the event of another housing crisis and changing the infrastructure for MBS. These are important developments, but not a full reform. In the meantime, the two firms remain linchpins of the U.S. housing finance system.

A key development of 2013 and 2014 is that Fannie and Freddie began to transfer some of the risk from their MBS guarantees to private investors, effectively bringing private capital into GSE securitization. These risk-sharing transactions, often referred to as "stacker" bonds, following the Freddie Mac terminology of Structured Agency Credit Risk (STACR) bonds, are much along the lines of what was envisioned in the Corker-Warner bill. Investors buy bonds from Fannie and Freddie that are associated with a reference pool of mortgages, and the returns on the securities decrease as credit losses are taken on the underlying loans over a specified period such as ten years. The initial risk-transfer securities were actually second-loss private capital, as the two GSEs took a modest amount of credit losses (30 bps) before private investors faced lower returns from further credit losses, with the private capital itself typically divided into tranches so that investors could take more or less exposure to housing risk. Subsequent transactions have transferred first-loss risk to the private investors. Much as with the MBS-level capital that was to be provided in the Corker-Warner and Johnson-Crapo bills, homeowner equity and any loan-level PMI stand in front of the risk-transfer transactions.

Private capital is coming back into housing finance in other ways. Fannie and Freddie have used reinsurance transactions to transfer some of their remaining credit risk, again with the coverage referencing specific pools of mortgages. Across the various approaches, some type of risk transfer applied to nearly half of the mortgages acquired by Fannie and Freddie in 2014. The firms are also reported to be considering allowing PMI firms to offer deeper loan-level coverage, such as by insuring losses on as much as half of the mortgage for borrowers with down payments of 5 percent, rather than the typical PMI policy, which covers around 25 percent of a mortgage for such borrowers.

The FHFA has also directed Fannie and Freddie to develop a single security to encompass MBS from both Fannie and Freddie, rather than the firms' now-distinct securities. If successful, a single security would allow all guaranteed MBS to trade in a common pool, in principle increasing liquidity and resulting in lower MBS yields and thus mortgage interest rates. This development would be especially beneficial for Freddie Mac, whose securities are less liquid than those of Fannie Mae and thus command lower prices (meaning that Freddie pays investors higher yields on MBS than Fannie does, even though the underlying mortgage interest rates are equalized between the two firms, resulting in lower profitability for Freddie). The FHFA has further instructed Fannie and Freddie to develop a common securitization platform on which both of their MBS would be issued. This new housing finance infrastructure was originally envisioned as a means to increase liquidity by unifying the pools for Fannie and Freddie MBS, and to facilitate entry by new guarantors. With legislation stuck, however, the prospect for new entrants has dimmed, and the common securitization platform is now being developed for the benefit of the two incumbent firms rather than in expectation of further competition.

The GSEs remain at the center of the U.S. housing finance system because mortgage securitization without a guarantee has been slow to rebound after collapsing in the financial crisis. The volume of such "private-label" securitization remains modest, although some nonguaranteed lending has migrated instead to bank balance sheets. Government-guaranteed mortgages remain by far the largest source of housing finance, reflecting both the funding advantage of Fannie and Freddie (and the FHA and other government-backed loans), with a now-explicit government backstop, and continued uncertainties about the legal framework for nonguaranteed mortgages.

U.S. taxpayers remain on the hook for catastrophic costs in the event of another foreclosure crisis, but private capital now takes on risk ahead of the GSEs through both loan-level and MBS-level channels. And as discussed above, in principle, the overall impact of this additional private capital on mortgage interest rates should be modest because the increased private capital should lead Fannie and Freddie to charge less for their insurance.

Bringing in private capital through risk-transfer transactions constitutes some progress toward protecting taxpayers but still falls well short of a full housing finance reform. Keeping the GSEs in government control with a taxpayer backstop, and thus funding advantage over potential competitors, will inevitably block development of private competitors, even as policy makers worry that the lack of private alternatives to securitization through Fannie and Freddie means that steps to limit the role of the two firms would crimp the availability of mortgage credit. A full housing finance reform is needed to break the stalemate between the progressives who want to ensure broad access to mortgage credit and conservatives who want to limit government involvement in mortgage markets. The success of the risk-transfer transactions is a hopeful step in this regard, as this development could illustrate that private capital can take on housing credit risk without constricting access to credit and leading to a socially unacceptable upward spike in mortgage interest rates. Over time, one possibility is that the experience with the risk-transfer securities allows the policy debate to return to models that feature both increased private capital and an improved market structure.

A natural next step in this regard would be for the FHFA as regulator to mandate that Fannie and Freddie arrange for credit risk transfer on all newly guaranteed mortgages going forward, rather than setting a goal that encompasses only some of the firms' mortgage production. Following the discussion above, the FHFA would need to decide on the amount of private capital, its quality, and how the requirement might vary with financial market conditions.

Whether reform moves forward depends on addressing the concerns of those who want to ensure broad mortgage access and those who are primarily concerned with limiting government involvement in mortgage markets. Until such a path is found, the housing finance system will remain dominated by the government—and there is a risk that given the political stalemate the conservatorship of Fannie Mae and Freddie Mac will continue indefinitely. The risk-transfer transactions could continue to increase in scope, reducing taxpayer exposure to housing credit risk and possibly paving the way for a revival in mortgage origination without a government guarantee. The housing finance system could evolve with such changes, perhaps in directions that are acceptable to both sides of the debate, although the prospects for comprehensive housing finance reform legislation remain challenging.

CHAPTER 2

The Capital and Governance of a Mortgage Securitization Utility

Patricia C. Mosser, Joseph Tracy, and Joshua Wright

In a previous paper, we proposed a utility structure for the securitization of high-quality, standardized residential mortgages as a replacement for the securitization infrastructure currently run by the housing government-sponsored enterprises (GSEs), Fannie Mae and Freddie Mac.[1] Using the approach of "keep what worked and change what didn't," the design of the utility was driven by several broad principles for reforming the residential mortgage finance system: more robust and sustainable credit access throughout the cycle, clear separation of affordable housing programs, and appropriate pricing of risk across the financing chain (borrowers, lenders, securitizers, investors, and the government). Three important elements in the design are explicit and priced government reinsurance for tail risks, greater alignment of incentives to prevent deterioration in underwriting ex ante, and more capital to absorb losses ex post. We preserve three beneficial aspects of the current system, which are "skin in the game" for originators and securitizers, standardization to exploit economies of scale, and the liquidity benefits of the to-be-announced (TBA) market for agency mortgage-backed securities (MBS).

Applying these principles led us to propose a securitization utility that both securitizes and guarantees standardized mortgage products—that is, a securitization platform with an in-house insurance function. To support robustness and availability of securitization through the cycle, the utility is required to purchase government reinsurance against systemic credit events for whole vintages of mortgage securities. The structure of the proposed utility better aligns incentives in a variety of ways, notably by decreasing incentives for excessive risk taking. Moreover, the ownership structure and business model of the utility are designed to minimize mortgage rates faced by homeowners, while still protecting taxpayers. Central to our approach is the notion that the system's source of capital goes hand in hand not only with its cost of capital but also with its ownership, incentive structure, and the nature of the market discipline it engenders.

In this chapter, we explore in more detail the utility's capital structure, governance model, and regulation. This discussion also raises numerous other questions of broader interest in the debate on mortgage finance reform. Specifically, this chapter is organized as follows.

- Section I ("Systemic Risk and Government Reinsurance") reviews the central debate in mortgage finance reform regarding the nature and extent of the government's role in addressing systemic risk. We argue that the government cannot credibly claim that it will not intervene in housing finance in the future and therefore must focus on managing its risk in the most effective way possible.

- Section II ("Vintage-Based Capital Structure") provides a more detailed description of how a vintage-based capital structure could mitigate the procyclicality of mortgage credit. In contrast to institution-level reinsurance, vintage-level reinsurance provides greater clarity about the timing and terms of government intervention, which helps maintain investors' and issuers' incentives to continue participating in the utility, thereby facilitating business continuity through a crisis and subsequent recovery. In addition, government reinsurance that is vintage- rather than security-based focuses more narrowly on truly systemic risk. We also discuss rules for releasing capital from high-performing vintages.

- Section III ("Pricing the Guarantee Fee and Building Capital") analyzes the relationships among the utility's guarantee fee (g-fee) charged to lenders, the government reinsurance fee charged to the utility, and various key assumptions, including the capital necessary to adequately cover unexpected mortgage credit losses, and the attachment point of the government tail risk reinsurance. We find that the g-fee—and therefore the mortgage rate faced by consumers—is most sensitive to the required capital ratio and the expected return on equity capital.

- Section IV ("Ownership and Governance") discusses at some length the incentive structure that mutualized ownership of the utility provides to lenders and why it is useful in the context of mortgage securitization. This includes discussions of incentive alignment, risk profile, internal governance, and comparisons to central counterparties and other financial market utilities (FMUs). We also discuss how a mortgage securitization utility meets some of the criteria for success laid out in the academic literature on co-operatives: members that are relatively homogenous; are in close proximity; possess sufficient sophistication, frequency of transaction, and economic interest at stake to exert effective monitoring power over their cooperative; and would otherwise be vulnerable to the exertion of market power by the utility if it were owned by outside third parties.

I. Systemic Risk and Government Reinsurance

The debate on the extent and nature of governmental involvement in the mortgage markets has been long running, but it received new urgency and fresh perspectives as the housing crisis evolved into a financial crisis over the course of 2007–2009. Observations and proposals have been published by a wide array of academics, industry trade groups, market analysts, and policy makers. Notable among the early discussants were Federal Reserve Chairman Ben Bernanke and former Treasury Secretary Henry Paulson, who each laid out a spectrum of options for the housing GSEs, from full privatization to full nationalization.

More recently, the U.S. Department of the Treasury and the Department of Housing and Urban Development (HUD) released a report on options for reforming the U.S. housing finance system, pursuant to Section 1074 of the Dodd-Frank Act (U.S. Department of the Treasury and U.S. Department of Housing and Urban Development 2011). The Treasury/HUD white paper laid out three options for long-term reform of the U.S. mortgage market: privatization (outside of the Federal Housing Administration and Veterans Administration programs), a countercyclical government backstop mechanism, and a government role through the provision of a reinsurance program for systemic risk. The white paper said little about the institutional design or ownership structure under any of these options. Instead, the options were presented in broad enough terms that a number of structures could be compatible with them.

On one end of the Treasury/HUD spectrum of choices is a fully private model with no government involvement, at least not for the core of the mortgage market.[2] Advocates for this approach typically suggest a phased transition by some combination of successively lowering the conforming loan limit over time and raising g-fees.[3] A fundamental question with this approach is whether the federal government can credibly commit to not intervening in housing finance in the future. History suggests that the answer is no. If pressures become serious enough, housing is too important—in terms of effects on both household wealth and systemic financial stability—for the government not to step in during a crisis.[4] If this is the case, then we argue that it is preferable for the government to be transparent and to make its backstop role explicit, define the terms on which it would intervene, and charge a price for the systemic risk reinsurance it provides. The alternative is a de facto implicit guarantee that is not priced and lacks transparency with respect to when and how the government would intervene.

Critics of government insurance raise concerns about the ability of governments to set appropriate prices for their insurance programs.[5] It could be that the fair value of government-provided reinsurance is much higher than the expected (i.e., probability-weighted) tail-event loss, because the reinsurance is paid out in the worst states of the world. However, we argue that the risk premium faced by strong-credit sovereigns is lower than that of private firms for true tail risk. More generally, while we acknowledge that governments have a history of mispricing guarantees, and that the technical and political challenges are indeed formidable, the degree of mispricing of an explicit guarantee relative to an implicit guarantee would likely be substantially smaller. That is, a positive price is preferable to a zero price for the government guarantee. In addition, defining ex ante the terms upon which the government will intervene (the "attachment point" of the reinsurance in a tail event) will likely lead to greater clarity and less uncertainty around the government's intervention as markets come under stress. This, in turn, would support asset prices and market functioning, both of which would support financial stability. Note, however, that the government reinsurance's attachment point must be credible, in that the government would not intervene ahead of this point, even as markets come under stress and political pressures mount.

Concerns over the ability of the government to properly price its reinsurance motivated a team of New York University researchers to propose a vertical risk-sharing role for the government.[6] In this model, the guarantee is fully priced in the market, and the government receives a pro rata share of the g-fees. Note, however, that with a vertical strip there is no effective government backstop, so mortgage guarantors can go out of business. Although in theory this should provide market discipline, in practice it might not; moreover, it raises the question of whether lending will remain robust in times of market stress. The NYU researchers rely on there being many guarantors in the market so that the failure of any one guarantor will not have a large impact on overall lending. However, the experience from the 2007–2009 financial crisis raises questions about this approach, because all guarantors would likely be adversely impacted at the same time by any truly systemic shock. As guarantors begin to fail, contagion could spread, resulting in a sharper contraction of lending.[7] The market discipline is eroded if guarantors anticipate that the government would in fact support them to prevent this credit contraction.

In evaluating the degree of concern over the pricing of the government backstop guarantee, it is important to keep in mind that in our utility, the guarantee is designed to be triggered only by a systemic shock—an event that is expected to happen only infrequently over time. The g-fee paid by a borrower consists of an annual fee with a component to compensate for the private capital that takes a first-loss position ahead of the government, and another component to cover the government reinsurance for tail-event losses. As we will show, the vast majority of this overall g-fee, then, is determined by the market and not by the government.[8] In addition, the degree to which the overall g-fee varies with the changing risks in the lending environment is entirely reflected by changes in the privately priced component of the g-fee. That is, the price for the government's reinsurance would not vary over the credit cycle, but rather would be priced to recoup the government's expected losses associated with very infrequent payouts—for example, once every thirty to fifty years.[9] Changes in the government's reinsurance fee would only occur infrequently based on new information accumulated over time about the nature of long-cycle systemic risks, not based on current market conditions. Consequently, the variation in the g-fee over the credit cycle is entirely market driven.

Numerous commentators have questioned whether a combination of private capital and a government backstop guarantee is more efficient than a pure private capital approach. Scharfstein and Sunderam (2011), for instance, argue that the combination approach is only more efficient if the government does not charge a risk premium for its guarantee. As pointed out by Arrow and Lind (1970), a risk premium is appropriate if taxpayers are required to cover any shortfalls in the government insurance fund at the same time as they have experienced an adverse shock to their income. This occurs if the government is required to have a balanced budget each year and to meet any shortfall between the available insurance funds and the claims on the fund by some combination of cutting current government expenditures and raising current taxes. However, the federal government can borrow against future g-fees from an international investor base to cover any shortfall. Experience also suggests that in this event the U.S. government's borrowing costs would not likely be elevated, due to flight-to-quality dynamics supporting demand for U.S. Treasury securities. As a result, the federal government can provide this reinsurance at a lower cost than private firms would through self-insurance. In this sense, the federal government is better able than the private sector to efficiently provide reinsurance for systemic risks.[10]

A related question is whether government reinsurance is important for maintaining a liquid secondary market in MBS. Following the second option contemplated by the Treasury/HUD 2011 white paper, several proposals incorporate some mechanism for expanding the government's role in the mortgage market during times of crisis.[11] Some have argued that a government backstop guarantee is not necessary in a normally functioning market. That is, the guarantee would only have value during periods of market stress.

However, this argument applies to all forms of insurance: the consumer of the insurance only receives a payout under specified scenarios. In the mortgage markets, an important point is that liquidity in the secondary market is enhanced by investors knowing that they do not face any credit risk regardless of current and future (foreseen or unforeseen) market conditions. Investors do not have the same faith in the credit protection provided by structured securities lacking government support. A goal of mortgage finance reform is to provide a robust system of finance even during periods of market stress. It is precisely during these stressed periods that the backstop guarantee serves to maintain liquidity. Absent a backstop guarantee, following a sufficiently adverse shock, a fully private lending market is prone to experiencing a severe contraction in credit availability with adverse consequences for the real economy.

Note that the liquidity benefits of the agency MBS market arise not only from the government backstop but also from the standardization of the products themselves, as detailed by Vickery and Wright (2013). Even in normal times, a private securitization market will not produce liquid standardized securities, because the security issuers have incentives to create differentiated products, not standardized ones. This is demonstrated by the long history of high product diversity and low liquidity in private-label mortgage securities, consumer credit securitizations, and corporate bonds. In times of market stress, nonstandard financial instruments demonstrate much less liquidity, greater price volatility, and a larger drop in issuance and credit formation.[12]

Scharfstein and Sunderam (2011) propose to deal with the problem of cyclicality in credit availability by having a government guarantor that would significantly increase its lending during periods when private lenders were reducing their credit exposure. In normal market conditions, the government guarantor would define its credit box and price its g-fee so as to maintain a modest market share of new originations. The expectation is that this would allow the government guarantor to be able to retain the expertise and systems necessary to perform its lending backstop role when required. The balance sheet of the government guarantor, consequently, would be very elastic over the credit cycle.

This alternative approach raises the question of whether it is more efficient and effective to support robust credit availability through a government reinsurer for private lending or through a government agency that provides backstop lending. Assuming that both approaches could be designed to maintain credit availability during periods of market stress, the question is which approach exposes the taxpayer to less risk. With the government reinsurer, the risk to the taxpayer takes the form of the potential for underpriced government g-fees. With the government backstop lender, the risks to the taxpayer take the form of a more direct exposure to credit and operational losses at the government lender that are not covered by its g-fee—that is, another form of underpricing.

In thinking about this comparison, it is instructive to look at the recent case of the Federal Housing Administration (FHA). The FHA has essentially been performing the role of a countercyclically scalable government securitization mechanism through the most recent housing cycle. At the height of the nonprime lending boom, the FHA's market share of originations fell below 5 percent. As house prices began to decline and nonprime lending collapsed, the FHA's market share more than tripled to over 15 percent, with the size of the FHA's insurance in force exceeding a trillion dollars. The last audit review estimates that the FHA's current books of business have a negative present value of $13.5 billion.[13] Recent analysis indicates that the resulting credit risk to the FHA insurance fund from increasing its lending has been significantly underestimated over the past several years and that the FHA may require taxpayer support for the first time in its history.[14] This experience of the FHA offers a caution to the countercyclically scalable government backstop approach.

An equally important issue in managing the systemic risk of housing finance channels is inherent tensions across agents in a securitization chain, tensions that are multiplied when securitization has access to even remote government reinsurance. The potential misalignments in incentives inherent in all securitizations are discussed in detail in Ashcraft and Schuermann (2008) and Adrian and Ashcraft (2012). The history of private-label securitization in the mid-2000s is a case study in how the breakdown of mechanisms to align incentives across mortgage lenders, securities issuers, and investors contributed to the housing bubble and the subsequent systemic crisis in housing finance. Similarly, Fannie Mae's and Freddie Mac's contributions to the financial crisis highlight the moral hazard risks of misaligned incentives between the government and the private sector, as well as their implications for systemic risk.

Addressing both types of incentive misalignments is the core argument for a mutualized securitization utility. The mutualization of ownership and risk would align incentives across private members to set and enforce high credit standards and reduce incentives to compete by lowering credit standards during boom times. Reducing incentives for a "race to the bottom" during good times can mitigate the procyclicality of mortgage credit availability. In addition, having securitization and credit standards set by the same entity that holds significant credit risk aligns members' incentives to monitor and manage risk over time. Compared to shareholder-owned financial firms, mutualized utilities have lower risk profiles, lower required profits, and much lower incentives to expand into new business areas, all of which are aligned with the policy imperative to manage tail risk in a careful way.

Most recent proposals, including our own to reform the housing finance system, and GSE-type securitization in particular, emphasize the sharply differentiated roles of private-sector participants and the government.[15] However, most alternative proposals are largely silent on how these roles intersect and the associated incentive alignment issues in securitized mortgage markets. Rather, there is a reliance on regulatory oversight with limited or no discussion of how government and regulators will address the information asymmetries and avoid being "gamed" over time by the private sector. In addition, there is little insight into how their proposals will limit a "race to the bottom" in credit standards during upswings in housing activity, when mortgage lending often degenerates into a volume-focused business model. In other words, a strong regulator may not be sufficient to make up for a poor mechanism design.

In order to avoid repeating the pitfalls of the recent crisis, housing finance reform, and securitization reform in particular, should directly address, in detail, the mechanisms to align incentives across all participants—private and public. However, the economics of housing finance are sufficiently complex that there likely is no ideal model. Rather, GSE reform realistically is an effort to identify the most workable options, not the first-best option—even on the economic merits, before considering the notoriously challenging political dimensions. Policy makers and analysts must therefore weigh the benefits and risks associated with each proposed model and focus on their trade-offs in both preventing and responding to systemic risk events.

II. Vintage-Based Capital Structure

In this section, we discuss a vintage-based capital structure for a mortgage-insuring securitization utility, including equity capital provided up front by the private sector.

As with Freddie and Fannie, the utility would receive g-fees on a flow basis from the loans underlying its MBS. These fees would compensate the government for the reinsurance of systemic risk, cover operating costs, generate a return on capital, and build loss absorption capacity within the utility. In our previous paper, we argued that the tail risk insurance would be optimally applied at the level of a "vintage," or a set of MBS pooled across issuers within the utility and originated over a particular time period—for example, the six-month period used for the ABX index, or a year.

A vintage approach has several attractive features. For instance, it is consistent with the insurance only being triggered by a systemic shock. Loan-level guarantees would be triggered by idiosyncratic factors that impact a borrower's ability to pay (such as unemployment, health shocks, and divorce), and security-level guarantees would be susceptible to regional shocks (as opposed to macroeconomic shocks). In either case, these are not systemic risks and so are not appropriate for government reinsurance.

The alternative of institution-level guarantees such as in Seidman et al. (2013) raises questions about continued credit availability amid solvency concerns. In a systemic event, all institutions taking mortgage credit risk ahead of the government would likely face growing credit losses simultaneously because of the monoline nature of their business models. As noted above, uncertainty about institutions' solvency can impair their ability to continue to provide private capital to mortgage securitization. This would likely impair market functioning, as well as add downward pressure to asset prices. Other solutions have been proposed to address these concerns about recovery and resolution planning, including minimum average debt maturity levels and contingent capital. However, these approaches generally require some impairment of the firm itself—apparently in an attempt to address concerns about "too big to fail" and to punish bad actors—which would still raise questions about market confidence and hence systemic risk and financial stability.

In contrast, a vintage-level guarantee would provide clarity around business continuity and the lighter operational burden and more appropriate risk profile of a guarantee narrowly focused on systemic risk. Note that the vintage-level attachment would therefore not fall neatly into either of the "issue-based" and "security-based" categories laid out by the FHFA.[16] A vintage is neither an individual security nor an issuer in the sense of a perpetual corporation. Rather, a vintage would be a limited-duration legal trust, a nonreplenishing aggregation of mortgage securities and their underlying loans.

Note that a vintage-level guarantee would assuage the concerns of MBS investors, lenders, and equity holders. It would help ensure that the utility can continue to provide access to mortgage credit even in periods of stress, as market participants need not speculate on whether or when the government will step in or on how newly originated mortgages will reach the secondary market. This would help to limit the procyclicality of the provision of residential mortgage credit, as the government tail risk insurance would provide a firebreak between losses on existing vintages and new lending, safeguarding that the utility's capital is never depleted to the point where market participants question the viability of the utility and the market it supports. Losses from an existing vintage would not eat into the fees supporting a new vintage. With vintage-level systemic risk reinsurance, there is no uncertainty over the maximum vintage losses that lenders selling to the utility may incur (Dechario et al. 2011). The members themselves would still have an incentive to continue participating in the utility, knowing that their return from originating mortgages into a new vintage is not impacted by their share of any losses incurred by an earlier vintage, and that the g-fee on new mortgages reflects the expected loss rate given the current lending environment.[17] In addition, they would have confidence that the institutional framework, or "rules of the game," is not about to change.

Although the vintage structure would mitigate some procyclical effects, it cannot eliminate them all. For instance, there would be certain start-up costs to capitalizing the first few vintages after losses from a systemic event wipe out the capital of one or more vintages and reduce the excess capital from nearby vintages. However, any uncertainty over the ultimate magnitude of losses for a vintage once it triggers the reinsurance would not hinder starting a new vintage. A transition period similar to that for the inaugural set of vintages (described more fully at the end of Section III) might be required to mitigate any procyclical dynamic in restarting the vintage capitalization cycle.

Historical data on cumulative default rates for prime conforming mortgages broken out by year of origination (see Figure 2.1) indicate that the performance of vintages appears stratified. Moreover, this stratification is typically apparent within three years of origination, suggesting that each vintage need adhere to a conservative capital ratio for only an initial few years, after which capital in excess of expected losses could begin to be released for distribution as dividends to participants in the vintage (or, as explained below, rolled over into start-up capital for new vintages). This stratification is also relevant for setting the attachment point of the government tail insurance, as discussed in the next section.

Members would be eligible to sell mortgages to the securitization utility after paying in some equity capital up front. Nonmembers could gain access to the securitization markets either on less preferable terms or by selling loans to members via what the industry calls correspondent relationships with aggregator banks. Participants in each vintage would contribute loss mitigation capital to vintage-specific loss pools—that is, separate legal trusts—in proportion to the volume of mortgage balances they securitized into each vintage. Charging fees proportional to the volume of balances they securitize would be analogous to the approach used within the Federal Home

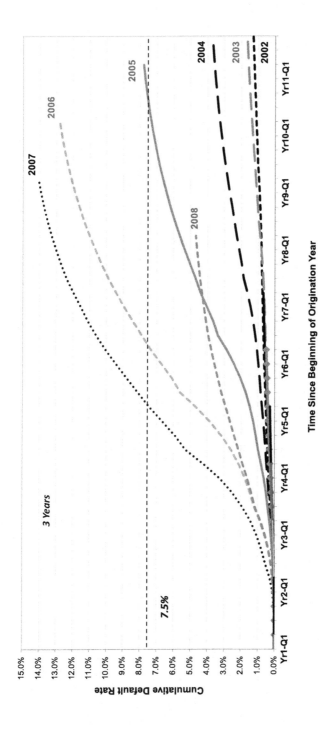

Figure 2.1. Agency vintage cumulative default rates. Data provided by Fannie Mae, reproduced with permission.

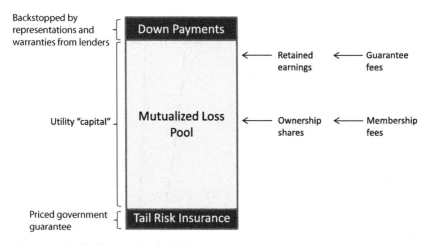

Figure 2.2. Utility's capital waterfall.

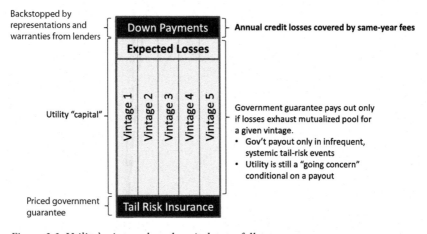

Figure 2.3. Utility's vintage-based capital waterfall.

Loan Bank (FHLB) system. As we discuss in more detail in Section IV, providing nonmembers multiple points of access to the securitization markets would help ensure equitable pricing for lenders.

An example of a capital waterfall for the utility is shown in Figure 2.2, and the vintage-level guarantee is illustrated in Figure 2.3.[18] After an initial transition period (described below), the utility would be expected to fully capitalize each new vintage once the originations into that vintage have been closed. As we discuss below, for each vintage the utility would be expected to hold a minimum percent of loss absorption capital—for example, 3 percent—against the total origination balance. This capital can be sourced from new capital, excess capital released from prior vintages, and fees paid by the vintage.[19]

The utility would be required to hold the full amount of loss absorption capital for the initial three years. At that point, a vintage-specific delinquency test would be performed, and if the vintage's performance at its three-year anniversary indicated that the vintage would be unlikely to trigger the government reinsurance, then the regulator could allow the utility to begin to release capital and, going forward, require the utility to hold capital against only the remaining balance in the vintage.

In order to accelerate the accumulation of capital in each vintage, the utility could—subject to regulatory approval—transfer excess capital from existing vintages into start-up capital for new vintages. Also, to preserve the countercyclical firebreak between existing vintages and new lending, capital from new vintages could not be used to absorb losses from older vintages. Note that this implies an important asymmetry: although excess capital from maturing old vintages could be rolled over to support new vintages, capital from new vintages could not be used to absorb losses from older vintages. This asymmetry would be critical for maintaining confidence and preventing the equivalent of a bank run. Otherwise, lenders might decline to participate in a new vintage if they fear having to pay for previous vintages' losses.

This description of vintage-based capital has so far focused on how the structure would function in a steady state. Reaching that steady state would first require a credible transition plan. To simplify the discussion, we can assume that any new utility would start off de novo, completely segregated from Fannie's and Freddie's legacy book of business.[20] This would facilitate the clearest assessment of the entity's business model. As a start-up, the utility would build securitization activity slowly in order to allow the business model; regulatory structure; and most importantly, operational infrastructure, to be tested and adjusted.[21]

There are several approaches that could be taken to provide sufficient loss absorption capital for a new vintage of mortgages during the transition phase. The most conservative approach is to require all of the capital backing up the vintage to be paid in up front. That is, each vintage starts out fully capitalized to absorb up to a 3 percent loss. To implement such a conservative approach would require that the members provide larger up-front equity capital to the utility, that significant share of the utility's capital structure is financed by junior bonds in capital markets, that originators capitalize some portion of expected g-fees up front to the utility, or some up-front capital is provided from past GSE securitization profits (i.e., from the government), to be repaid in subsequent years. The alternative approach would be for the regulatory authority to allow the utility to build up the capital for each vintage over time.[22] Given that losses typically occur over time, this approach could be designed in such a way as to ensure that sufficient capital is in place in time to absorb required losses ahead of the government reinsurance.

III. Pricing the Guarantee Fee and Building Capital

Key questions for any mortgage market reform model include what level of g-fees a government-reinsured securitization utility would require and the resulting impact on fixed mortgage rates. In this section, we present calculations that illustrate the relationships among capital and other factors that affect the utility's g-fees and the government reinsurance fee. Our intention here is not to present a capital model, but rather to illustrate the dynamics and sensitivities of capital and g-fees to several key variables. A comprehensive, risk-based capital modeling exercise is beyond the scope of this chapter.[23]

We assume that the utility initially will securitize mortgages that adhere to credit and other standards currently in use by the existing GSEs. This is advantageous from a transition standpoint, because it will not require changes to MBS characteristics or TBA trading conventions, and because it will facilitate the continued flow of mortgage credit across all types of lenders who are likely to have underwriting systems geared to current GSE standards. In addition, using current GSE standards will simplify the regulator's job of setting initial capital standards, risk management standards, and the pricing of the government reinsurance, since it can rely on a large quantity of historical information on the performance of mortgages securitized by the agencies.[24]

We derive the implied g-fee needed to cover all costs and provide an expected return using a simple model based on the Basel framework used for bank capital. Under the Basel requirements, a regulated financial institution must hold loss absorption capital in proportion to the aggregate risk exposure of its assets.[25] To account for variation in riskiness across assets—and therefore the amount of loss absorption capacity a regulated institution needs—the Basel standards apply "risk weightings" to different asset classes. The required capital ratio is thus a simple ratio of the institution's aggregate loss-absorbing capital to a risk-weighted sum of its assets. As a definitional matter, it is important to note that the capital calculations below refer to loss absorption capital that is held in each vintage's mutualized loss pool in the steady state (later we discuss the dynamics around building capital in a transition to the new structure). Under this model, the main two drivers of the g-fee are the utility's required capital ratio and its assumed return on equity. A third driver of pricing is the assumption of how frequently the reinsurance is triggered, while a marginal contributing factor is the administrative costs. The g-fee consists of the following components:

$$Guarantee\ fee = Capital\ charge + Administrative\ cost \\ + Expected\ losses + Reinsurance\ fee$$

The specifications for the capital charge and the reinsurance fee are as follows:

$$Capital\ charge = (Capital\ ratio\ {}^* (Expected\ return - After\text{-}tax\ interest \\ income\ on\ capital)/(1 - Tax\ rate)$$

$$Reinsurance\ fee = (Expected\ tail\ loss - Expected\ loss - Capital) \\ /(Total\ notional\ {}^* years)$$

Prior to the Housing and Economic Recovery Act of 2008, the GSEs were subject to a regulatory regime completely separate from depository institutions. They were required to hold capital against off–balance sheet assets sufficient to meet an idiosyncratic minimum leverage ratio of 45 basis points.[26] To translate this into a bank-like Basel-based capital ratio, we assume a Basel I risk weighting of 50 percent for the credit risk of prime residential mortgage loans. This represents the "floor" on Basel III risk weights for U.S. banks and so is a useful comparator for the capital cost to originators of holding mortgages on their own balance sheets rather than securitizing them.[27] Applying this risk weighting to a balance sheet composed entirely of mortgage assets, the minimum leverage requirement for the GSEs of 45 basis points would correspond to an effective capital ratio of only 0.9 percent.[28]

Like other commentators, we believe recent history has proved that this level was insufficient, and therefore we use a higher capital ratio as a starting point.

A. Required Capital Ratios

Below we walk through the details of the capital calculations and discuss the sensitivity of the derived g-fee to assumptions about capital, losses, and other variables. We assume a required capital ratio of 3 percent as a base case, and later consider the impact of higher capital standards on g-fees. At the 3 percent capital ratio level, the GSE's $4.4 trillion book of business would have required $132 billion of capital for credit losses, which contrasts sharply with the mere $20 billion of capital required under the previous GSE regime.

The level of cumulative defaults for a vintage that would exhaust the utility's loss absorption capital and trigger the government reinsurance depends on the average loss severity. Assuming a 40 percent loss severity,[29] an effective capital ratio of 3 percent would imply a government tail insurance trigger at a 7.5 percent cumulative default rate for a vintage. Turning again to Figure 2.1, if vintages were defined by calendar year, the 2006 and 2007 vintages would have triggered the government reinsurance, but not the 2005 or the 2008 vintages.[30]

The 2006 and 2007 vintages of GSE-guaranteed mortgage loans reflected a significant deterioration in underwriting standards, but because their cumulative default rates have exceeded the 7.5 percent threshold by several percentage points, it is possible that higher-quality vintages would also have breached this trigger—albeit somewhat later—if they went through the recent housing price cycle. Although we anticipate that proper governance and pricing could prevent or reduce deterioration in underwriting, this is far from guaranteed.[31] The larger point is that this 3 percent attachment point is conservative in that it would make triggering the government reinsurance relatively unlikely.

B. Other Assumptions

We assume that the fee would continue to be collected as a spread on mortgage rates and would be used to fund operating expenses, expected losses, and a required return on capital for the owners of the mortgage securitizer-insurer.

Given the conservative underwriting standards mentioned above, we assume expected credit losses of 10 basis points per year, although given the historical performance of prime conforming mortgages that the GSEs traditionally guaranteed, the expected loss rate could actually be lower.[32] In addition, we assume administrative costs of 10 basis points per year, a 35 percent tax rate, and a 2 percent after-tax interest income on capital reserves.

In our base case, we also assume a 10 percent return on the utility's equity capital and a tail event that is expected to occur every thirty years. For guidance on an appropriate expected return on equity capital (in terms of earnings, not interest income), we looked at several industries. Although the historical average return on equity for financial companies in the S&P 500 that have stayed in business over 1993–2011 has been 15 percent, calculations by Damodaran (n.d.) indicate that insurance companies and physical utilities (i.e., for power and water) tend to provide returns in the range of 4 to 12 percent.[33] In their model for catastrophe insurance, Harrington and Niehaus (2003) have also used 10 percent as a hurdle rate.[34] However, some financial mutuals have historically provided returns well below 10 percent,[35] and financial market utilities have occasionally operated on a profitless, breakeven basis.

Indeed, in the following section, we argue that members of a mutualized securitization utility may have reason to accept lower returns on their paid-in capital if they view the utility as a mechanism for lowering funding costs and increasing the volume of origination fees rather than a profit center in its own right. Furthermore, calculations for utilities' returns are sometimes based on the much smaller members' equity capital, not the entire loss absorption capacity of the firm. In the calculations below, the assumed returns are calculated as the return on the entire loss-absorption capital base. In light of the comparative evidence, it seems likely that a mortgage securitization utility would not need to provide 15 percent return on equity capital, but it is prudent to assume it would need to earn more than other types of cooperatively owned financial utilities.

C. Access to Government Tail Insurance

In Table 2.1, we calculate the g-fee for several scenarios, changing assumptions regarding the presence of priced government reinsurance, the capital requirement, the return on equity, and the frequency of tail events (later, we provide sensitivity analyses for several variables, then explore risk syndication

Table 2.1. Scenario Analysis

	Assumptions				
	No Reinsurance	*3% Capital*	*4% Capital*	*15% ROE*	*50 Years*
Total loss in tail event	6%	**6%**	6%	6%	6%
Required private capital	6%	**3%**	4%	3%	3%
Expected return on capital	10%	**10%**	10%	15%	10%
Period between tail events	30 years	**30 years**	30 years	30 years	50 years
After-tax interest income			2%		
Tax rate			35%		

	Fee Breakdown (basis points/year)				
	No Reinsurance	*3% Capital*	*4% Capital*	*15% ROE*	*50 Years*
Expected losses	10				
Administrative cost	10				
Reinsurance fee	0	**10**	6	10	6
Net income	75	**37**	50	60	37
Guarantee fee	**94**	**67**	**76**	**90**	**63**

via junior bond issuance). In each of these cases, we assume that in a tail event the expected loss for a vintage is 6 percent—twice the loss level that triggers the government reinsurance—and that this occurs at regular intervals specified in the model. Assuming a loss given default of 40 percent, a 6 percent expected tail loss implies a 15 percent cumulative default ratio, which is above the approximately 14 percent cumulative default ratio that Fannie Mae's 2007 vintage has reached so far. These are very conservative assumptions, especially as we are also assuming substantially higher-quality underwriting than Fannie Mae's 2007 vintage.

Among other things, this conservatism is meant to address the concern that the risk-neutral fair value of government-provided reinsurance could be much higher than the expected tail-event loss, because the reinsurance is paid out in the worst states of the world. As noted above, we would argue that the risk premium faced by strong-credit sovereigns is lower than that of private firms, particularly in times of market stress. Nevertheless, our use across scenarios of a single high-stress tail-event loss assumption is meant to account for this discrepancy between the reinsurance's risk-neutral expected value and its actual (or assumed) fair value. That is, we implicitly build in a risk premium in setting the reinsurance fee by assuming that if cumulative losses exceed 3 percent, they will always reach 6 percent cumulative loss rather than an expected cumulative loss, which is likely to be lower than 6 percent.

In a fully privatized structure, the utility would be required to hold capital sufficient to absorb entirely on its own the full 6 percent expected tail-scenario losses for any vintage. This is consistent with a pledge by the government never to intervene. With these assumptions, we estimate that the total g-fee would then need to be 94 basis points. This is at least four to five times the size of the pre-conservatorship g-fee charged by the GSEs.

In the next scenario, the utility has access to government reinsurance. In that case, the government absorbs any losses on a specific vintage beyond the utility's required 3 percent capital and receives a fee as compensation. In our base case, the fee is calculated to compensate the government for absorbing the residual 300 basis points of losses in the expected tail-event loss of 6 percent occurring over our thirty-year horizon, and our model produces a g-fee of 67 basis points. Even though the government would be expected to pay out on this reinsurance only rarely, the government backstop reduces the annual g-fee for mortgages by almost 29 percent. This reflects the efficiency gain from moving from private to public provision of the tail insurance.

The access to government reinsurance significantly lowers the overall g-fee because the reinsurance fee paid to the government as compensation for tail-event losses is only assumed to break even over the entire credit cycle, and its losses need not be covered up front (in contrast, the owners of a private firm pay in capital up front, although subsequently this initial private capital may be supplemented by retained earnings).[36] The baseline pricing without and with government tail-risk reinsurance is summarized below. Note that the reinsurance fee only varies with assumptions that affect the government's risk exposure: the tail-event loss rate, the tail-event frequency, and the level of private capital. Note also that if the utility securitized more risky, nonstandardized mortgage products—for example, mortgages with a low down payment—higher g-fees would result from both a higher required capital ratio and a higher tail-loss assumption.

As Table 2.1 demonstrates, the implied g-fee is a linear function of most of the variables. For example, if the expected loss rate on a vintage increases from 10 to 15 basis points due to weaker economic fundamentals, the g-fee would increase by 5 basis points.[37] Consequently, forecasted cyclical fluctuations in credit risk would be fully priced. Because this repricing would be done by the private-sector participants and not by the government (although changes to the g-fee, particularly reductions, would require regulatory approval, as discussed below), credit risk should not be shifted to the government guarantee—in contrast to a concern raised by Frame, Hancock, and Passmore (2012).

D. Junior Bonds: Outside Capital and Market Discipline

A number of proposals and commentators have called for more private capital to stand in front of any government reinsurance of mortgage risk. In the utility described above, private capital comes from borrowers through down payments, from lenders and originators through paid-in capital, and from the utility's retained earnings (i.e., accumulated g-fees). However, as the FHFA and many commentators have noted, there may be several advantages to attracting supplemental sources of private capital and providing a variety of structures for sharing credit risk in the new system.

One way to do this within the proposed utility would be to allow for the sale of junior bonds with direct credit risk exposure to specific vintages securitized by the utility and subordinated to the utility's equity capital. Such junior bonds could allow for diversification of credit risk to investors beyond the utility, reducing the concentration of risk. If junior bonds attracted investors who would otherwise not be willing to invest in mortgage risk indirectly (i.e., by investing in the lenders themselves), then these bonds could replace a portion of the private capital, thus broadening the capital base available for mortgage credit and potentially reducing the cost of mortgage credit. In addition, sales of junior bonds to a broader marketplace could provide both the utility and its regulator with a market assessment of the credit risk in each vintage.

However, if not structured properly, there are also potential disadvantages to diversifying the utility's capital structure. We review four potential pitfalls and then explain how junior bonds can be designed to mitigate them.

First, it is important not to rely on facile assertions about market discipline. A major problem in private-label mortgage securitization prior to the crisis was the spectacular failure of credit investors to impose market discipline on issuers.[38] Many private mortgage securitizations relied on bond structures whose sole purpose was to achieve particular credit ratings (often related to risk weightings for regulatory capital standards). These targeted credit ratings were typically investment grade—high enough that many investors felt overconfident that their credit risk exposure was low.[39] Such investors relied excessively on the ratings agencies' opinions rather than conducting independent due diligence on the credit risk. Investment patterns in risky bonds—both structured credit bonds and corporate bonds— suggest that investors who conduct appropriate due diligence are those who invest in instruments with expected losses, loss distributions, and yields consistent with speculative or "high-yield" credit ratings.

In addition, because investment in risky bonds tends to be highly procyclical, an overreliance on junior bonds as a source of credit protection could reduce the utility's robustness during a market downturn. Although there is an inherent cyclicality to the lender community's behavior as well, during a period of tight credit availability, lenders will likely be willing to undertake some lending for securitization (at a price), whereas many credit investors may withdraw from the housing sector altogether, just as we have seen in recent years.

A third concern is that excess leverage and insufficient diversification of capital sources could exacerbate procyclicality. Junior bonds could be used by levered mortgage-lending or -insuring institutions to increase their earnings by "doubling down" on their exposure to credit risks. Not only would this fail to diversify sources of mortgage funding, but it could increase aggregate leverage in the mortgage system. Leverage and concentration risks are particular concerns if the credit risk is distributed through insurance or derivatives, because these mechanisms would add additional long-term counterparty risks and are likely to be particularly attractive instruments to levered financial institutions that may already hold significant amounts of mortgage credit risk. Importantly, in a housing downturn, the ability of insurance and derivatives counterparties to perform on their obligations and provide loss absorption capacity is likely to be impaired.

Finally, it is important to bear in mind that syndicating risk through the capital markets has implications for the incentive alignment in the securitization chain. The more credit risk that is sold into the market, the less "skin in the game" retained by the utility. At some point, increasing the issuance of junior bonds could erode incentives for robust underwriting. This would increase the risk to the government, even with the same attachment point for the tail reinsurance.

These risks imply at least four design features for junior bonds. First, if market discipline is an important goal for the junior bonds, then they need to be sufficiently risky—preferably speculative-grade or high-yield bonds— such that investors with the appropriate skill sets will have the incentive to conduct independent due diligence on the credit risk in the bonds. If we continue to assume relatively conservative underwriting standards, then the notional size of the speculative-grade junior bond would be relatively small, or the underlying pool's few credit losses would not be able to generate a loss rate high enough to incent rigorous credit evaluation.

Small-scale syndication of risky bonds would have two additional benefits. Ensuring that the junior bonds bear sufficient risk is a mechanism for diversifying demand away from the regulated, levered financial firms that may already have substantial exposure to the residential mortgage credit risk. Also, reducing the system's reliance on syndications could reduce the overall cyclicality of the system, given the cyclical nature of credit bond investing. The utility should not be expected to sell off junior bonds at all points in the credit cycle.

Second, in order to preserve incentives to robustly monitor and enforce its securitization credit standards, the utility should be required to retain significant credit risk in the underlying pools it securitizes. This is important to address the incentive alignment issues. As noted above, completely separating those who hold credit risk from those who set the credit risk standards can lead to a breakdown in incentives to monitor and control risk. This is what occurred in the private-label securitization market in the mid-2000s and to some forms of subprime lending during prior housing cycles. The addition of government reinsurance makes it particularly important to align incentives across the private-sector participants in securitization, because the government will bear the risk of failure by the private sector to appropriately manage and monitor credit risk. In addition, if the utility is allowed to sell off investment-grade junior bonds, even greater risk retention by the utility is called for as investor discipline is likely to be weaker.

Third, to address the concerns about leverage and counterparty risks, any external capital raised by the utility to support mortgage credit risk should come in the form of cash paid up front. The utility should be prohibited from selling off credit risk to the private sector in the form of either insurance or derivatives.

Finally, the fourth consideration for junior bonds concerns structure and issuance patterns. If the utility and its regulator wish to use junior bond pricing as an independent market assessment of credit risk, then the bonds need to be structured in a way that promotes market liquidity and transparency in pricing by relying on actual transactions, not just indicative marks by dealers. Because high-risk credit products are typically not liquid instruments, the utility's junior bonds should be highly standardized and with relatively simple structures. Moreover, fixed-income products generally tend to have highest liquidity and price transparency immediately after they are issued. Market discipline will therefore be larger if the utility issues such bonds at regular intervals (assuming that demand for risky bonds exists).[40]

As long as the junior bond provides a high yield or comprises a small fraction of the overall capital structure, its impact on the pricing of the g-fee would be limited. The speculative-grade yields required to induce true market discipline would probably be only modestly lower than the utility's expected return on equity—for example, 8 percent compared to 10 percent.[41] In that case, even issuing as much par value of junior bonds as to cover a full 1 percent of a vintage's outstanding notional would result in limited reduction of the g-fee. Issuing a more senior investment grade risk-bearing bond, as Fannie Mae and Freddie Mac have done in recent years, would lower the g-fee more, but it would provide less market discipline than the riskier bond, still contribute to procyclicality, and further erode the alignment of the utility's incentives for effective risk management and sound underwriting.

IV. Ownership and Governance

If the government provides a backstop to mortgage credit to address systemic crises of sufficient magnitude, then the future institutional arrangements must reduce both the likelihood and the consequences of intervention. This includes not just the capital structure and price but also the utility's governance, to address the incentive alignment problems laid out in the first section of this chapter and thereby reduce the deterioration in underwriting that leads to tail events. Prevention therefore requires a careful analysis of the incentive structure embedded in the institutional framework.

A cooperative or mutualized ownership structure is one way of addressing the incentive misalignments inherent in both government insurance and securitization itself. The misalignments arising from government reinsurance are classic "moral hazard" externalities, where government interventions shield private citizens from the full impact of their actions, such as in deposit insurance, pension benefit insurance, flood insurance, terrorism insurance, and bailouts of "too big to fail" financial institutions.[42] The misalignments in all types of securitization consist of a series of conflicts of interest generated by the parceling out of the various steps of the lending process, as documented by Ashcraft and Schuermann (2008) and Adrian and Ashcraft (2012).

The solution in both types of misalignments involves improved regulation, but it should not rely solely on regulation. Any external regulatory regime, no matter how well designed and implemented, faces daunting challenges in terms of both technical difficulty and political vulnerability. Therefore, the risk-bearing institutions themselves should be redesigned to have incentives for better risk management. One institutional feature that would align lenders' incentives with prudent underwriting is risk retention. Having the lenders mutually own the securitization utility would be consistent with this approach, vertically reintegrating the lending process and mitigating the conflicts of interest that are inherent across the chain of production in securitization. Note that this applies to both the origination process and the loss mitigation process, where the breakdown in securitization governance has arguably been even more severe.[43] However, the virtues of mutualization extend beyond the much-rehearsed arguments about risk retention. The literature on cooperatives suggests that a mortgage securitization utility would match both the theoretical criteria for the appropriateness of mutualization and the empirical characteristics of certain well-known financial cooperatives.

A. Cooperatives and Financial Market Utilities

Both cooperatives and mutuals have a long history among U.S. firms. Outside of the financial sector, cooperatives have been common in agriculture, housing, and utilities for physical infrastructure (such as electricity or water). Among financial institutions, savings mutuals, credit unions, thrifts, and mutual funds are all well represented. Most pertinent to our discussion, though, are clearinghouses and central counterparties. These are institutions through which other financial firms have advanced their shared private interests—as well as broader public ones—by providing the infrastructure that enables other, more narrowly private enterprise. Notable examples of current or former mutually owned utilities include clearing and settlement institutions such as the Chicago Mercantile Exchange, the London Clearing House, the Depository Trust & Clearing Corporation (DTCC), and the CLS Group (originally Continuous Linked Settlement). These financial market utilities (FMUs) centralize settlement and manage multilateral counterparty risk for transactions that are fundamental to the financial system, simultaneously reducing systemic risk—that is, risk to taxpayers—and enabling risk taking among nonsystemic private firms.[44]

A mortgage securitization utility would in some respects resemble other FMUs: it would provide a public good (a low-cost channel for mortgage funding) that has economies of scale. If structured as a cooperative, it could manage its risks through a mutualized loss pool funded by fees from its members. However, the nature of the goods provided and the risks incurred would differ from typical FMUs.

Most FMUs assume the credit or operational risk associated with clearing and settling trades, and the duration of these exposures often extends no more than a few days.[45] Securitization, of course, entails long-term exposures. Although a purely mechanical securitization platform that executes the pooling of loans and issuance of securities might entail exposures of just a few weeks or a few months, a mortgage security guarantor assumes risk exposures that last years. As such, a mortgage securitization utility would have a sui generis credit risk profile closer to that of a bank or financial guarantor, with the latter's monoline risk profile but the former's exposure to the majority portion of each loan.

B. Criteria for Cooperatives and Mutuals

Cooperative and mutual structures have not enjoyed a strong following in academic circles in recent decades, having been criticized as providing lower returns, less innovation, less efficient decision making, and more limited access to capital markets. Their standing in industry has declined as well: a number of financial institutions with mutual ownership have been demutualized, or transformed into shareholder corporations.[46]

However, Murphy (2012) has argued that in the unique context of a utility for mortgage securitization, many of these common criticisms of cooperatives and mutuals either would not apply or may actually be virtues. In particular, he notes that some critics have pointed to governance challenges in agricultural and workers' cooperatives in rural communities despite the fact that a mortgage securitization cooperative would differ in numerous important ways, perhaps most notably by drawing from a fundamentally different membership, one which would have crucial advantages in governance. Moreover, there is nothing in a mutualized structure that would prevent it from adopting the best practices of corporate America to address some of the criticisms, and Murphy provides a useful overview of some of these as well as some of the best practices specific to cooperatives, particularly with regard to their legal form.

Furthermore, a mortgage securitization utility seems to meet criteria laid out by Hansmann (1996 and 1999) for an effective cooperative. Hansmann argues that the entire range of organization types can be understood as expressing the same underlying principle about how to optimize a firm's efficiency. Hansmann articulates this principle as the minimization of the sum total of all transaction costs across the stakeholders in a firm's business activities, including both the aggregate costs of ownership itself (such as monitoring, risk bearing, and collective decision making) and the aggregate costs of market contracting (such as information asymmetries and market power relationships). Given the same underlying principles, differences in ownership are then attributable to differences in a firm's objectives, its business process, or its industry's market structure.

Hansmann notes that the design of ownership can reduce or eliminate the conflict of interest between buyer and seller—precisely one of the concerns policy makers have enunciated with respect to securitization and shadow banking (Hansmann 1999: 389, 391–92). More generally, Hansmann argues that cooperatives are most appropriate when the members satisfy the following criteria: they are a relatively homogenous group in close proximity and possess sufficient sophistication, frequency of transaction, and economic interest at stake to exert effective monitoring power over their cooperative; and they would otherwise be vulnerable to the exertion of market power by the institution if it were owned by outside third parties. A mortgage-insuring securitization utility would seem to satisfy most of these criteria, and for those that it does not, remedial mechanisms are readily available.

Certainly, lenders participating in the mortgage cooperative would be a relatively knowledgeable and sophisticated set of owners and would participate in frequent transactions that would comprise a large proportion of the owners' businesses. These two characteristics would facilitate monitoring and internal oversight of the cooperative, thus providing a forum for lenders to monitor one another's contributions. Effective monitoring would in turn reduce the risk that mutualization would give rise to free riders—a risk due to the costs of risk taking being diffused across individual members of the cooperative. Here the literature on cooperatives agrees with the literature on industrial organization, which finds that repeated interaction and mutual observation increase the likelihood of long-term cooperation among firms.[47]

Note that in these respects, participants in a mortgage securitization resemble the participants in other common cooperatives, such as housing, where the owners' detailed knowledge and frequent observation of the operations facilitates monitoring. At the same time, the greater managerial sophistication of mortgage-lending firms would provide an added advantage in monitoring commensurate with what would clearly be a more complex business model. Unlike many other financial mutuals, such as savings mutuals—which are among those that have been held up as examples of less efficient governance[48]—mortgage lenders would be both expert and actively engaged in the securitization utility's business because they would supply its raw materials of residential mortgage loans. They would also have powerful incentives to see the cooperative run well, due to the crucial service and large business exposure it would provide by lowering capital costs and helping them generate their origination fees.[49] Lenders, both large and small, participating in the mortgage cooperative would be a relatively homogenous group with respect to their interests in two objectives: maintaining access to a common low-cost funding channel and avoiding exploitation by monopolistic or oligopolistic securitizers and credit enhancers. This homogeneity is important primarily because it would reduce the challenges of collective decision making, which some commentators have considered one of the primary weaknesses of cooperatives.[50] Larger members' interests may diverge from smaller members to the extent that their greater use of the cooperative would leave them with more capital at risk and likely provide them with more voting rights. This raises important questions about governance, which we will discuss below, but it does not change the shared interest of lenders of numerous types. In this sense, the monoline nature of the securitization utility supports its mutualization.

C. Mutualizing Mortgage Securitization

In addition to these traditional criteria for cooperatives, there are a number of other ways mutualization may be particularly well suited to the peculiarities of a mortgage securitization utility and to address common perceptions of what went wrong in the previous institutional arrangement. A broader point is that cooperative and mutual structures provide a *different set of trade-offs* relative to a shareholder-owned corporation, and it is critical to evaluate those trade-offs in the context of the utility's mission.

For instance, some studies note that the historically lower rate of return provided by cooperatives relative to shareholder corporations indicates weaknesses in governance.[51] However, as Murphy (2012) notes, there is a trade-off here in that cooperatives also tend to take less risk and as a consequence fail less frequently. The reason is simple: by diffusing the profits across members, cooperatives also diffuse the returns to risk taking.[52] In fact, this dynamic highlights a fundamental difference between the incentives faced by shareholder corporations and cooperatives. Third-party shareholders invest in a company primarily to obtain a rate of return or diversify the risk profile of their investment portfolios, whereas the members of a cooperative may have other goals in addition to or instead of using the mutual as a profit center unto itself.

For instance, a cooperative may be seen as a service provider for its members, helping them to gain access to higher-quality or lower-cost products or services that they then use as inputs to their more explicitly revenue-generating business lines.[53] In the case of mortgage securitization, the service provided to members consists of access to the low-cost funding channel of securitization markets, particularly via the TBA market, and lower capital costs associated with holding mortgage-related assets. The return to the members may take the form of efficiency gains from stable funding and cost minimization, rather than dividends, capital appreciation, or the expansion of products and market share. Given these supplementary value propositions, the modest historical returns on equity cited in the previous section may overestimate the return on equity lenders would require to participate in such a cooperative structure. And as noted in a previous section, the mortgage utility's return on equity is among the most important variables for determining g-fees and thus the primary mortgage rate.

In fact, critical infrastructure can benefit from the conservative approach of a cooperative. In many cases, infrastructure-providing utilities of various types provide modest but steady returns. If the securitization utility maintains relatively conservative underwriting standards, both the risk it assumes and the return demanded by its investors will be moderated—and lower mortgage rates should result.

However, innovation, expansion, and risk taking would not be among the mortgage utility's primary goals and would, in fact, stand in tension with the objective of providing a specific service or critical infrastructure (Holmstrom 1999: 411–14). Although innovation may remain a vital activity in this market, the point is that it should occur outside of the central infrastructure, which should take on new duties only after careful deliberation.[54] For an FMU, financial stability—the ability to avoid failure—is more crucial than the ability to innovate, especially where the product offering is mature.

Indeed, an overemphasis on profit making and innovation likely contributed to the GSEs' excessive size, risk, and ultimately their failure. Many analysts have reached the conclusion that one of the most significant factors contributing to the GSEs' failure was their decision to guarantee lower-quality mortgages in 2005–2007 in a bid to regain market share that they had lost to the private-label securitization market.[55] Many have likewise suggested that the broader proliferation of mortgage loan types and mortgage-related securities in the 2004–2007 period constituted a socially inefficient substitution of product differentiation for price competition. [56] In the long run, placing less emphasis on the introduction of new mortgage products through a government-reinsured entity could be an advantage of a cooperative structure.

The members of a lender-owned cooperative would most likely see aggressive innovation in securitizing new mortgage products as cannibalizing their own proprietary business lines conducted outside the cooperative. Although the cooperative would remit the profits to its owners, that diffuses the profits (as well as the control of the product line), reducing a member's ability to gain competitive advantage. Thus, cooperative owners would be significantly less likely than outside shareholders to encourage expansion of business lines. Instead, the owners would likely seek to keep this cooperative focused on a narrow mission of providing securitization services for standardized mortgage products. Innovation could occur outside the cooperative and over time lead to a lagged adoption within the cooperative.

Note that having a common purpose with a relatively narrow scope is one form of the homogeneity that appears to be crucial to the success of a cooperative or a mutual. Innovation tends to expose divergences in the interests of members of a cooperative and make governance more difficult.[57] Maintaining focus on a narrow mission of efficiently providing a specific service, rather than aggressive profit growth, would also yield several benefits from a public policy perspective. First, it would be consistent with prioritizing financial stability over innovation at a funding utility. Second, it would allow for more accurate modeling and pricing of the government reinsurance on vintages. Finally, it would also facilitate the effective oversight and monitoring of the cooperative by both the owners and regulatory authorities.[58]

D. Access and Market Structure

Some commentators have raised concerns about the risk of a few large lenders dominating a cooperative and controlling access to the TBA market, which some consider to be prima facie grounds for rejecting a cooperative structure.[59] The risk of the larger lenders using the cooperative to amplify their market power could put both smaller lenders and consumers at a disadvantage.

However, though a cooperative might reflect preexisting market concentration among mortgage lenders, it would not necessarily exacerbate them. As long as there is robust competition among the largest, most influential members of the cooperative, they will have strong incentives to monitor one another. Nevertheless, both governance structure and the regulatory structure should be set to minimize collusion among the larger members. As Murphy (2012) and Hansmann (1999) explain, there are several best practices in standard corporate governance that could be readily adapted for a mortgage cooperative. The objective of these practices would be to facilitate not only fair and open access but broad participation in the cooperative, including by smaller lenders. With such practices in place, the potential market power derived from control over a major funding channel would arguably be better distributed across even an imperfectly competitive landscape than the previous duopoly. Indeed, diffusing such market power is what Hansmann means by lowering the aggregate costs of contracting and reducing economic actors' vulnerability to market power.

The most intuitive guiding principle would be to keep barriers to entry low. For example, policies regarding volume-based discounts on g-fees could be set to encourage small lender participation.[60] For a cooperative, this principle could also apply to the membership fees (i.e., the paid-in capital). In practice, both smaller lenders and the cooperative itself may prefer for smaller lenders to pass their mortgages to the cooperative via correspondent relationships with larger, aggregator banks, for several reasons (operational/ logistical, relationship management, etc.). That is, the larger banks would buy the loans from the smaller lenders before selling them on to the cooperative.

To supplement the external force of regulation, structural incentives could also be incorporated in the institutional design. The literature on industrial organization indicates that, in order to obtain good pricing on these correspondent transactions, smaller lenders could exercise influence in the utility either by direct participation and voting or by leaving the cooperative and using an outside funding mechanisms. [61] Note that homogeneity of membership is important for the cooperative to lower the costs of collective decision making and therefore voting.

What would be the smaller lenders' outside option? Multiple utilities could be established, potentially even individually designed to accommodate different segments of lenders. Alternatively, smaller lenders might establish a conduit of their own or obtain funding from an existing institution where they already enjoy influence, such as the Federal Home Loan Bank System (FHLBs).[62] In designing the remedy, two of the key questions are precisely how much larger and smaller lenders' interests are aligned with respect to a utility for mortgage securitization and insurance, and how the relative costs of voice and exit for each of these sets of institutions may shift over time.[63]

Aside from price regulation and sound outside options, there are a number of other mechanisms that can increase the responsiveness of cooperatives to the full breadth of their membership. One is a federated structure or multilevel mutualization, with governance mutualized among specific classes of constituents. [64] This may be particularly useful in light of the challenges presented by a large number of members, which can lead to the coordination difficulties some critics of cooperatives have attributed to diffuse ownership.[65]

In addition, to strengthen the bargaining position of smaller institutions, board structure, regulatory remedies, and voting structures such as cumulative voting could be employed.[66] Other alternatives include reserving seats on the cooperative's board of directors as well as its membership and risk committees, such that smaller members could ensure that their views on access are incorporated and that risk management is not used as an oblique way of limiting their access.

Finally, membership stakes may be monitored and updated. Some retained earnings may be earmarked for individual members before the periods in which they are distributed as dividends. Because they reflect previous years' activity, over time these capital accounts may diverge from current patterns of usage if dividends are not distributed frequently enough. This would be a particularly acute concern if members' voting rights were linked to their capital accounts.[67]

E. Market Access and TBA Trading

As we noted in our earlier paper, scale economies in securitization of standardized products and scale economies in banking suggest the proposed securitization utility may be a natural monopoly.[68] Moreover, access to the TBA market where liquidity, fungibility, and homogeneity of securities is paramount would be the primary attraction for lenders to participate in a mortgage securitization cooperative.[69] Both imply the optimal number of utilities is likely to be quite small.

Some commentators have raised concerns about the risk of a limited number of large mortgage securitization utilities being too big to fail.[70] However, nearly all types of financial market infrastructures—including the clearing and settlement utilities noted earlier—are highly concentrated, with exceptionally large market shares.[71] The large size and concentrated market share of FMUs—including the structure proposed in this chapter—reflect large economies of scale or "natural monopolies" in their industries. In addition, for the securitization utility proposed here, the vintage structure for managing credit risk and for the provision of explicit government tail risk insurance is designed to address the too-big-to-fail concern by ensuring that the cooperative is still viable even when the tail insurance triggers.

There are also drawbacks to the alternative of having a large number of mortgage security issuers. As noted earlier, a large number of securitization issuers would encourage product differentiation and likely fragment the TBA market, reducing the liquidity benefit in secondary MBS trading, and thus raise primary mortgage rates. [72] Not only would fewer utilities reduce the risk of such fragmentation, but they would have incentives to create larger and more diversified pools of mortgages across regions and across lenders. This would likely reduce the degree of adverse selection in the current TBA market, enhance liquidity, and potentially reduce mortgage costs to households.

Also, as we argued in Section I of this chapter, a large number of national mortgage security issuers would be unlikely to reduce systemic risk or protect the taxpayer, because the correlations of their financial conditions would likely be very high for a systemic event that triggered the government-backed reinsurance. All of the mortgage security issuers would have similar risk profiles. In short, there would be few if any systemic risk benefits to a large number of similar monoline securitization firms, whereas there might be a cost to borrowers in the form of higher primary mortgage rates.

F. Mutualizing Credit Risk: Capital Versus Representations and Warranties

Mortgage securitization entails a system of repeated transfers of credit risk over extended periods of time. Although mutualization provides members with incentives to enforce a set of credit standards, it also runs the risk of free rider problems. One solution to mitigate this risk is to limit the degree of mutualization through the use of representations and warranties, such that members are forced to internalize more of the consequences of their behavior. Member-specific reserve accounts are a possible solution, although those could pose a challenge for true-sale accounting, which is needed to make securitization viable.

G. Oversight by Boards

One of the fundamental governance questions regarding this regime is how to structure the board of directors and its committees. Drawing on best practices in corporate governance as laid out by several industry groups, Murphy (2012) has several recommendations for the board of directors that would help ensure that the interests of smaller lender-members would be effectively represented.[73] These include a requirement that the chairman and at least one-third of the cooperative board members be independent (in the sense that they are not employed by any of the lender-member-owners) as well as that an independent board member hold the swing vote on the committee for selecting new board members. As an empirical matter, cooperatives frequently require that a majority of their board members be drawn from institutions that are members of the cooperative, apparently to reduce principal-agent problems. Cooperatives also frequently prohibit or limit participation on the board by the cooperative's managers—which differs markedly from shareholder-owned firms. Members could also be given the ability to remove appointed board members.

V. Conclusion

In this chapter, we have explored in detail the capital structure and governance model of a financial market utility for mortgage securitization and how it interacts with the question of government reinsurance for systemic risk. We have argued that the government is ineluctably exposed to the full depth of true tail losses, and there are only four ways to improve its risk profile: (1) charge a price for bearing that risk; (2) attract and maintain the participation of private capital in sharing risk; (3) establish a clear mechanism for reducing government involvement following intervention; and (4) prevent tail events by addressing the conflicts of interest inherent in government reinsurance and in securitization itself. These constraints have led us to explore the unique features of a vintage-based guarantee and a mortgage securitization utility that would itself have a unique function. A vintage-based capital structure could mitigate the procyclicality of mortgage credit, providing greater clarity about the timing and terms of intervention than institution-level reinsurance and thereby giving investors and issuers robust incentives to continue participating in the utility. In addition, vintages would also help focus the government reinsurance more narrowly on truly systemic risk than a security-based attachment point would.

To frame the question of capitalization, we presented several examples to analyze the relationships among g-fees and various key assumptions. We demonstrated how selling off an appropriately risky junior bond to the capital markets would have only a modest impact on the g-fee, and how the informational and market discipline value of these transactions may vary with the level of risk transfer. In contrast, in exploring the sensitivity of the g-fee to other key parameters, we found that the g-fee—and therefore the mortgage rate faced by consumers—is most sensitive to the required capital ratio and the expected return on equity capital. The importance of the return on equity underlines the importance of ownership structure: mutuals have lower risk and lower returns on equity. The system's source of capital goes hand in hand not only with its cost of capital but also with its incentive structure and the nature of the market discipline it engenders.

We have explored the appropriateness of a mutualized ownership structure to align the private incentives with the public interest, to employ more than just external regulation to address the incentive misalignments inherent in government reinsurance and in securitization itself. The vertical integration of the utility would help address the conflicts of interest along the chain of production (as well as loss mitigation) in securitization. As for moral hazard, if the government provides a backstop to mortgage credit on the downside of a systemic event, then the future institutional structure must both mitigate the consequences of intervention and decrease the likelihood (or frequency) of intervention. Thus, the utility's governance and regulation should be designed to align incentives and prevent deterioration in underwriting in advance.

We discuss a number of ways mutualization may be particularly well suited for the peculiarities of a mortgage securitization utility. Notably, such an institution meets some of the criteria for successful cooperatives as laid out in the academic literature. In addition, the weaker incentives for innovation found in cooperatives go hand in hand with a reduced tendency to take risk. Much as with a centralized counterparty or clearinghouse, low risk and less focus on innovation are actually virtues for this critical infrastructure. More practically speaking, cooperatives' reduced emphasis on earnings and market share seem to respond to many observers' diagnosis of what went wrong in the previous institutional arrangement. We suggest that a mutual utility, with incentive alignment and appropriate governance controls, could allow robust competition among lenders for mortgage origination, although a full assessment of the competitive dynamics in the market for mortgage lending is beyond the scope of this chapter.

We have explored how the governance structure for the cooperative could be designed to address the typical concerns raised in the literature. Though certainly not riskless, our proposed utility structure is less risky than most alternatives. The economics of housing finance are sufficiently complex that there may be no ideal model. Indeed, in several cases, key objectives for the system, such as market discipline and systemic robustness, stand in tension with each other.

GSE reform is likely a question of identifying the most workable, not the first-best, design—even on the economic merits—before considering the notoriously challenging political dimensions. If that's so, policy makers will have to weigh the benefits and risks associated with each proposed model and focus on their preferred trade-offs. We hope that our diagnosis of the most urgent policy risks and our formulation of potential remedies will stimulate and inform precisely such reflection and debate.

CHAPTER 3

Macroprudential Mortgage-Backed Securitization: Can It Work?

Diana Hancock and Wayne Passmore

I. Introduction

In early 2011, the Obama administration indicated that the government's primary role in the U.S. housing finance market "should be limited to robust oversight and consumer protection, targeted assistance for low- and moderate-income homeowners and renters, and carefully designed support for market stability and crisis response" (U.S. Department of Treasury and U.S. Department of Housing and Urban Development 2011). In its housing finance white paper, the Obama administration put forth three options for long-term reform.

Under the first option, the government's role in insuring or guaranteeing mortgages would be dramatically reduced by limiting it to the Federal Housing Administration (FHA) and other programs targeted to creditworthy lower- and moderate-income borrowers.[1] Although the government would continue to provide access for this targeted segment of borrowers, it would leave the vast majority of the mortgage market to the private sector (e.g., mortgages financed using balance-sheet funding by originators or mortgage pools financed using private-label securitization).

Under the second option, the government would also provide a guarantee mechanism that would normally have a minimal presence but would stand ready to scale up to a larger share of the mortgage market as private capital withdraws in times of financial stress (see also Scharfstein and

Sunderam 2011). To implement this backstop government guarantee mechanism, the guarantee fee for securitizations could be set at a sufficiently high level that it would only be competitive in the absence of private capital, or alternatively there could potentially be a restriction on the amount of public insurance that would be sold to the private market in normal conditions that could be relaxed to stabilize the mortgage market in times of stress.

Under the third option, the government would add to the first option the provision of catastrophic reinsurance for a targeted range of eligible mortgages, with the private capital taking the primary credit risk (see Hancock and Passmore 2011a). This catastrophic reinsurance for securitizations would be provided by the government for an explicit guarantee fee. To implement either a government-provided backstop guarantee mechanism (option 2) or government-provided catastrophic reinsurance for securitizations (option 3), what we classify as "hybrid securitizations," it would be necessary to determine the guarantee fee (g-fee) used for access to a full faith and credit guarantee by the government, as well as the amount of private capital that would take the primary (first-loss) credit risk during normal conditions and during periods when the mortgage market is stressed. The Obama administration was silent on the appropriate g-fee and private capitalization levels that are necessary to implement a hybrid securitization system with macroprudential features, a gap we seek to address.

Before previewing our results, it is useful to consider recent legislative efforts to implement the three options described above.[2] Several bills to reform the U.S. housing finance system have been put forth by legislators in both the House of Representatives and the Senate. The bill most consistent with the first option, which narrowly delimits the government's role, is the Protecting American Taxpayers and Homeowners (PATH) Act. This act would redefine the mission of the FHA and would establish a nongovernmental, not-for-profit National Mortgage Market Utility to develop "best practice" standards for the private origination, servicing, pooling and securitizing of mortgages.[3] This utility would also operate a publicly accessible securitization outlet to match loan originators with investors and serve as a repository for mortgage data. Proponents of this act argue that no government backstop is needed for securitizations because liquidity in the secondary market for mortgages would result from uniform standards, public disclosures and transparency. Opponents argue this approach would leave the government with too few tools to ensure sufficient mortgage credit availability in a severe housing downturn.

The housing reform bill introduced by Senate Banking Chairman Tim Johnson and Senator Mike Crapo during the last Congress would have implemented a hybrid securitization system.[4] Under this bill, a federal mortgage insurer would provide a government backstop for eligible mortgage pools that have secured a private first-loss piece equal to 10 percent, through approved risk-sharing mechanisms (e.g., senior-subordinated structures or credit-linked notes). This 10 percent first-loss position, however, could be reduced in periods of exigent circumstances. Issuers of government-backed MBS would pay a g-fee for catastrophic insurance on the eligible mortgage pools consisting of mortgages with an 80 percent loan-to-value ratio (using either a homeowner's down payment or some form of credit enhancement) and a minimum down payment of 3.5 percent for first-time homebuyers or a minimum down payment of 5 percent for other homebuyers. Depending on how the g-fee is priced, the design of this hybrid securitization system could range from a crisis-driven government backstop (option 2 above) to the facilitation of government-backed securitization during normal conditions (option 3 above). Proponents of this bill argue that government support can help promote financial stability by ensuring the flow of credit through periods of economic stress; opponents argue that any time the government stands behind a loan, it takes on some degree of risk, a risk that is difficult for the government to price.

Although these options for GSE reform are debated, private-sector securitization of mortgages has virtually disappeared since the onset of the financial crisis, and private-sector securitization of conforming mortgages has always been small proportionally relative to securitization of conforming mortgages by the government. Figure 3.1 describes the recent evolution of the U.S. conforming mortgage market (i.e., the market for mortgages that are eligible for GSE purchase and that are not FHA loans). As shown in the upper left panel, there are generally between $1 trillion and $2 trillion of conforming mortgages originated each year. In the upper right panel, the dollar amount of MBS issuance by Fannie Mae and Freddie Mac is similar in magnitude to conforming originations since 2008. Almost all conforming mortgages have been purchased and securitized by the GSEs since 2001 (lower left panel). Moreover, Fannie Mae and Freddie Mac currently securitize over 60 percent of all mortgages origi-

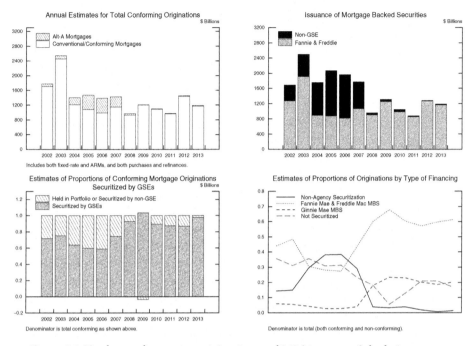

Figure 3.1. Total annual mortgage originations and MBS issuance. Calculations based on Inside Mortgage Finance (2014a, 2014c).

nated (lower right panel). In recent years, the remainder are securitized by Ginnie Mae (FHA mortgages) or held in banks' portfolios (at about 20 percent each).

II. Our Analysis of Hybrid Securitization

In this study, we consider the following three questions about a hybrid securitization system under options 2 and 3 from a financial stability perspective:

1. How does the government set a guarantee fee (i.e., g-fee) where the private sector bears some losses but where the government provides a full faith and credit backstop (i.e., the government provides catastrophic reinsurance)?

2. How much mortgage credit risk would the private sector bear (i.e., how much private equity capital can be put at risk) before the government guarantee would kick in?
3. Under what conditions is hybrid securitization feasible?

In today's mortgage market, the answers to the above questions are as follows. First, the g-fee is set based on the views of policy makers about the appropriate role of government-sponsored enterprises, Fannie Mae and Freddie Mac, in the mortgage market and is not directly related to calculations of expected loss. Second, the private sector bears little or no risk with government securitizations, and the government bears almost all the credit risks associated with government-sponsored enterprises (GSEs) mortgage-backed securities (MBS). Finally, the current system is viable only with open-ended government assistance to Fannie Mae and Freddie Mac.

Hybrid securitization supposedly resolves these problems by inducing the private sector to participate in government-backed securitizations. With hybrid securitizations, the goal is to set g-fees and private first-loss capital positions to provide private-sector discipline in pricing and underwriting while meeting policy-maker macroprudential objectives. By macroprudential, we mean policies that are designed to make the macroeconomy more stable and that limit the need for government bailouts.

The second and third policy options described above invoke different approaches toward increasing macroeconomic stability. The second option envisions a government securitization program that is idle during boom times but active during a housing bust, when supposedly private securitization has ceased to function. This type of program increases macroeconomic stability because a securitization outlet for banks is still available during a financial crisis, thereby encouraging mortgage lending by banks when the private sector has withdrawn from the secondary markets. However, investors who participated in private securitization during the boom may suffer large losses, and the economy might falter from any spillover effects created by these losses.

The third option provides a government securitization outlet and catastrophic insurance through both booms and busts. In this case, investors in mortgage-backed securities are protected from catastrophic losses during the bust, limiting the spillover effects created by losses imposed on them. If the spillover effects from investor losses are large, then the third option might provide greater stability. If the spillover effects are small or if the government insurance program creates additional market distortions during the boom, then the second option might be preferred.

Of course, if market distortions created by either government securitization or insurance are large enough, then option 1 might dominate both options 2 and 3. We do not address this issue here, but the first-loss position held by private-sector participants has to be "large enough" to induce appropriate mortgage underwriting for home purchases.

Below, we use data collected over the recent U.S. residential real estate boom and bust to analyze outcomes had the government required the private sector to cover the losses associated with mortgage defaults in all but a catastrophic financial crisis. Our analysis demonstrates that a hybrid securitization system under option 2 would have been essentially unused during the real estate boom because the first-loss capital requirement would have made government-sponsored securitization uncompetitive relative to private-sector securitization during that period. With the insurance program unused, the government may be "on the hook" to bail out failing mortgage-related institutions.

As for option 3, the historical data from the previous cycle suggest the funding of the government insurance program will be too little. Again, the government may be "on the hook" to bail out failing mortgage-related institutions. Overall, if policy makers want to (1) retain the ubiquity of the thirty-year fixed-rate mortgage (FRM) in the United States, (2) insure all private-sector investors against catastrophic outcome and minimize spillover effects during a financial crisis, and (3) build a sufficiently large private-sector insurance fund to ensure that the government is only "on the hook" for mortgage losses when there is a catastrophic outcome, then the government may need to require that all mortgages, whether securitized privately or through a government-backed program, be insured against catastrophic risk.

III. Simulating Hybrid Securitization Over the Last Housing Boom and Bust

As outlined in the introduction, many policy makers would like to encourage a minimum amount of private capital to be available to absorb the first losses from mortgage defaults in any government-backed program of mortgage securitization. What is different with hybrid securitization relative to purely private securitization is that after the first losses from mortgage defaults are covered by private investors, the government backstop kicks in and covers mortgage default losses when such losses are catastrophic. Hybrid securitization is basically GSE securitization with a higher cost of funding because of the capital costs associated with the private-sector first-loss position and g-fees designed to build a fund to cover catastrophic default losses. But would GSE securitization be used with these design features in the presence of purely private securitization?

From the perspective of the investor holding a hybrid public–private security, the securitization is government backed. With hybrid securitization, the government sets two policy parameters: (1) the size of the "first-loss position" (which will define what is a catastrophe and what is not) and (2) the government g-fee.[5] Thus, the MBS investor effectively has to pay two guarantee fees: one for the private-sector backing of the first-loss position and another for the coverage of any additional catastrophic losses born by the government. We assume that both of these fees are set in an actuarially fair manner, that is:

$$g_{PG} = \gamma_{Mez}(\phi_{PG} - \theta) + \gamma_e \theta$$

$$g_{GOV} = \gamma_{AAA}(1 - \phi_{PG})\,(1 - \text{CDF}(\phi_{PG}))$$

The first premium, g_{PG}, is paid to the private guarantor of the MBS security. It has two components: the expected loss θ and the loss that is incurred if the loss outcome exceeds the expected loss but is smaller than a catastrophe—that is, smaller than the loss outcome threshold set by the government, ϕ_{PG}. The private guarantor is assumed to have to provide a competitive return on equity to the capital (γ_e) that is raised to cover expected losses, and a competitive return on a more senior mezzanine tranche (γ_{Mez}) for the unexpected, noncatastrophic loss outcomes. We estimate the return on equity using a forward-looking stock-market return and the return on the mezzanine tranche using the BBB corporate bond rate.[6] We judge that these are realistic alternative investments for the types of risks investors would face under a hybrid-securitization structure. A table of variable definitions is provided at the end of this chapter in Table 3.5.

The government's catastrophic insurance is priced in a similar manner; the expected loss is based on the cumulative distribution function of loss outcomes, $(1 - \text{CDF}(\phi_{PG}))$. If a tail event occurs, the government only pays out the portion of the loss that exceeds the first-loss position of the private guarantor, $(1 - \phi_{PG})$. The government's opportunity cost of the funds disbursed is assumed to be the AAA corporate rate (effectively, the Treasury rate plus a very small spread that accounts for a small probability of loss).[7]

We consider the two alternative government policy options described earlier. First, we formalize the treatment of the Obama administration's option 2. The government might want to pursue a "through-the-cycle" macroprudential policy, where it structures a constant first-loss position so that it covers the average credit loss over the housing cycle. During a financial crisis, the government wants government-sponsored securitization to be used if private securitization is not available, but prior to a crisis (i.e., during a housing "boom") the program sits idle because the capital costs seem too high to private-market participants. Private-sector investors bear the losses during the bust from investments made during the boom, but mortgage securitization remains available through the government at the average "through-the-cycle" price.[8]

As for option 3, suppose that the government sets its g-fee during "normal times" in a manner so that the private sector would be indifferent between private-sector and GSE securitization.[9] In other words, the government would not directly provide a subsidy to the private-sector participants, but the government would set the g-fee and first-loss capital requirement so that the estimated benefits to MBS investors would be equal to the costs of the guarantee fees. Under this policy, the government would need to cover more than catastrophic mortgage losses during a crisis (the private-sector first-loss position will be insufficient during the bust, and if the securitizer purchased the government insurance, the government will bear some of the non-catastrophic losses). In addition, some private-market firms and households would go bankrupt (those that did not participate in the government-backed securitization product), albeit fewer than under option 2 if the government does not bail out holders of mortgage-backed securities.

IV. Loss Outcomes for Portfolios of Conforming Mortgages

Zandi and deRitis (2013) have calculated the actual average lifetime loss on a GSE mortgage during the most recent economic crisis as 2.7 percent.[10] This approximation of the losses to mortgages that were originated in 2007 was calculated by dividing all GSE-realized residential mortgage loan losses during 2006–2012 by the outstanding debt in 2007.

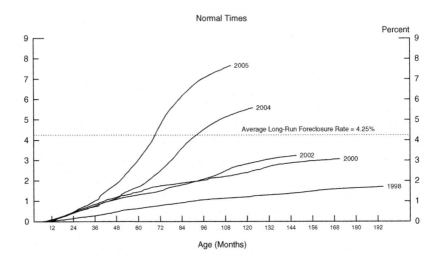

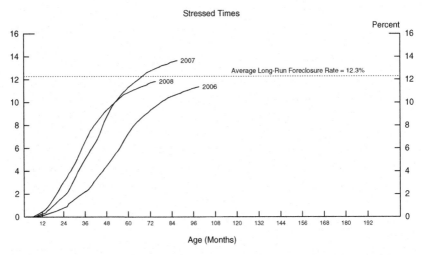

Figure 3.2. Cumulative foreclosure rates for "conforming" mortgages (single-family, first-lien, conventional 30-year fixed, all FICO scores) by year of origination. Calculations based on Black Knight Financial Services (2014).

In contrast, for our assessment of the feasibility of alternative options for housing finance reform, we created an expected loss distribution for conforming mortgages using a three-step process. In the first step, we constructed an estimate of expected losses for mortgages using loan-level mortgage data from Lender Processing Services Inc. (LPS). More specifically, we calculated annual cumulative foreclosure rates for conforming mortgages stratified by year of origination. In Figure 3.2, these cumulative foreclosure rates are provided for "normal" times (top panel) and for "stressed times" (bottom panel), where these "stressed times" are defined as the years in which the household would experience the financial crisis soon after their mortgage was originated. For conforming loans originated between 1998 and 2005—the years when the financial crisis was not experienced early on—cumulative foreclosure rates averaged 4.25 percent (upper panel). However, mortgage borrowers that experienced "stressed times" early in the life of their mortgage had cumulative foreclosure rates that averaged 12.3 percent (bottom panel), an average cumulative foreclosure rate more than 2.8 times the "normal" average cumulative foreclosure rate.

In the second step, we considered losses given default and constructed expected lifetime mortgage default rates during "normal" and "stressed" periods. Historical loss-given-default data for conforming mortgages are both difficult to find and difficult to calculate. Fannie Mae has reported a "single-family initial charge-off severity rate" in their annual report (10-K) since 2008. We would argue that the loss severity rates for mortgages originated in the years 2008 through 2013 reflected mortgage cohorts with relatively tight underwriting standards. In these years, the expected loss severity rates for foreclosures had values around 25 percent.

The peak for Fannie Mae's reported initial loss severity measure was 37.2 percent. This loss severity rate, which likely reflected mortgages under-written in 2006 and 2007, probably represents the peak of Fannie Mae's losses given default, given the loose underwriting standards prior to the crisis combined with the extreme depth of the financial crisis itself.

With an expected lifetime mortgage default rate for a cohort of mortgages and the loss severities associated with those mortgages, we then calculated expected losses. Based on a "normal" foreclosure rate of 4.25 percent and a loss given default of 25 percent, the expected losses were approximately 1.06 percent for the mortgages that defaulted but did not experience a financial crisis soon after origination. Similarly, we calculated "stressed" expected losses for the years 2006–2008 of 4.3%, which were based on a 12.3 percent foreclosure rate and a 35 percent loss given default.

The third step entails the calculation of value at risk; this step requires information about the frequency of financial crises. To generate a distribution of expected losses, we assumed that expected losses follow a log-normal distribution. Such an assumption is common and is embedded in the Basel

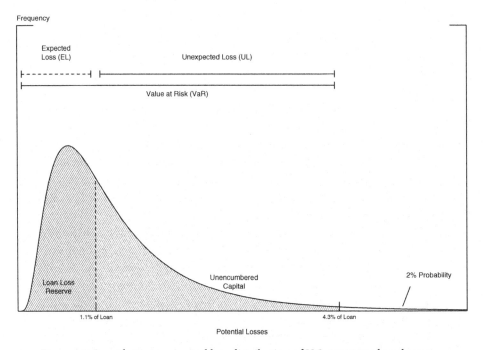

Figure 3.3. Long-horizon expected loss distribution of U.S. mortgage loan losses.

II capital standards (see Jones and Mingo 1999). Then, we set the typical loss of 1.06 percent to the median value of our distribution, assumed that the financial crisis is a "1-in-50" event, and placed 4.3 percent loss rate at the 98th percentile of the loss distribution. The resulting distribution of implied mortgage loan losses is shown in Figure 3.3. This long horizon expected loss distribution is roughly consistent with the Basel assumptions concerning mortgage risk. The standard Basel risk weight on a conforming mortgage is 4.0 percent, and with our distribution, 4.0 percent additional capital would cover slightly less than 98 percent of the expected loss outcomes. More detail on the variations in the calculation of "through-the-cycle" first-loss capital requirements (along with the private-sector "g-fee" and the government "g-fee") are provided in Table 3.1.

But with so little information about potential mortgage losses available, the calculation of an appropriate first-loss position is very difficult as small changes in the estimates of the "tail" of the expected loss distribution can result in substantial changes in the first-loss capital needed for the private

Table 3.1. Variation in "Through-The-Cycle" First-Loss Capital Requirements, Private Sector G-Fees, and Government G-Fees using Alternative Assumptions on Frequency of Crises and Loss Scenarios

Estimated Underlying Loss Distributions

First Loss Position [Private Guarantee Fee] {Government Guarantee Fee}		*Assuming the Recent Financial Crisis was a 1-in-50 Event*			*Assuming the Recent Financial Crisis was a 1-in-20 event*		
		(1)	*(2)*	*(3)*	*(4)*	*(5)*	*(6)*
Extreme loss standard set by government	95%	2.88 [21] {18}	3.26 [23] {18}	3.62 [25] {18}	3.69 [25] {18}	4.30 [28] {18}	4.91 [31] {18}
	98%	3.69 [25] {7}	4.30 [28] {7}	4.91 [31] {7}	5.02 [32] {7}	6.09 [37] {7}	7.19 [43] {7}
	99%	4.35 [28] {4}	5.18 [33] {4}	6.02 [37] {4}	6.17 [38] {4}	7.67 [45] {3}	9.27 [53] {3}
	99.5%	5.06 [32] {2}	6.13 [37] {2}	7.25 [43] {2}	7.45 [44] {2}	9.48 [54] {2}	11.69 [65] {2}
	99.9%	6.90 [41] {0}	8.71 [50] {0}	10.6 [60] {0}	11.0 [61] {0}	14.68 [80] {0}	18.87 [101] {0}

Assumes median loss rate of 1.1%=(4.25% foreclosure rate ['98–'05] * 25% Loss Given Default) and a "stressed" foreclosure rate of 12.3% ('06–'08).

"Low" Expected Loss Scenario assumes a 30% Loss Given Default.	"Mid" Expected Loss Scenario assumes a 35% Loss Given Default.	"High" Expected Loss Scenario assumes a 40% Loss Given Default

sector to cover most expected loss outcomes. As a result, we provide a time series for calculations for the needed first-loss capital requirement based on (1) variations in the expected frequency of financial crises and (2) variations in the acceptable strike point for government intervention during a financial crisis (Table 3.1). These simulations demonstrate that either a higher frequency of crises or standards that would require a higher proportion of loss outcomes covered by the private sector, or both, can result in very high levels of private-sector capital needed to avoid a government intervention—sometimes more than 15 percent.

Returning to the second policy option described earlier, we estimate that a government guarantor who uses the standard that private-sector capital must cover 99.9 percent of expected loss outcomes would require a first-loss position of 8.7 percent (the horizontal line with long dashes shown in Figure 3.4); if this expected loss coverage threshold was lowered to 95 percent, then the government guarantor would require only a 3.3 percent first-loss position (indicated by the dashed horizontal line). Consequently, small changes in the expected loss coverage threshold combined with the uncertainty of the loss data can yield meaningful differences in the amount of first-loss capital required by the government guarantor. This makes a "through-the-cycle" macroprudential first-loss position difficult to construct. If the government backstop is to "spring to life" during a financial crisis, policy makers will need to decide the degree and rationale for the capital subsidy given to mortgage securitizations during the crisis, using limited and highly uncertain loss information.

Under the third policy option, the government would set the first-loss positions and g-fees for government securitization to be competitive with private-sector securitizations. The size of the first-loss position shifts over time depending on the estimate of the government benefit and the cost of capital. As a result of the widespread use of government catastrophic insurance during the boom, the spillover effects of mortgage defaults are mitigated during a housing bust. We now turn to how to measure the benefits of government securitization over the previous housing cycle.

V. Measuring the Historical Benefits of GSE MBS to the Private Sector (Option 3)

To analyze hybrid securitization under option 3, where the government is concerned that private-sector securitizers of conforming mortgages voluntarily use the government insurance program, we will first need to understand why private securitization of conforming mortgages was dominated by government securitization before the crisis and is currently nonexistent after the crisis. The underlying capital structures of private securitization and hybrid securitization are similar, and thus understanding the failure of private

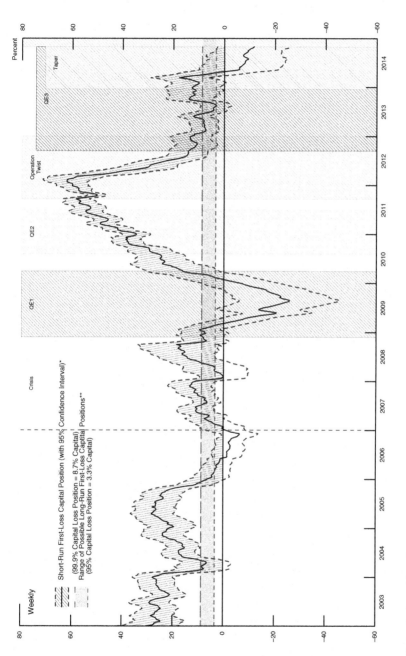

*Short-run first-loss positions adjust private sector capital holdings to equate GSE benefit and GSE Guarantee Fees.
**Long-run first-loss positions are constant throughout housing cycle. The variation is created by deflating government standards for "catastrophic losses."

Figure 3.4. Estimates of private-sector, first-loss positions for 30-year fixed-rate mortgage pools with confidence intervals.

securitization might help us understand the relative potential success, or failure, of hybrid securitization.

A. The Return to the Bank from Holding the Mortgage Directly

The return to the bank from holding the mortgage credit risk directly
would be

$$\gamma_{PORT} = \gamma_M - s - \gamma_e\, \theta + -[[\![\gamma_{mez}\, \phi_M + \gamma_D(1-\phi)]\!]_M)](1-\theta) - \gamma_{swap}(\gamma_T - \gamma_{repo})\, \alpha\delta_M$$

where the mortgage rate is denoted by γ_M, which we assume is set in a competitive market; the cost of servicing the mortgage is denoted by s; the bank's
cost of financing the mortgage is the weighted average of the desired return
on equity, γ_e, and the cost of deposits and other liabilities (the cost of funds),
which is denoted γ_D; the risk-weighted capital requirements are ϕ_M for mortgages; the regulatory risk weight is set to a value-at-risk (VaR) standard so
that all but the most improbable losses will be covered by capital, whereas
the loan loss reserve portion of capital is set to cover the average loss rate;
and the mean expected loss over the lifetime of a representative mortgage
portfolio is denoted by θ.

If the bank chooses to hold the mortgage in its portfolio, it bears both the
credit and interest rate risks of the mortgage. It funds a loan loss reserve of $\gamma_e\theta$
to cover expected credit losses. A loan loss reserve is simply an allocation of
capital that is expected to bear losses over the life of the loan. It is usually set
to cover the average losses observed across the bank's mortgage portfolios.

Standing behind the loan loss reserve is the unencumbered capital generated either by market expectations concerning capitalization of the bank
or by binding regulatory capital requirements. Because of its "second loss"
position, we assume that the expected yield needed to attract this capital is
similar to the yield that exists on high-yield corporate debt or on mezzanine
debt in a securitization, and we denote this yield as γ_{mez}.

To offset interest rate risk, the bank purchases a swap with equal duration to the expected duration of the mortgage. This swap hedges interest rate
risk but leaves the bank holding the prepayment risk associated with the
swap. Thus, the bank may purchase another financial derivative (such as options or swaps with options) to hedge prepayment risk. We denote the net
cost of the financial derivatives needed to hedge a bank's portfolio against
interest rate risk by γ_{swap}. We include in γ_{swap} all of the transactions that would

be needed to hedge against prepayment risks and other risks (e.g., the basis risks incurred when hedging instruments with different reference rates from the underlying instruments).

Finally, the bank is required by regulators to hold a liquidity portfolio. Let α denote the thirty-day runoff rate of liabilities during a financial panic. We assume that the bank meets its liquidity holdings requirement by financing a government Treasury portfolio with reverse repurchase obligations, which has a spread, $(\gamma_T - \gamma_{repo})$. Holding the mortgages in portfolio is treated less favorably than holding GSE mortgage-backed securities (MBS), which are perceived as being more liquid during a financial panic. The liquidity haircut applied to holding mortgages is δ_M.

On its balance sheet, the bank holds mortgages and Treasury securities funded by deposits and equity. Equity is divided into a loan loss reserve and into unencumbered capital, which is sufficient to meet regulatory requirements and can also be used to finance additional mortgages. In this analysis, we assume other regulatory capital requirements, such as the bank leverage ratio, are not binding.

B. The Return to the Bank from Selling the Mortgage

If the bank sells its mortgage portfolio to the private sector, the return is

$$\gamma_{PLS} = \gamma_M - s + b_{pls} - [\gamma_{MBS}(1 - \phi_M) + \gamma_{Mez}\,\phi_M]\,(1 - \theta) - \gamma_e\,\theta$$

The first-loss reserve ($\gamma_i e\,\theta$), or residual part of a private-sector mortgage securitization is like the loan loss reserve at the bank. It is assumed to be large enough so that expected credit losses are covered. Beyond the residential tranche, the mortgage can be broken into two components: a low-risk component that has little default risk (the AAA component, which can be made equivalent to a GSE MBS security with enough loss protection, and thus yields γ_{MBS}, and a higher-risk component that bears the expected loss (the "subordinated" component, or $\gamma_{Mez}\phi_M$). Using this tranching scheme, the subordinated component bears all normal credit losses, whereas the AAA component bears credit losses that occur only under the most catastrophic conditions. The subordinated (i.e., junior) portion of the security is similar to the unencumbered capital at the bank, and this portion is only expected to take losses if losses run above the average expected level. By providing mortgages for private mortgage securitization, the bank may also capture some of the benefits that such securitization gives to other market participants (e.g., higher liquidity), denoted by b_{pls}.

However, historically, conforming mortgages were rarely sold into the private market. Instead, most banks, particularly the largest banks that originated the bulk of all mortgages, swapped their mortgages for GSE MBS. The return in this case is

$$\gamma_{GSE} = [\![\gamma]\!]_M + b_{gse} - s - \gamma_{MBS}] - [[\![\gamma_{mez}\,\phi_{MBS} + \gamma_D(1-\phi)]\!]_{MBS})] \\ + \gamma_{MBS} - \gamma_{swap} + (\gamma_T - \gamma_{repo})\,\alpha\delta_{MBS}$$

The yield on MBS, γ_{MBS}, is the current-coupon yield. This is the hypothetical coupon associated with an MBS pool that trades at par value (i.e., the MBS trades at a price of $100 for $100 of mortgages in the pool).[11] The bank financing for the GSE MBS is a combination of bank deposits and capital, where the capital earns a return that is equivalent to mezzanine financing, γ_{mez}, because the GSEs' capital bears the first-loss position, and the bank only suffers losses if the GSE fails and the government does not bail out the GSE. (Of course, the U.S. government did bail out GSE MBS investors in 2008, but this outcome was not certain prior to that bailout).

C. Estimating the Benefits of GSE Securitization

The difference in returns from GSE securitization and private securitization is

$$\gamma_{PLS} - \gamma_{GSE} = b_{pls} - b_{gse} + g_{gse} - [\gamma_{MBS}(1-\phi_M) + \gamma_{mez}\,\phi_M](1-\theta) - \gamma_e\,\theta + \gamma_{swap} \\ + [[\![\gamma_{mez}\,\phi_{MBS} + \gamma_D(1-\phi)]\!]_{MBS})] - (\gamma_T - \gamma_{repo})\,\alpha\delta_{MBS}$$

If banks strive to equate the returns from selling mortgages to either private securitizers or to the GSEs, then the following relationship can be deduced:

$$\gamma_{MBS} = \frac{1}{(1-\phi_M)(1-\theta)}(\gamma_{swap} + (1-\phi_{MBS})\gamma_D + [\phi_{MBS} - (1-\theta)\phi_M]\gamma_{mez} \\ - \gamma_e\theta - (\gamma_T - \gamma_{repo})\alpha\delta_{MBS} + b_{pls} - b_{gse})$$

Thus, we estimate the equation:

$$\gamma_{MBS} = c_0 + c_1\,\gamma_{swap} + c_2\,\gamma_D + c_2\,r_{mez} + c_4\,(\gamma_T - \gamma_{repo}) + \varepsilon$$

where $b_{pls} - b_{gse} = c_0 + \varepsilon$ is an estimate of the extent to which the benefits of private securitization must exceed the benefits of GSE securitization for private securitization to be feasible. The constant term is the expected value of the government advantage to MBS investors. It is the amount of extra return the private sector must offer the originator to equate the implied mortgage rate financed by private-sector securitization to the implied mortgage rate financed by government-backed (GSE) securitization. The larger the advantage of government-sponsored MBS over privately sponsored MBS is, the larger the constant term in the above equation will become.

In other words, the regression attempts to equate the mortgage rate created by the government-sponsored entity to a hypothetical mortgage rate created by summing the banks' cost of funds and a weighted average of private-sector yields that capture three types of risk: interest rate risk (proxied by the yields on interest rate swaps and by bond volatility), credit risk (proxied by the yields on BBB debt), and liquidity risk (proxied by the Treasury-repo spread). In normal times, we would expect the constant to be positive because the liquidity benefits and regulatory capital savings of government sponsorship of MBS are positive. But as our analysis shows below, when hedging costs are high, when private-sector capital is especially cheap, or when the value of government-backing or government policy is in question, the relative benefits of government sponsorship of MBS are diminished, and this constant term can become small or even negative.

Our regression estimates for the γ_{MBS} specification over the past fourteen years are provided in Table 3.2. The coefficients are generally significant and suggest that the average benefit of GSE securitization over private-sector securitization is 87 basis points over the July 2000 to March 2014 period.[12] As shown in Figure 3.5, the regression residual is stationary, and there is no unit root. Note that the variation in the residual can be large relative to the constant, especially during the financial crisis. However, the expected value of the residual is zero, so we focus on the constant estimate as the long-run average value of the GSE benefit advantage.

As suggested above, the estimated constant in this regression likely varies over time. A more appropriate estimation technique for our estimate of the relative value of the GSE advantage to investors is to use rolling regressions (the intercept coefficients of these rolling regressions are shown in Figure 3.6). These rolling regressions update the coefficients in the γ_{MBS} specification to reflect the evolving views of market participants. They also allow the underlying regulatory and loss distribution parameters to evolve over time. Here, we use a two-year rolling window to estimate each regression.[13]

Table 3.2. MBS Yield Determinants Where the Intercept Measures the GSE Benefit Relative to Private Sector Securitizations

Dependent Variable:	
MBS Yield	
Independent Variable	*Parameter Estimate*
(1) Long Swap	0.78***
(2) Short Swap	-0.03**
(3) Bond Volatility	0.65***
(4) Cost of Funds	0.09***
(5) BBB Yield	0.05***
(6) Treasury—Repo Spread	-0.10***
(7) Intercept	0.87***
Adjusted R-squared = 0.989	
Weekly Data from July 7, 2000, to September 26, 2014 (n = 743)	

Asterisks represent significance *** at the 99% confidence level, ** at the 95% level, and * at the 90% level.

Private securitization—most of the time—was unable to compete with GSE securitization because the constant term is positive and statistically significant from zero during most of the rolling windows. The exceptions are during the end of 2006 and beginning of 2007, as well as during the financial crisis, where the private benefits dominated the GSE benefits on average. Private-label securitizations would have been perhaps very valuable to investors during this period of GSE MBS market chaos because of the abnormally low MBS yields, but private-label securitizers themselves were in turmoil, making them unable to take advantage of the abnormally high prices and low yields for mortgage risk found in the government-backed MBS market during 2009.

During the financial crisis of 2008 and 2009, our estimates suggest that market participants would have benefited from private securitization. Fannie Mae and Freddie Mac were in conservatorship and the Federal Reserve's QE1 MBS purchases were rapidly driving down MBS yields. However, the private market was in such disarray that such an alternative was not actually available. Our rolling regressions highlight this point; our model yields stationary regressions except during the turmoil of 2009 (Figure 3.7). In that year, we likely have failed to account for an important common factor in our regression, which is the Federal Reserve's QE1 pro-

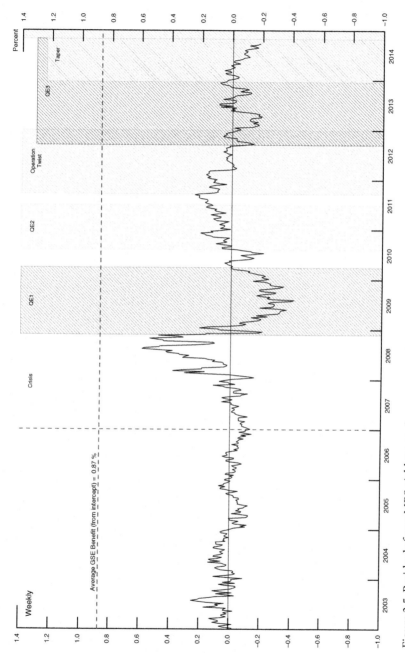

Figure 3.5. Residuals from MBS yield regression.

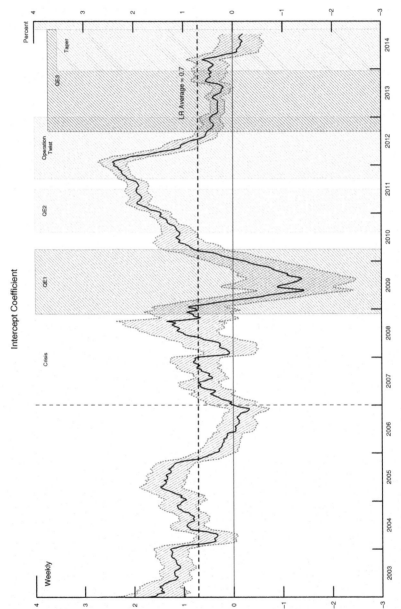

Figure 3.6. GSE benefit advantage (based on rolling regression intercept coefficients).

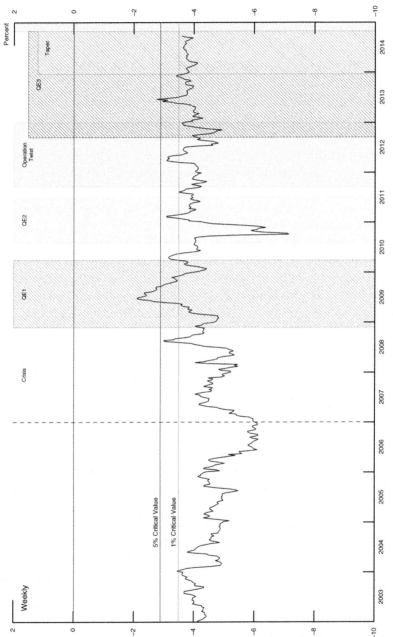

Figure 3.7. Test for stationarity using rolling regressions. Based on augmented Dickey-Fuller unit root *t*-tests.

gram (see Hancock and Passmore, 2011b; Hancock and Passmore forthcoming).

VI. Macroprudential Policy with Hybrid Securitization

If the government follows the "through-the-cycle" policy (option 2), private securitization would dominate government securitization some of the time. For example, if the private sector uses the "normal times" expected loss distribution in a boom period, the capital backing of many private mortgage pools will prove to be inadequate during stressed times. The government might be indifferent to this outcome. But if many private mortgage pools are undercapitalized, then the government may actually bear the resulting credit risks if mortgage pools become distressed and financial institutions fail (as did occur in 2008).

As for the third policy option (i.e., where the government would set the first-loss position to be competitive with requirements that are set in the private sector), the government would select the first-loss private-sector position such that the cost of capital equals all of the benefits received by the private sector when using the government-backed system (using the rolling regression estimates from above). Under this policy, the benefits of private-label securitization are set equal to the benefits of government securitization. The size of the first-loss position shifts over time, depending on the estimate of the government benefit and the cost of capital (the solid line in Figure 3.4 that is surrounded by the standard error band indicated by dashed lines). This is the highest requirement of first-loss capital (and the lowest level of the government g-fee, which is set to zero) that is consistent with private-sector participation in the hybrid securitization program. If the first-loss private-sector capital requirement is set higher than what is specified by the upper bound for the solid line, then private-sector participation in the third policy option would likely cease.

Under the third option, the government can solve the problem of private-market participants not using the government insurance program by making the government program "competitive" and lowering the amount of capital needed to meet the first-loss capital requirements. But if it meets the competition, it creates a new problem: the amount of capital collected for the first-loss position will be inadequate to cover all losses in a catastrophe because many mortgages will be privately securitized rather than flow through the hybrid securitization system.

Hybrid securitization under option 3 is difficult to implement because the benefits of government-backed securitization relative to the cost of the "first-loss" capital position vary a lot. Why are these benefits of government-backed securitization so volatile?

Recall that banks are assumed to be the marginal investors in MBS, and one key element of their return calculation for holding mortgages versus holding MBS is the cost of hedging interest rate risk. We have assumed that thirty-year FRMs underlie the GSE MBS in our estimate of GSE benefits. As a result, when hedging costs are high, the benefit of government securitization decreases. The banking industry may "disgorge" the thirty-year fixed-rate MBS into the GSE MBS secondary market when these hedging costs are too high, where they might be purchased by nonhedging entities (e.g. foreign sovereigns).

Turning to Figure 3.8, it is apparent that hedging costs were relatively high and the cost of equity was relatively cheap compared to a bank's cost of funds during the 2006–2007 period, which resulted in much lower estimates of the GSE benefit advantage than were needed on average to equate MBS yields to a hypothetical current-coupon, private-sector MBS. Our results suggest that banks might find private securitization more appealing than hybrid securitization if these historical conditions were ever repeated.

We can measure the importance of the hedging costs using the following thought experiment. Suppose the dominant mortgage was an adjustable-rate mortgage tied to the bank's cost of funds rather than a thirty-year FRM. If that were the case, then the return to a bank from a hybrid securitization would exclude the cost of hedging; the mortgage pool is naturally hedged because it is based on a bank's cost of funds.

In Table 3.3, we re-estimate the government advantage excluding hedging costs. Without the need to hedge, the resulting estimate of the government advantage is almost three times as large, at 2.48 on average. As shown in Figure 3.9, the government is outcompeted by private-sector securitization in 2008, when the lagging investor expectations of a low cost of BBB capital are out of sync with the rapid increases in interest rates. Our two-year rolling regression does not update itself rapidly enough to capture the shift in rates, and thus underestimates the cost of capital for private securitization. Similarly, the rolling regression structure misses the (smaller) uptick in 2013. Otherwise, the government could have set the macroprudential level of "first-loss" capital for hybrid securitizations based on cost of funds mortgages at a level that limits the government liability without having

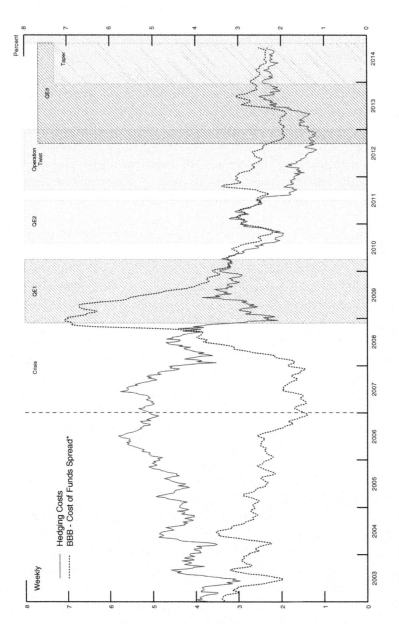

*Using 5-year BBB yield.

Figure 3.8. Hedging and capital costs. Hedging costs estimated using data from Reuters Ltd. BBB yield calculations based on Merrill Lynch (2015). Cost of funds calculation based on Federal Financial Institutions Examination Council (2015).

Table 3.3. Estimate of Government Advantage Using Cost of Funds and No Hedging Costs (Intercept)

Dependent Variable:	
MBS Yield	
Independent Variable	*Parameter Estimate*
(1) Cost of Funds	0.83 ***
(2) BBB Yield	0.15 ***
(3) Treasury—Repo Spread	1.14 ***
(4) Intercept	2.48 ***

Adjusted R-squared = 0.868
Weekly data from June 30, 2000 to September 26, 2014 (n = 744)

Asterisks represent significance *** at the 99% confidence level, ** at the 95% level, and * at the 90% level.

mortgages flow into the private securitization markets. Policy makers, however, have shown a strong preference for maintaining the thirty-year FRM. Because moving away from the thirty-year FRM may be politically infeasible, another approach might be for government backstop insurance to be required also for pools purchased by private-label MBS investors. Based on historical experience, the government could have kept the government catastrophic insurance competitive if it had levied an insurance premium on all mortgage securitizations regardless of whether the securitization was in the purely private sector or government sponsored. The mortgage insurance premium in this case would be structured like an FDIC premium, which capitalizes the FDIC insurance fund by taxing deposits regardless of whether the bank engages in very risky or very safe lending. As shown in Figure 3.10, our estimates suggest that this premium would vary between 5 and 35 basis points, depending on the size of the first-loss capital position carried by private-market MBS guarantors. Of course, if the frequency of crisis was higher, or the government standard to avoid losses set tighter, then a higher premium might be necessary (recall the resulting first-loss capital positions and average premiums shown in Table 3.2). On the other hand, this government premium could be reduced even further if the catastrophic insurance program was designed with deductibles and/or mandatory paybacks of government outlays by industry participants. Similar to the Terrorism Risk Insurance Act (TRIA) or the structure of the

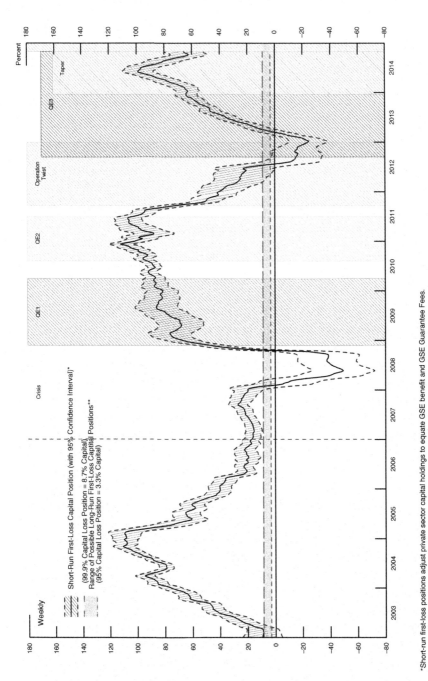

*Short-run first-loss positions adjust private sector capital holdings to equate GSE benefit and GSE Guarantee Fees.

**Long-run first-loss positions are constant throughout housing cycle. The variation is created by deflating government standards for "catastrophic losses."

Figure 3.9. Estimates of private-sector, first-loss positions for 30-year fixed-rate mortgage pools with confidence intervals without hedging cost (basis points).

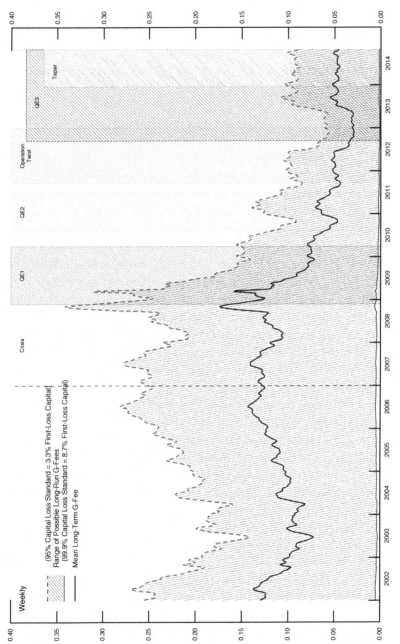

Figure 3.10. Estimates of insurance premium under a catastrophic insurance regime.

FDIC's line of credit from the Department of the Treasury for its insurance fund, these types of insurance pricing methods (along with mandatory premiums) could create a low-cost government backstop that would credibly insure both GSE and private-label MBS investors against mortgage credit risks, while maintaining a thirty-year FRM for mortgage borrowers.

VII. A Discussion of Our Results

Mirroring the forgoing alternative visions to reform and recapitalize the U.S. housing system are two alternative views of what went wrong with securitization. One explanation for the demise of securitization is that agency problems were endemic. Proponents of this view point to evidence that lending standards were progressively lowered in the years leading up to the financial crisis (see Mian and Sufi 2009; Keys et al. 2010; Demyanyk and van Hemert 2011; Duca, Muellbauer, and Murphy 2011; Rajan 2005; and Kashyap, Rajan, and Stein 2008). In addition, information frictions have been identified in the securitization process. Ashcraft and Schuermann (2008) provide a taxonomy of such frictions, including information frictions between the borrower and the originator, or between the originator and the issuer of securities. Uniform standards, public disclosure, and transparency proposed by those who favor "pure privatization" are viewed as mitigating agency problems and information frictions.

Alternatively, one can argue that securitization affects the housing boom and/or the housing bust. Shin (2009) argues that securitization shifts the mix between internal and external funding by banks and other originators of mortgages. This shift toward securitization results in greater aggregate lending to borrowers even if the leverage of individual banks or originators remains unchanged. In turn, the increased lending, which is made feasible through securitization, results in a higher asset price (i.e., house price) and a lower probability of default for the borrower (i.e., the mortgagor). In this manner, securitization can kick-start and then amplify a lending boom. In addition, Brunnermeier and Sannikov (2014) argue that risk sharing among experts (via securitization) reduces inefficiencies from idiosyncratic risk on one hand, but on the other hand emboldens them to maintain smaller net worth buffers and attain higher leverage. Finally, as recently shown by Gorton and Ordoñez (2014), very small shocks (e.g., small reductions in valuations for mortgage-backed securities) can encourage investors in information-insensitive debt to require more information regarding their collateralized debt. Inevitably, more information requirements lead to a decline in output (e.g., a real estate bust) and possibly a large financial crisis. These three elements—a lending boom, low capitalization of financial intermediaries, and run-prone capital investors—are seen as the toxic mix that generated the last financial crisis.

Hybrid securitization is often regarded as a way to "thread the needle" between these views and policy positions. A high first-loss capital position held by MBS guarantors creates a set of institutions that have a strong incentive to monitor the securitization process and resolve agency problems. A very limited catastrophic insurance program might provide just enough government backing to limit the most harmful outcome of a securitization-driven lending boom. Moreover, as argued in Hancock and Passmore (2011a), explicitly priced government-backed catastrophic insurance on mortgage pools comprised of only eligible mortgages would improve financial stability compared to the GSE reinsurance scheme that was in place before the financial crisis. This is because *explicit* pricing of a government-backed guarantee combined with a substantial private-sector loss position would mitigate market distortions that were created by *implicit* government guarantees during prosperity. Moreover, an explicitly priced fully government-backed catastrophic insurance program would help ensure that mortgage credit is provided at reasonable cost both in times of prosperity and during downturns because guarantee-sensitive investors in securitized mortgage pools would not engage in a "run" if they would be certain that their money would be repaid with interest.

One recent development that may indicate that hybrid securities are feasible are the credit risk sharing securities issued by Fannie Mae under Connecticut Avenue Securities (C-deals) and by Freddie Mac under Structured Agency Credit Risk (STACR) debt securities. C-deals and STACR debt securities are credit risk sharing securities that provide an opportunity to invest in a portion of the credit risk that the GSE retains when it guarantees single-family MBS. (More details are provided in Table 3.4.) The C-deals and STACR securities are neither guaranteed nor secured, with the payments based on the performance of the mortgage loans in a *reference pool* of recently securitized MBS. *Reference pools* are large, diversified pools of fully amortizing, full documentation, and single-family mortgage loans with a loan-to-value within the range of 60–97 percent; they are composed of a random sample of one quarter's single-family loan acquisitions deemed to be

Table 3.4. Fannie Mae C-Deal and Freddie Mac STACR Initial Offerings

Date	July 26, 2013	Oct. 16, 2013	Nov. 12, 2013	Jan. 27, 2014	Feb. 12, 2014	Apr. 9, 2014	May 27, 2014	Aug. 11, 2014	Oct. 28, 2014
Security Issuer	STACR (Freddie Mac)	C-Deal (Fannie Mae)	STACR (Freddie Mac)	C-Deal (Fannie Mae)	STACR (Freddie Mac)	STACR (Freddie Mac)	C-Deal (Fannie Mae)	STACR (Freddie Mac)	STACR (Freddie Mac)
Total Volume	$500 Million	$675 Million	$630 Million	$750 Million	$1 Billion	$966 Million	$2 Billion	$675 Million	$611 Million
M-1 Coupon (spread over LIBOR)	3.59% (340 bps)	2.18% (200 bps)	1.62% (145 bps)	1.77% (160 bps)	1.15% (100 bps)	1% (85 bps)	1.10% (95 bps)	1.51% (135 bps)	1.55% (140 bps)
M-1 Rating	Not rated	BBB- (Fitch)	BBB— (Fitch) Baa1 (Moody's)	BBB— (Fitch) Baa2 (Moody's)	A1 (Moody's) A (Kroll)	A (Fitch) A (Kroll)	BBB (Fitch) BBB— (S&P)	A—(Fitch) A1 (Moody's)	A—(Fitch) A1 (Moody's)
M-2 Coupon (spread over LIBOR)	7.34	5.43	4.42% (425 bps)	4.57% (440 bps)	2.35% (220 bps)	1.80% (165 bps)	2.75% (260 bps)	2.56% (240 bps)	2.55% (240 bps)
M-2 Rating	Not rated	Not rated	Not rated	Not rated	Baa1 (Moody's) BBB (Kroll)	BBB— (Fitch) BBB (Kroll)	Not rated	BBB— (Fitch) A3 (Moody's)	BBB— (Fitch) A3 (Moody's)

Information from market source compiled by authors.

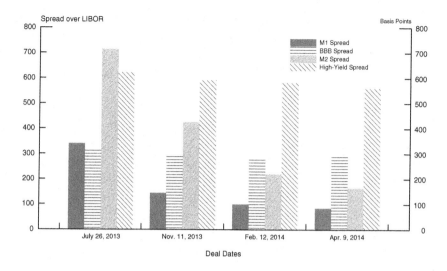

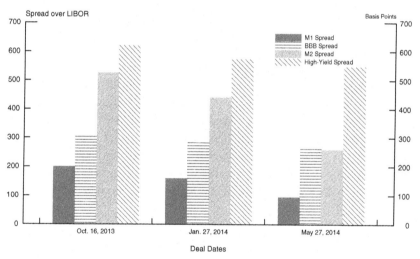

Figure 3.11. Freddie Mac STACR M1 and M2 tranches spread over LIBOR compared to BBB and high-yield corporate bond spreads over LIBOR (above). Fannie Mae C-deal M1 and M2 tranches spread over LIBOR compared to BBB and high-yield corporate bond spreads over LIBOR (below). Information from market source compiled by authors.

representative of recently securitized MBS. The crucial difference between these securities and other debt securities that have been issued by Fannie Mae and Freddie Mac is that if loans in the reference pool experience credit defaults, the investors in the credit risk sharing securities could bear losses and may not even recoup their principal.

Despite the design of the securities to transfer credit risk, the market prices of these securities issued by Fannie Mae and Freddie Mac may indicate that investors do not believe that they are truly bearing the risk associated with mortgage defaults (Figure 3.11). The declining spread of the most recent offerings relative to benchmark spreads suggests that investors may assume they are not taking on the credit risks associated with these securities, despite Fannie Mae and Freddie Mac's stated position that these securities are not guaranteed. For such securities to truly convince the private sector that private investors would actually bear the credit risk, an institutional structure may be needed that makes clear that no mechanism exists for bailing out such investors.

But ultimately the Achilles heel of hybrid securitization proposals may be the thirty-year FRM. As shown above, establishing a sizable first-loss private-sector position in government-backed securitizations when the underlying collateral is thirty-year FRMs may be difficult, except when a catastrophe has recently occurred. The consequences of this problem depend on whether or not under private securitization the losses during a financial crisis are purely borne by the private sector. If the government is perceived to be likely to engage in a bailout, then a mandatory insurance fund or a known method of collecting revenues to recover the costs of a bailout may be a more efficient, and more equitable, approach to covering such losses.

VIII. Conclusion

This chapter seeks to provide an empirical analysis of the appropriate guarantee fee (g-fee) and private-sector first loss (i.e., capitalization levels) that would be necessary to implement a hybrid securitization system. Mortgage originators consider the government g-fee, as well as other government requirements such as capital requirements, when deciding whether to securitize a mortgage. Hybrid-securitization systems, proposed as possible replacements for Fannie Mae and Freddie Mac by U.S. legislators, would require more private capital to back the housing finance system than the capital that backed traditional GSE securitization as it would explicitly provide government backing of catastrophic losses. However, hybrid securitization may be difficult to successfully implement without considering the competitive and regulatory environment in place for mortgage securitization.

Hybrid securitization lowers the cost of capital and adds liquidity to privately backed securitizations. But if the government follows a macroprudential policy of always having enough first-loss capital in place to cover almost all (expected) losses, the program may be uncompetitive during normal economic times. If private-sector investors do not use the program, then government insurance will not cover their losses during a financial crisis. If private investors are unable to bear the mortgage-related losses associated with a financial crisis without significant bankruptcies and nonpayment on private-label MBS, which would be similar to the most recent financial crisis, then other government interventions or bailouts may be necessary to prevent a persistent decline in economic activity.

Our study of the historical evidence suggests that the benefits of the hybrid securitization system would be too small to create a constant first-loss capital position for private-sector participants that would be both competitive and adequate for generating a pool that would cover most mortgage loss outcomes. This low level of benefits associated with a hypothetical hybrid-securitization program seems to be caused by the substantial interest rate risk associated with the thirty-year FRM. Thus to achieve policy makers' desired goal of creating a sufficiently large insurance fund that could be used to smooth out the boom and bust cycles in U.S. real estate markets while maintaining the provision of the thirty-year FRM, the government might need to require that all mortgages be insured against catastrophic mortgage outcomes regardless of whether they are securitized with the government-backed catastrophic insurance.

Table 3.5. Table of Variables

Symbol	Variable	Details/Source
γ_{PORT}	Return to bank from holding mortgage in portfolio	Endogenous
γ_{GSE}	Return to bank from private securitization	Endogenous
γ_{PLS}	Return to bank from private securitization	Endogenous
γ_M	30-year fixed conventional mortgage rate	Federal Reserve—Housing and Real Estate Finance Section
S	Cost of servicing	Mortgage market convention
γ_{swap}	Net hedging costs for interest rate, prepayment, and basis risks	Swap rates: Federal Reserve—H.15; Bond volatility: Bloomberg, Federal Reserve staff calculations
γ_{mez}	Return on mezzanine financing	Corporate BBB 5-year yield: Computed using the Nelson Siegel yield curve model and data from the Bank of America Merrill Lynch Bond Indexes
ϕ_M, ϕ_{MBS}	Risk-weighted capital requirements for mortgages and MBS	Regulatory constants
θ	The mean expected loss over the lifetime of a representative mortgage portfolio, as fraction of principal	Derived from estimating the expected loss distribution
γ_D	Cost of funds	Interest expense divided by interest-bearing liability for all commercial banks: Federal Reserve—Banking Analysis Section
γ_e	Equity return	DDDM model: 10-year horizon
$\gamma_T - \gamma_{repo}$	Treasury repo spread	3-month Treasury Rate minus Overnight Repo Rate: Federal Reserve—H.15
α	Amount of runoff of liabilities during the first 30 days of a financial **panic**	Assumed to be 5%, based on required Basel III liquidity holdings

(*continued*)

Table 3.5 (*continued*)

Symbol	Variable	Details/Source
δ_M	Percent of MBS holdings that the bank can count toward its liquidity requirement	Regulatory requirement, assumed to be 85%
γ_{GSE}^{ES}	Excess servicing	Derived from the difference between mortgage and the MBS yield plus servicing plus the GSE guarantee fee
b_{gse}, b_{pls}	Benefits of GSE and private sector securitization respectively	The difference between the two benefits estimated using the regression described in the text
γ_{MBS}	Current coupon MBS yield	Authors' calculations using Bloomberg MBS coupon price data; see Hancock and Passmore (2014)
ϕ_{PG}	The first-loss capital position held by the private sector in a hybrid-securitization system	Set by policymakers and estimated using the distribution of expected losses

PART II

Housing Finance: Beyond
the Basics

CHAPTER 4

Reforms for a System That Works:
Multifamily Housing Finance

Mark A. Willis and John Griffith

I. Introduction

Since 2008, when a foreclosure crisis in the subprime mortgage market triggered the worst economic downturn since the Great Depression, dozens of
proposals have been offered to establish a more stable and responsible system of housing finance in the United States (Griffith 2013). Understandably,
most reform efforts have focused on the single-family mortgage market, with
a particular focus on Fannie Mae and Freddie Mac (collectively the Enterprises), two companies that were placed under federal government conservatorship in the early days of the financial crisis.[1]

Although the bulk of their businesses support homeownership, the
Enterprises also play a major role in financing homes for the more than one-
third of Americans who rent. Through their multifamily businesses, which
finance apartment buildings with five or more rental units, the Enterprises
are part of a much broader system that makes capital available to building
owners so that they can build new rental units, recapitalize existing properties, and pay for rehabilitation projects and major capital improvements.
Within this system, the Enterprises own or guarantee almost one-third of
all outstanding multifamily mortgages in the United States (Fannie Mae
2015a: 4).

In the wake of the housing crisis and subsequent Great Recession, demand for rental housing in the United States has increased and may well

continue to grow faster than the demand for homeownership (Joint Center for Housing Studies of Harvard University 2014: 22). That also translates into more demand for multifamily buildings, which comprise a significant share of the rental stock and a meaningful portion of the rental units that are most affordable. As more households delay or forgo homeownership and look to the rental market, it is increasingly important to ensure that there is a stable, liquid, and affordable system for financing multifamily housing.

This chapter lays out an approach toward possible reforms in the multifamily mortgage finance market. It focuses on a single premise: despite the problems in the single-family market during the crisis, the multifamily housing finance system has proven to work relatively well. Given that fact, the primary goal in multifamily reform must be to "do no harm" while improving the system's shortcomings.[2]

Section II provides some background on the important role multifamily housing plays in ensuring a healthy rental market. Section III highlights the varied sources of capital and liquidity in the market today, as well as the key role played by the Enterprises. Section IV examines the lessons learned from the most recent housing crisis, with a focus on what worked and what did not in the multifamily finance market. Section V explores some of the challenges posed by the government's involvement in the financing of multifamily properties, with a focus on the risk of moral hazard, crowding out private capital, and political pressure to lower underwriting standards. Section VI lays out opportunities to strengthen the multifamily finance system as part of any broader housing finance reform effort. Section VII explores some additional options for reform that could be viable, but only after additional analysis and testing. Finally, Section VIII concludes by reiterating the need to "do no harm" and exercise caution when moving forward with any effort to reform the multifamily housing finance system.

II. The Importance of Multifamily Rental Housing as the Demand for Rental Housing Grows

More than 100 million Americans—about 36 percent of the population— rent their homes (U.S. Census Bureau 2015a). The percentage of households who rent has risen steadily in recent years, up from a low of 32 percent in 2001 (U.S. Census Bureau 2015b; U.S. Census Bureau 2002: Figure 1). In fact, the 2000s saw the sharpest increase in rental housing of any decade in the past half century, and the trend is expected to continue as homeownership rates have fallen "across a broad spectrum of the population," according to the Joint Center for Housing Studies (Joint Center for Housing Studies of Harvard University 2011: 17–18; Joint Center for Housing Studies of Harvard University 2013: 1).

Meanwhile, the demand for rental housing is growing faster than the demand for homeownership, especially for lower-income households (Joint Center for Housing Studies of Harvard University 2013: 2). In fact, scholars have predicted that the continued growth in rental demand will be a fundamental shift in the American housing market on the scale of America's post-World War II suburbanization (Nelson 2009: 192; Center for American Progress 2010). There are several reasons for this. First, credit standards for single-family mortgages are tight today compared to historic norms, which is locking many working and traditionally creditworthy borrowers out of the homeownership market.[3] In addition, today's young people tend to favor apartments, even after marriage (Joint Center for Housing Studies of Harvard University 2011: 2; Joint Center for Housing Studies of Harvard University 2013: 3; Kinney 2013: 64). The nation's increasing diversity is also expected to increase rental demand, because black and Hispanic families have much lower homeownership rates than non-Hispanic whites and Asians (Kinney 2013: 64; Joint Center for Housing Studies of Harvard University 2011: 3).

Meeting this increased demand will require both the production of new units and the rehabilitation of the existing rental stock, which will require reasonably priced short- and long-term financing. Analysts expect an average of 400,000 new renter households to enter the market each year over the next decade (Joint Center for Housing Studies of Harvard University 2013: 2),[4] and the industry constructs about 300,000 new rental units annually.[5] The rental vacancy rate has also been declining since 2009—albeit at a slower rate more recently—indicating a relative shortage of units (Joint Center for Housing Studies of Harvard University 2013: 5). Meanwhile, America's rental housing stock has a median age of thirty-eight years (Joint Center for Housing Studies of Harvard University 2011: 6), and one-third of the occupied stock is over fifty years old (Joint Center for Housing Studies of Harvard University 2013: 15). According to the Joint Center for Housing Studies, "nearly half of all unassisted housing with rents under $400 were built before 1960," whereas "many of the homes renting in the $400–599 range were built between 1960 and 1979" (Joint Center for Housing Studies of Harvard University 2013:

19). If a significant portion of these buildings disappeared or became dilapidated, much of our affordable housing stock could be lost at a time when lower-income renters in particular face a shortfall of affordable housing options (Joint Center for Housing Studies of Harvard University 2013: 16).[6] Already today, 27 percent of renters pay more than half of their monthly income on housing (Joint Center for Housing Studies of Harvard University 2014: 27), up from 20 percent in 2000 and 12 percent in 1960 (Joint Center for Housing Studies of Harvard University 2011: 29).

Multifamily properties, meaning buildings with five or more units, are a major source of rental housing, representing 14 percent of the nation's total housing stock (Fannie Mae 2012a: 13–14). Multifamily rental units generally serve lower-income households, with 91 percent of the units in 2009 affordable to households earning the area median income (Fannie Mae 2012a: 13). Access to affordable rental housing is particularly important for low-income workers, who have seen their incomes fall in recent years while rents and utility prices (e.g., energy and water) have steadily increased (Joint Center for Housing Studies of Harvard University 2011: 33).

III. Capital for Financing for Multifamily Housing Comes from a Number of Sources, with the Enterprises Playing a Major Role

Today there is roughly $1 trillion in residential multifamily mortgage debt outstanding (Federal Reserve Bank of the United States 2015b). Capital flows to the multifamily mortgage market from several sources, including banks and thrifts, Fannie Mae and Freddie Mac, Ginnie Mae, state and local credit agencies, conduits for commercial MBS, and life insurance companies.

Banks and thrifts, which account for 33 percent of multifamily debt outstanding, typically offer floating-rate, non-amortizing loans with three- to five-year maturities serving a broad range of lender needs (Federal Reserve Bank of the United States 2015b). Some banks also both issue mortgage-backed securities (MBS) backed by loans they have originated or purchased and purchase MBS that they hold in portfolio. Like most private sources of capital in the multifamily market, bank lending can be highly sensitive to overall economic conditions and tends to dry up during market downturns.

Fannie Mae and Freddie Mac collectively account for about 32 percent of multifamily debt outstanding (Federal Reserve Bank of the United States 2015b). The Enterprises purchase loans originated by other financial institutions and either package them into MBS or hold them in their own investment portfolios.[7] Since 2008, when the Enterprises were placed under the conservatorship of the federal government, Fannie and Freddie have had access to a capped line of credit with the U.S. Treasury, meaning they are effectively backed by taxpayers. Due in part to the government guarantee, the Enterprises are able to access a large pool of low-cost capital, offer mortgages with terms longer than typical for banks when originating for their own portfolios, and fund mortgages even during economic and housing downturns when risk-taking capital becomes scarce. The existence of a ready market for trading Enterprise multifamily securities also helps to provide liquidity to the multifamily mortgage market as a whole.

The federal government accounts for 10 percent of multifamily debt outstanding (Federal Reserve Bank of the United States 2015b). This includes Ginnie Mae securities, which are backed mainly by mortgages insured by the Federal Housing Administration (FHA), as well as the much smaller amount of multifamily mortgages guaranteed by the Department of Agriculture (Ginnie Mae 2014). With the backing of the federal government, FHA is able to make favorable pricing available for high-leverage loans with terms of up to forty years and for construction financing as part of the permanent loan.[8]

Commercial mortgage-backed securities (CMBS) account for 7 percent of multifamily debt outstanding (Federal Reserve Bank of the United States 2015b). These are securities issued by so-called conduits—which are often financial institutions—made up of multifamily, office, retail, and other loans that are not backed by the federal government. The CMBS market was a major source of capital during the recent housing bubble before it practically shut down in the years immediately following the crisis. As the multifamily market has recovered, CMBS issuances have substantially rebounded in recent years (see below) (Geiger 2014).

Life insurance companies account for another 6 percent of multifamily debt outstanding (Federal Reserve Bank of the United States 2015b). As part of their investment portfolios, life insurance companies have a limited appetite for high-quality, long-term assets that match their long-term liabilities to policyholders. Historically, life insurance companies have preferred to directly finance only "Class A" multifamily assets, such as luxury apartment

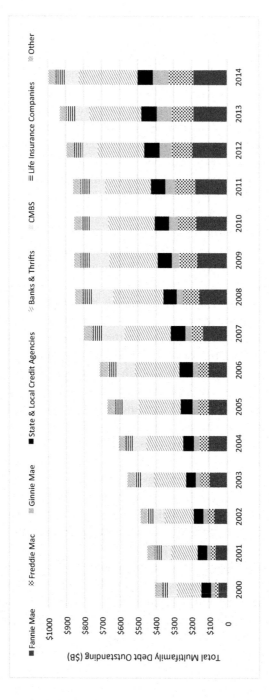

Figure 4.1. Multifamily mortgage debt outstanding by source of capital, 2000–2014. Fannie Mae (2015a) analysis of Federal Reserve data.

buildings in top-tier housing markets. These companies also support the mortgage market by holding in portfolio MBS guaranteed by the agencies and by Ginnie Mae.

Other sources account for the remaining 12 percent of multifamily debt outstanding (Federal Reserve Bank of the United States 2015b). The bulk of this debt is owned by state and local credit agencies and other government entities that issue mortgage-related bonds to finance the construction and preservation of affordable rental housing. This total also includes private pension funds, state and local government retirement funds, Real Estate Investment Trusts, nonbank corporate businesses, and individuals.

Although the relative size of these different sources has varied over time, they all remain active today, providing broad liquidity to the multifamily market. See Figure 4.1 for how each source's share of the market has changed over the past fifteen years.

As the figure shows, the total amount of multifamily debt outstanding gradually doubled between 2000 and 2007, driven largely by an increase in lending by banks, thrifts, and CMBS conduits. When the housing crisis hit in 2007 and 2008, the multifamily market continued to grow—albeit at a much slower clip—undergirded largely by government-backed capital provided by Ginnie Mae, Fannie Mae, and Freddie Mac. Over the whole period from 2000 to 2014, the share attributable to these government-backed sources grew significantly from less than 25 percent to more than 40 percent.

IV. Lessons from the Housing Crisis:
The Multifamily System Works

The recent housing and economic downturn prompted many private sources of capital to retreat from funding new mortgages or MBS not backed by the government. However, the Enterprises and other government-backed sources ensured the continued availability of capital, thus helping to avoid a total collapse of the funding for the new multifamily mortgages and preventing asset prices from falling even further.[9] In 2006, the Enterprises combined for 32 percent of multifamily debt acquisitions. By 2008, the year Fannie and Freddie were placed under government conservatorship, the Enterprises' share of the market more than doubled, to 79 percent, as investors were leery of putting their money into housing without a government guarantee

(Fannie Mae 2015a: 6). Between 2007 and 2009, non-Enterprise issuances of multifamily MBS dropped by 92 percent (Fannie Mae 2015a: 6).

The Enterprises were able to provide this countercyclical support in part because they were backed by the federal government, which allowed them to maintain access to capital markets for the securities they guaranteed and to fund the mortgages they purchased and held in portfolio.[10] Another factor that allowed Fannie and Freddie to stay in the market was the high credit quality of the multifamily loans that they had been guaranteed and which had much lower delinquency rates and losses than the rest of the market, as shown in Figure 4.2 below.[11] The Enterprises' multifamily businesses remained steadily profitable, even as the single-family sides of their businesses required billions of dollars in support from the federal government to stay solvent.[12]

The multifamily business of both Enterprises had been able to avoid a "race to the bottom" on underwriting standards. In 1988, Fannie Mae instituted a risk-sharing program with a highly selective group of Delegated Underwriting and Servicing (DUS) lenders (Fannie Mae 2015b; Segal and Szymanoski 1998: 59, 69). Under this business model, only a limited number of so-called DUS lenders are authorized to commit Fannie Mae to acquire multifamily loans, which are underwritten, originated, and serviced according to Fannie's standards. In exchange for this authority, DUS lenders must share the risk of loss over the life of the loan, generally retaining, on a pari passu basis, one-third of the underlying credit risk on each loan sold to Fannie Mae.[13] This risk sharing aligns the interests between Fannie and its delegated underwriters to ensure that loans are properly underwritten.

As for Freddie Mac, a high level of losses caused the company to drop out of the multifamily market for three years in the early 1990s. When Freddie reentered the market, it would only work with a highly selective group of "Program Plus Seller/Servicer" lenders. Moreover, the company brought all underwriting for these loans totally in-house (Segal and Szymanoski 1998: 70).[14] More recently, Freddie's underwriting undergoes further scrutiny from investors who are required to take the first losses on the multifamily securities. Under so-called K-Deals, which Freddie began issuing in 2009, the security is divided into tranches, with investors in the "senior" tranches receiving payment first and investors in the "subordinate" tranches being the first to absorb any losses (Brickman 2013). Although the senior tranches benefit from a Freddie guarantee, the subordinate tranches do not, thus aligning the incentives of both Freddie and the investors in the subordinate

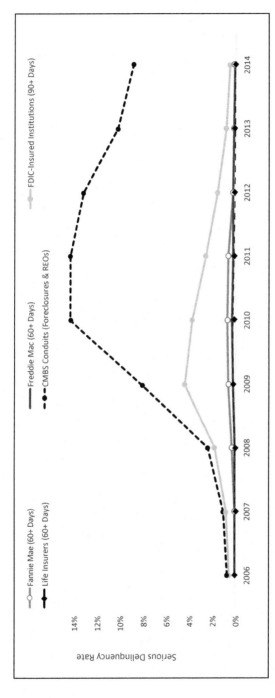

Figure 4.2. Multifamily mortgage delinquency rates by source of capital, 2006–2014. (Not all delinquency rates are comparable between investor groups. GSE and life insurance data reflect 60+ delinquency rates. FDIC bank data reflect 90+ day delinquency rates [the 60+ day rate would presumably be higher]. For CMBS, the threshold being measured is presumably even more restrictive because it only includes properties that are in foreclosures or REO.) Fannie Mae (2015a) analysis of multifamily finance data.

tranches for each to independently and carefully underwrite these loans (Goodman and Parsons 2012: 80).[15] The ability of Freddie to issue K-Deal securities depends on its ability to market the subordinate tranches, thus potentially limiting its flexibility to serve markets where credit risk is not well understood by investors. As of September 2013, the current loan delinquency rate on mortgages in K-deals was just 0.06 percent, and the losses to investors in the subordinate tranches appear to be very small and well short of the 15 percent losses that would have to happen before the senior bonds that Freddie guarantees would be at risk (Brickman 2013).

In addition to countercyclical support, the Enterprises have been an important source of credit over the course of the business cycle for buildings that offer rents affordable to low-income households—meaning they earn below 80 percent of the area median income—and for projects being built under the Low Income Housing Tax Credit program (Gould Ellen, Tye, and Willis 2010: 8–9, 20). As shown in Figure 4.3 below, according to the Federal Housing Finance Agency (FHFA), at least 75 percent of the multifamily units financed by the Enterprises in 2013 were affordable to low-income households, and 17 percent were affordable to households earning less than half of the area median income (FHFA 2014a).

As overall economic and housing conditions have continued to improve, the other sources of mortgage capital have bounced back to more traditional levels, in contrast to the continued depressed levels of the private-label securities (PLS) market on the single-family side. As a result, the Enterprises' share of multifamily originations is beginning to fall back to pre-recession levels. As shown in Figure 4.4, the Enterprises combined for 31 percent of originations in 2013. Meanwhile, banks, life insurance companies, CMBS conduits, and other private sources have gradually returned to the market in recent years, combining for 58 percent of the multifamily market in 2013 (FHFA 2014a: 491). Today new multifamily construction has returned to historical levels while that for single family remains subdued (Sparshott and Hudson 2015).

One key factor that accounts for the relative resiliency of the multifamily market is the very nature of multifamily lending, which differs in important ways from single-family lending. Although multifamily loans are generally nonrecourse to the borrower, careful underwriting is required to assess the sufficiency of the cash flow generated by the property to cover the debt payments and to assess a borrower's creditworthiness and ability to successfully operate the apartment property that acts as collateral for the loan.[16] The loan

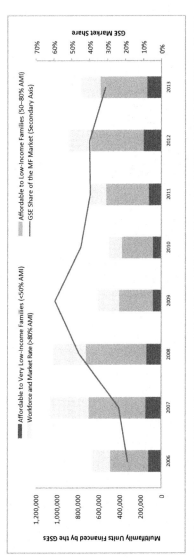

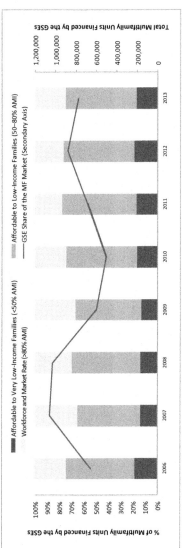

Figure 4.3. Affordability of multifamily units financed by the enterprises by year, 2006–2013. Federal Housing Finance Agency (2014a).

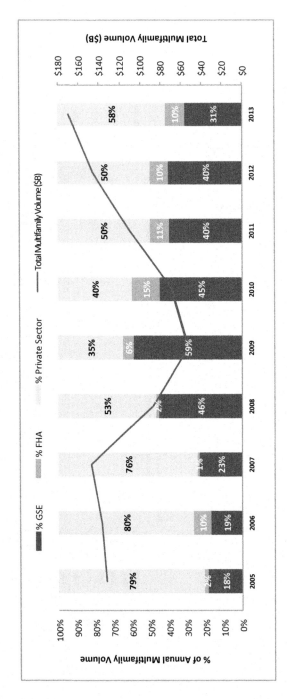

Figure 4.4. Share of the multifamily originations market by source of capital, 2005–2013. Federal Housing Finance Agency (2014a).

evaluation process includes an examination of such quantitative and qualitative data as liquid assets, net worth, number of units owned, experience in a market and/or property type, multifamily portfolio performance, access to additional liquidity, debt maturities, asset/property management platform, senior management experience, reputation and lender exposure (Fannie Mae 2012b: 4). In addition, the relatively large loan sizes in the multifamily market and the limited number of loans in a security—at times a security may include as few as one loan—allows investors to do their own underwriting (in contrast to the large number of small loans in a single-family MBS).[17] Moreover, servicing of multifamily loans that become delinquent is handled by specialists (so-called "special servicers").[18] The combination of the limited number of loans for investors to underwrite and "high-touch" servicing allowed investors to gain the comfort necessary to reenter the CMBS market.

V. Government Involvement Brings Challenges

Government involvement in the multifamily housing finance system brings three challenges: (1) how to avoid elevated risk due to moral hazard, (2) how to prevent the Enterprises from crowding out private capital that would otherwise well serve the market (White and Wilkins 2013: 3), and (3) how to protect the Enterprises from the inevitable political pressure from government officials and politicians to make decisions that could underprice the actual riskiness of loans. Fortunately, the multifamily finance market seems to have resisted the worst of these, but as discussed later in this chapter, a number of steps can be taken to further guard against these concerns.

A. Moral Hazard

The combination of private ownership with an implicit government guarantee of corporate obligations can create moral hazard, with the Enterprises taking on extra risk to increase their profits. With their relationship to the government allowing them to access low-cost capital, regardless of the riskiness of their mortgage purchases and the perception that the government will bail them out if they get into trouble, the outcome can lead to what has been referred to as the "privatization of gain and socialization of losses"—an outcome which has been attributed to the single-family side of the Enterprises businesses (Morgenson and Rosner 2011; Boyack 2011).

Fortunately, the multifamily businesses of the Enterprises appears to have held to high standards and do not appear to have taken excessive risks, as evidenced by their low delinquency rates. As explained above, the multifamily programs at both Enterprises incorporate risk sharing with the private sector, resulting in high underwriting standards. A noted above, the DUS model aligned originators' incentives with those of Fannie, to carefully underwrite the loans. As for Freddie, it kept its underwriting in-house and now has the added oversight of the investors of its subordinate tranches in its K-Deals.

B. Crowding out Private Capital

Another concern is that access to low-cost capital would allow the Enterprises to "crowd out" private capital. In two areas at least, this would not seem to be a problem. The first is during market downturns—such as the period between 2008 and 2012—when private sources of capital tend to retreat from the mortgage market, leaving few options other than government-backed sources. The second concerns multifamily properties that serve low-income families.

As mentioned earlier, a significant portion of Enterprise-backed multifamily mortgages serve low-income families—including many properties receiving subsidies through the Low-Income Housing Tax Credit, Section 8 project-based rental assistance and other programs—while serving many secondary and tertiary housing markets (Fannie Mae 2015a: 14). Traditionally, these segments of the market are less attractive to the private sector, in part because the profit margins are relatively small. For example, insurance companies tend to finance higher-end properties, and CMBS conduits look to finance standard types of deals, not those with layers of government subsidy. Although there may well be more of an issue of crowding out in the middle and upper ends of the multifamily market, especially when the housing market is strong, competition is less likely in the more affordable segments of the market.

Nevertheless, it may still be true that the Enterprises are crowding out private sources of capital because the government backing does give them extra pricing power, which they can use to cream higher quality deals. Later in this chapter we propose a way to test the willingness and ability of the private market to backfill markets now served by the Enterprises. One important concern with anything that reduces the footprint of the Enterprises would be a loss of liquidity and reasonably priced capital to the multifamily finance system, especially during economic downturns. The challenge is to make sure that the Enterprises pass on to borrowers the savings from having access to low-cost capital throughout the business cycle, as well as allow them to serve the parts of the market that otherwise would be underserved. At the same time, it is important that the Enterprises are not able to crowd out private capital that could serve the same customers or capture some of the savings for themselves for the benefit of their management and investors.[19]

C. Political Pressure

A third challenge is to prevent government officials and politicians from trying to use the Enterprises to carry out agendas that may weaken the quality of their underwriting. In the single-family market, some critics have claimed that politically motivated efforts to expand homeownership encouraged the Enterprises to lower their underwriting standards in the mid- and late-2000s, leading to significant losses when the foreclosure crisis took hold.[20]

Regardless of whether this occurred in the single-family market—and there is considerable room for debate on that issue—it is not clear that any such pressure existed in the multifamily market because so much of the political attention was on homeownership and not on rental housing. In short, there does not seem to be evidence that the Enterprises offered risky multifamily mortgages.

VI. Opportunities for Reforming the Multifamily Housing Finance System

Over the past six years, dozens of proposals have been offered to reform America's housing finance system, including four comprehensive reform bills introduced in the 113th Congress alone (Enterprise Community Partners 2015).[21] The proposals range from nationalizing Fannie Mae and

Freddie Mac as official government entities, to eliminating the Enterprises and fully privatizing the U.S. mortgage market, to establishing a hybrid approach of privately issued, government-insured securities.

Reform should follow a simple maxim: Do no harm. The burden of proof should be on those who propose such a major change to show either that the existing system is untenable or that a better way exists that will not significantly disrupt the supply of multifamily rental housing throughout the business cycle.[22] It makes no sense to automatically impose the same reforms on the multifamily businesses as the single-family businesses.

Doing no harm does not necessarily mean that the Enterprises themselves must be preserved in their current forms, nor does it preclude Congress from winding down the Enterprises over time (see Section VII below). Three areas for reform exist: (1) The government guarantee should be made explicit, priced, separated from the Enterprises, and more widely available to other entities that may want to enter the market; (2) the multifamily businesses now part of the Enterprises should be spun off in order to allow them to continue to serve the market while also promoting more competition; and (3) to ensure that the government's involvement benefits as much of the market as possible, those securitizers benefiting from the government guarantee need to offer mortgages on viable projects that other players in the market tend to ignore or underserve.

A. Make the Government Guarantee Explicit, Priced, Separate from the Enterprises, and Widely Available

One way to further reduce the dangers of moral hazard and limit taxpayer exposure without disrupting the market would be to make the guarantee explicit and have its provision overseen by a separate government entity.[23] To further protect taxpayers, the guaranteeing entity (called the public guarantor) should charge a premium for providing this coverage, using the proceeds to build a loss reserve.[24] To lower risk in the whole system, this entity should also set standards and monitor performance for the underwriting and servicing of the loans, and make the guarantee more generally available to other issuers of qualifying securities.

An additional step to limit the the public guarantor's (and the taxpayer's) exposure to loss would be to ensure that a sufficient amount of private capital is required to be at risk ahead of the government guarantee. The private capital should be sufficient to cover losses during periods of all but the most extreme economic or housing distress—that is, the government guarantee would only be triggered in the case of catastrophic economic conditions. The responsibility for requiring and monitoring the level of private capital would be under the purview of the public guarantor. In the case of a DUS lender system, it would be necessary to set and monitor the capital levels of both the lenders and the issuer/insurer of the securities that is sharing the risk on a pari passu basis. In the case of the Freddie Mac model, the subordinate tranches need to be large enough, and the issuer and insurer of the senior bonds will have to have sufficent capital to cover losses where a disproportionately large number of defaults occur within a single pool of mortgages (Goodman and Zhu 2014b).

B. Preserve the Current Multifamily Businesses in Some Form, but Also Promote More Competition

One way to minimize disruption to the multifamily housing market resulting from reform of the single-family sides of the Enterprises would be to separate out the existing multifamily businesses into self-contained subsidiaries, which could ultimately be sold off to private investors if the Enterprises are phased out.[25] Initially, these subsidiaries could pay their respective holding companies for continuing to provide the government guarantee. Once the public guarantor is up and running, the now fully explicit guarantee for the multifamily business would be purchased from this new entity whether or not these entities have been sold off or remain with the Enterprises.[26] The guarantee would only cover the qualifying securities issued by the new entities, not their corporate debt.[27]

In order to promote competition and efficiency in the guaranteed segment of the market, over time the catastrophic guarantee should be made available to other issuers of qualifying multifamily securities beyond the Enterprises. Each new issuer should be subject to approval by the regulator and guarantor to ensure, for example, that it meets minimum risk-sharing and capital requirements and that it monitors the quality of both the servicing and underwriting by its originators. If more competitors do not enter the market place, then it may be necessary for the government to impose regulations to ensure that the benefits of low-cost capital flow to borrowers.[28]

C. Continue the Commitment to Serving Underserved Market Segments

To ensure continued service to segments of the multifamily market that have been traditionally underserved, the government could require securitizers that benefit from the government guarantee to devote a certain percentage of their business to those segments of the market. Under this approach, securitizers benefiting from a government guarantee would still be able to do business in other markets—for example, those with rents only affordable to higher-income households, such as those making more than 120 percent of Area Median Income (AMI). However, they could only do so if they finance a corresponding amount of units from the designated markets that have been historically underserved. Stated another way, the more units that are financed in market segments that are not traditionally well served, the more overall business the securitizer can do.

With such a rule in place, regulators could ensure that the government guarantee is serving a clear social purpose: building and preserving affordable rental housing in underserved markets. Of course, the specified minimum shares should not preclude the securitizers from having a reasonable chance of making a profit. Otherwise, no entity will avail itself of the government guarantee. One place to start in determining these shares would be to look at the recent experience of these entities to serve these markets and still make a profit.[29] The recent track records of the Enterprises show an ability to sustain a mix of business profitably: some 75 percent of the units funded are able to serve tenants earning 80 percent of AMI and for 17 percent able to serve tenants at 50 percent of AMI (FHFA 2014a). Other submarkets such as rural multifamily housing could also have a specified minimum share.[30]

Another approach—which could be done in addition to the mandate described above—would be to divert some of the profit that the government guarantee allows the securitizers to earn as a result of access to low-cost capital. One example would be a surcharge on all multifamily mortgages securitized with a government guarantee; another would be just to impose the surcharge on multifamily projects that contain a high proportion of higher-rent units. These funds could then be channelled to the entities focused on serving underserved markets, such as the existing Housing Trust Fund and the Capital Magnet Fund as well as the proposed Market Access Fund (Narasimhan 2013). For example, an annual assessment of 10 basis points on the total mortgage principal outstanding in securities with a government guarantee—single and multifamily, including securities guaranteed by Ginnie Mae—could generate up to $6 billion each year for the three funds, once fully phased in.[31]

VII. Some Ideas for Testing—Can the Scope of the Market Backed by Government Guarantee Be Cut Back Without Doing Harm?

The increased presence of the Enterprises in the market has not been universally welcomed. As mentioned above, critics claim that the Enterprises have crowded out other sources of capital and are not needed to maintain a healthy multifamily mortgage market (White and Wilkins 2013: 12). As a result, some have proposed to eliminate the Enterprises' multifamily businesses entirely as part of any housing finance reform effort and to discontinue a government guarantee beyond that offered by Ginnie Mae (Committee on Financial Services 2013).

Although it is important to maintain a sufficient government presence in the multifamily housing finance system to ensure the availability of funding for new mortgages during economic downturns, it might be possible to reduce its presence during good economic times. As a condition for determining if a reduction is sensible, it is important to assess whether the securitizers or other sources of capital would be able to provide the market support necessary during the down cycles to be able to fill in the gap left by a reduction in the share of the market supported by the government guarantee. It is this latter question to which we now turn.

A. What Is the Ability of Other Sources of Capital to Fill a Gap Caused by a Reduction in the Government Guarantee?

One way to assess the ability of other major sources of multifamily mortgage capital to fill the gap caused by a retrenchment in the government guarantee is to look at what determines their current volume and how much and how quickly they could expand if the Enterprises were simply phased out over a five-year period, as has been often proposed (Enterprise Community Partners 2015). Some, if not all, of the private sources of capital—including banks, life companies, CMBS conduits, and Ginnie Mae—seemingly would face significant constraints on their ability to respond in a timely manner to such a phase-out.

In order for banks, life companies, and other private sources to fill the gap left by the Enterprises, they would have to meaningfully increase the share of their assets devoted to this asset class. For most of these types of entities, maintaining diversified portfolios is part of prudent financial management, resulting in being able to devote only a portion of investment assets to mortgages. Prudent management for banks, for example, calls for them to diversify their assets across classes with different risk profiles from those of mortgages.[32] As a result, although banks could increase the share of mortgages within their portfolios, their overall capacity to do so is limited by their ability to grow their assets overall.

Already, almost 30 percent of bank portfolios consist of residential and commercial mortgages, and of the mortgages they hold, only about 8 percent are multifamily (Federal Reserve Bank of the United States 2015b).[33] In an extreme scenario, if banks were relied upon to be the sole source of funding for mortgages, they would have to devote their whole portfolios to that asset class—an outcome that no prudential bank regulator would allow.

Similarly, life insurance companies and private pension funds now devote only about 9 percent (Federal Reserve Bank of the United States 2015b: 91) and 0.2 percent (Federal Reserve Board 2015a: 93) of their respective portfolios to mortgages, and only a fraction of those numbers are multifamily mortgages. They do hold mortgages backed by the government, but unless they were willing to increase their holdings of mortgages alone or invest in CMBS, they might not be much help. Over time, presumably, their mortgage holdings would likely grow, but only at the rate of growth of their overall portfolios.

Another possible source of capital would be a vastly expanded role for CMBS conduits. Although the market for new CMBS business disappeared for a period during the recent economic downturn as private investors exited the market, it had grown significantly before the financial crisis, and with new issuances rising again, its share of outstanding mortgages could bounce back to earlier levels. Even so, its share of the total of mortgage debt obligations outstanding never exceeded 15 percent of the market, or about $124 billion (Federal Reserve Bank of the United States 2015c: 118).[34]

Ginnie Mae multifamily securities also tap the rate-investor market and so could conceivably be expanded, but their growth is limited by the capacity of FHA to endorse a larger number of individual loans. Further expansion of FHA's capacity would require an increase in congressional appropriations and would increase the taxpayers' potential exposure to losses because both FHA and Ginnie Mae are backed by the U.S. government.[35]

In summary, it is hard to see how these alternative sources of capital could expand fast enough, either individually or collectively, to substitute for the Enterprises, particularly within a five-year timeline. Doing so would require major increases in portfolio allocations of banks, insurance companies, and pension funds, or a fast scale-up of the CMBS market to record highs. The resulting decrease in financing could significantly hurt the multifamily housing market. Developers would not be able to build as many multifamily units. Owners would also have trouble recapitalizing or raising cash to make major repairs, which could force certain owners to disinvest from or not properly maintain their properties. It could also make the property market less liquid, leaving investors locked into their investments and unable to take cash out.

Moreover, the loss of Fannie Mae and Freddie Mac could have a disproportionately negative impact on the availability of longer-term loans,[36] thus leaving borrowers with more interest rate risk.[37] To compensate, owners would have to build higher financing costs into their cost base, resulting in higher rents, higher abandonment, and less supply. All of these changes could very well have a disproportionately large effect on the supply and maintenance of older, privately owned stock, which is a key part of the Enterprises' multifamily business (Freddie Mac 2012: 7).

B. Testing the Waters

Given these questions as to the willingness and ability of the mortgage finance market to fill any gaps if the Enterprises should simply go away, it seems prudent to proceed carefully, testing along the way for any serious disruptions of the multifamily housing market. One approach might be to gradually lower the amount of multifamily business the Enterprises can do by setting a volume cap that then can be lowered in stages.[38] To do this, the cap would have to be lowered very slowly to ensure that it would not create too big a gap in the market for others to fill, thereby undermining the market's ability to expand the supply of new multifamily buildings to meet the increasing demand. Perhaps more of a problem is that a cap that works one year may be totally inappropriate the next year as the demand for mortgages fluctuates widely with economic and real estate cycles.

Alternatively, the Enterprises could simply be made less competitive in some or all of its market, thereby testing whether other sources of finance can be "crowded in." Such an approach would be unlikely to leave gaps in the market (although it could cause the cost of mortgages to rise) and so would provide a relatively low-risk way to test the overall availability of mortgage credit. Such a test might involve increasing, in stages, the guarantee fee for a small subset of securities, such as those that contain properties that serve higher-income households. The threshold for determining which securities are subject to a surcharge could be based on a combination of the income level being served (using the standard of 30 percent of income being devoted to housing) and the percent of units with rents that exceed that limit. This test would provide evidence of (1) how easy it would be to "crowd in" more portfolio lending or nonguaranteed CMBS and (2) the possible impact of such changes on the mix of products that would be available to finance multifamily rental units.

The previously discussed idea of requiring that minimum proportions of the business serve traditionally underserved markets could also be used as a vehicle to test the ability of other players to fill any gap resulting from a reduction in the overall level of multifamily finance business done by those securitizers that benefit from a government guarantee. By raising the required share of their business that must go to historically underserved markets, the ability of these securitizers to capture market share will be reduced. Participating securitizers will be forced to either grow the business in traditionally underserved markets or cut back their financing of units that serve households at higher incomes. Moreover, because the traditionally underserved market is thought to be less profitable, forcing them to cut back on the share of their business that can come from the more profitable market segments will both reduce their penetration of those markets and cause them to have to raise the fees. Whichever action they take, the effect will be to make it easier for other sources of capital to compete for a higher share of the multifamily finance business, thus limiting the ability of those securitizers benefiting from the government guarantee to crowd out the competition by underpricing them. Again, care must be taken not to make the overall business unprofitable, or no securitizers will avail themselves of the government guarantee.

If in either or both of these cases the other sources of capital step up, and the impact on the availability and product mix of mortgages for multifamily properties were acceptable—for example, no significant negative impact on the supply, quality, or affordability of multifamily units—then further steps can be taken in the same direction by increasing the types of properties subject to the surcharge or requiring that the underserved segments receive an even higher share of the overall number of units being financed.

VIII. Conclusion

The construction of multifamily housing is now back to pre-crisis levels, and the multifamily housing finance system seems to have recovered as well. Even during the downturn, money for new mortgages remained available as a result of government backing of the MBS of Fannie, Freddie, and Ginnie Mae. The multifamily housing finance system worked in contrast to the near collapse of the Enterprises' single-family businesses, which required a massive government bailout and sparked calls for termination of the Enterprises.[39] The single-family mortgage market has still not fully recovered.

The Enterprise's multifamily businesses, in part a result of their access to a government guarantee, have been able to (1) provide countercyclical support to the rental market by funding new mortgages throughout the recent housing and economic downturn, (2) offer longer-term mortgages than generally available from banks, and (3) ensure that the vast majority of the mortgages they fund offer rents affordable to low-income households.

Reform should be careful not to lessen these benefits; nevertheless, some steps seem appropriate to take at this time. The government guarantee could be made explicit, offered separately by a government entity, priced appropriately, and made available to competitors originating MBS backed by qualified mortgages. In addition, in order not to disrupt the availability of mortgage financing even if the Enterprises are eliminated, their multifamily housing finance businesses could be placed into self-contained subsidiaries and available to be spun off in the future as private entities. Those securitizers that continue to benefit from the government guarantee should have a requirement to serve those segments of the multifamily market that have traditionally been ignored or underserved by other sources of capital. As a general rule, any steps to lower the share of the market served now by the multifamily businesses backed by a government guarantee should only be carried out as part of a careful testing of the ability of the other sources of capital to fill the gap.

CHAPTER 5

The Once and Future Federal Housing Administration

Kevin A. Park and Roberto G. Quercia

I. Introduction

In the depths of the Great Depression, Congress enacted the National Housing Act of 1934 that created a new federal agency, the Federal Housing Administration (FHA), to provide mortgage lenders insurance against credit losses. In the half century that followed, the FHA was instrumental in increasing the homeownership rate in the United States and responsible for developing the thirty-year fixed-rate, prepayable mortgage that came to dominate the American housing finance market.[1]

Yet the FHA appeared to be a vestigial part of America's housing finance system near the end of the twentieth century. Faced with the growth of the government-sponsored enterprises (GSEs), Fannie Mae and Freddie Mac, and competition from the private mortgage insurance industry, the FHA was relegated to a niche market of first-time homebuyers and underserved borrowers.

The housing crisis that accompanied the Great Recession thrust the agency back to prominence and demonstrated the value of an explicit government guarantee to stabilize a distressed housing market. Losses suffered in performing this countercyclical role prompted the first draw on the U.S. Treasury in the FHA's history. However, the agency has undertaken a variety of reforms and premium increases designed to increase the economic value of recent books of business. The challenge is balancing the financial

health of the Mutual Mortgage Insurance (MMI) Fund with the social purpose of the FHA's mortgage insurance program.

Eventually, its market share will fall closer to historical norms, and the
FHA will return to a targeted program for low wealth and underserved borrowers. But with its reverse mortgage program catering to an aging Baby
Boom generation and new housing demand projected to disproportionately
come from minority households, the FHA is likely to play an important role
well into the twenty-first century.

II. The FHA in the Great Recession

The FHA's underwriting standards are generally less sensitive to the housing cycle than those of the conventional market (Ambrose, Pennington-
Cross, and Yezer 2002). Consequently, the FHA activity is often directly
correlated with housing risks such as mortgage defaults, house price declines,
and house price volatility (Holmes and Horvitz 1994; Ambrose, Pennington-
Cross, and Yezer 2002; Immergluck 2011). At the peak of the most recent
housing cycle, FHA accounted for less than 2 percent of new loan originations by dollar volume. Within three years, as house prices plummeted, the
FHA's market share spiked to over 20 percent overall and even more among
home purchase loans. Figure 5.1 clearly shows the FHA's countercyclical
market share.

Only some of the increase in the FHA's market share was due to an increase in maximum loan amount that the FHA could insure. Loan limits are
adjusted annually according to local median sales prices, but the Housing
and Economic Recovery Act of 2008 temporarily increased the loan limit
"floor" for a single-family unit from $200,160 to $271,050.[2] Yet only 29 percent
of the FHA endorsements by dollar volume (16 percent by loan count) since
2008 has been for loan amounts above the previously applicable limits. Moreover, the higher loan amounts were disproportionately refinancings rather
than home purchase mortgage originations. Since March 2008, the FHA has
helped refinance over 1.4 million conventional mortgages, allowing borrowers otherwise shut out by declining home equity levels to take advantage of
lower mortgage interest rates and ease their debt burden.

Although loan limits are tailored to local market conditions, FHA insurance premiums do not vary by geography. By contrast, private market participants increase prices or tighten underwriting in response to a declining

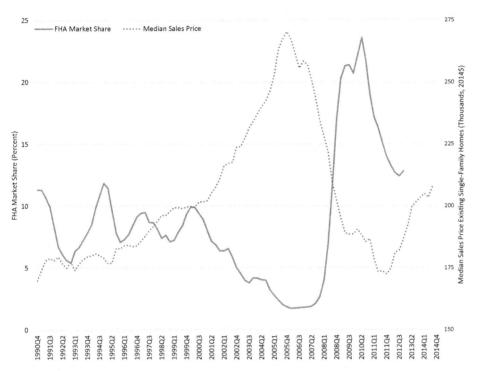

Figure 5.1. The Federal Housing Administration's countercyclical market share.
Note: Four-quarter moving market share. Inside Mortgage Finance (2004, 2006, 2008, 2010, 2012, 2013); National Association of Realtors Metro Home Prices/State Resales, Moody's Economy.com.

market. Consequently, the FHA's market share tends to increase disproportionately in areas most distressed. Figure 5.2 plots the change in the FHA's market share between 2006 and 2009 by county against the inflation-adjusted median sales price of existing homes. The geographic cross-section reveals the same countercyclical phenomenon as the previous time series. A line of best fit indicates that for every 10 percent decline in house prices in this time period, the FHA's market share increased by roughly two percentage points. The change in house prices alone explains 10 percent of the variation in FHA activity.

The FHA's countercyclical role was under-appreciated at the height of the housing bubble. Moody's Analytics estimates that if the FHA had suddenly stopped endorsing new loans in October 2010, conventional mortgage interest rates would have spiked, further depressing the housing market. New and existing home sales would have fallen an additional 2.4 million in 2011, and

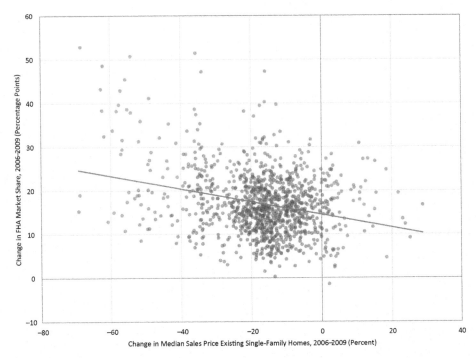

Figure 5.2. The Federal Housing Administration's countercyclical market share by county. Inside Mortgage Finance (2004, 2006, 2008, 2010, 2012, 2013); National Association of Realtors Metro Home Prices/State Resales, Moody's Economy.com; authors' tabulation of data from the Home Mortgage Disclosure Act.

median sales prices plunged by another $40,800, or roughly 19 percent. "The collapse in the housing market and resulting foreclosure crisis would have been measurably more severe if not for the unprecedented government response to stem the free fall. . . . Arguably the most important policy response to the housing crash has been the dramatic expansion of Federal Housing Administration lending" (Zandi and deRitis 2010).

Not even the GSEs in conservatorship can function as effectively as a buffer against a collapse in housing given their statutory requirement for private credit enhancement in order to purchase loans with low down payments. The most common form of credit enhancement is private mortgage insurance and the private mortgage insurance industry is facing its own financial problems. Three private mortgage insurance companies were forced into run-off by their state regulators and could not insure new loans.

The FHA's market share has gradually begun falling from its peak in 2009 and 2010, but the losses on these books of business related to the housing crisis continue to plague the MMI Fund.

III. The Financial Condition of the Mutual Mortgage Insurance Fund

There are three ways to evaluate the financial health of the FHA's MMI Fund.

The first approach simply examines the available capital resources and cash flow in the program. The most recent independent actuarial review finds that the MMI Fund has a net $28.4 billion in capital resources at the end of FY2014, down 22 percent from FY2010 (IFE 2014a, IFE 2014b, IFE 2010a, IFE 2010b). Further, claims continue to exceed revenue from premiums, property sale receipts and note sale proceeds. In total, the Fund lost $4 billion in FY2014. At the current rate, the FHA's capital resources would be exhausted in seven years.

Yet recent history may not be the best guide for future performance. Rather, the stream of premium revenue, prepayments, and claims can be modeled based on the credit quality of each book of business and projected economic conditions. Then the estimated value of total income and expense can be recorded on an accrual basis. The National Housing Act of 1990 requires an annual independent actuarial review to estimate the economic value of the MMI Fund, consisting of "the current cash available to the Fund, plus the net present value of all future cash inflows and outflows expected to result from the outstanding mortgages in the Fund." The National Housing Act also requires the MMI Fund to maintain a capital ratio (defined as the economic value as a share of the insurance in-force) of at least 2 percent. Using the amortized value of insurance in-force, the capital ratio was 7.4 percent as recently as FY2006 but fell below the 2 percent threshold three years later. In FY2012, the actuarial review had projected costs would exceed projected revenue and current capital resources by over $16 billion, meaning the economic value and capital ratio were negative (IFE 2012) (see Figure 5.3).

The financial health of the MMI Fund is also evaluated in a similar but separate process for budgetary purposes. Under the rules of the Federal Credit Reform Act of 1990 (FCRA), the negative economic value found at the end of the fiscal year by the Office of Management and Budget required

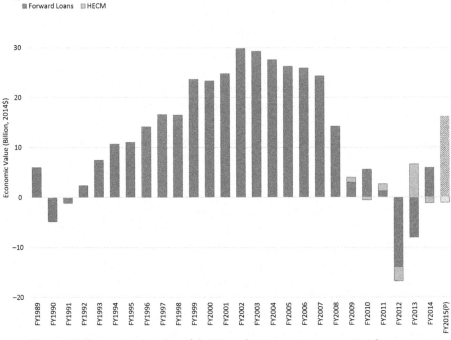

Figure 5.3. The economic value of the Mutual Mortgage Insurance Fund.
Independent actuarial reviews; Szymanoski et al. (2012).

the U.S. Treasury to transfer $1.7 billion to the MMI Fund in September
2013. It was the first time the FHA had to act on the authorization granted at
its founding to draw on taxpayer money to cover credit related losses.

A number of assumptions about the rate of prepayment and default are
required to estimate future cash flows. In addition, calculating the net
present value requires discounting future revenue and expenditures. FCRA
requires using discount rates based on the yield of Treasury securities of
comparable maturities at the time of endorsement; the actuarial review in
FY2014 based their discount rates on only the most recent yield curve, resulting in different estimates of the economic value. The actuarial review estimated the net present value of future cash flows at −$23.7 billion while the
result of using the discount rate required under FCRA results in an estimate
of −$20.6 billion. Applied to the current $28.4 billion in capital resources
yields an estimated economic value of $4.8 billion or $7.8 billion, respectively, and a capital ratio of 0.4 percent or 0.7 percent (U.S. Department of

Housing and Urban Development 2014). The discrepancy is unrelated to the projected rates of default and prepayment that will ultimately determine the true cost to the MMI Fund.

There is, however, uncertainty regarding future prepayment and claims. Risk-averse investors often demand a premium to compensate for this uncertainty. Consequently, some members of Congress have been pushing for an alternative approach known as fair-value accounting in addition to or instead of accrual accounting. For example, under the Protecting American Taxpayers and Homeowners (PATH) Act (H.R. 2767, 113th Cong. [2013]) "the executive branch and Congress would be required to use fair-value accounting in calculating the costs of FHA insurance programs that consider not only the borrowing costs of the federal government, but also the costs of the market risk the federal government is incurring by issuing FHA mortgage insurance or mortgage insurance commitments." Market risk is the correlation between the return on an investment and growth in the overall economy.

The Congressional Budget Office (CBO) compared FHA's mortgage insurance prices with those of private mortgage insurers, adjusting for differences in coverage, and with the combined cost of private mortgage insurance premiums and guarantee fees charged by the GSEs, and came to an estimate of the market risk premium of 115 basis points in 2014.[3] Using this premium, CBO estimates that FHA endorsements of forward loans between FY1992 and FY2014 with outstanding balances have a fair-value accounting cost of $64 billion, corresponding to a 5.2 percent subsidy rate. By contrast, under FCRA accounting, these books of business would cost roughly $5 billion and have a subsidy rate of just 0.4 percent (Castelli et al. 2014). Projecting endorsements over the next decade, CBO estimates that the FHA will generate budgetary savings of $63 billion (–2.8 percent subsidy rate) under FCRA accounting but cost $30 billion (1.3 percent subsidy rate) under fair-value accounting (Remy 2014).

The esoteric issue of discount rates has substantial consequences for estimating the value of the MMI Fund, which in turn has important ramifications for housing policy. Political and public support will be difficult for a program that appears to be bleeding taxpayer money, even if those losses will never be realized in the federal budget. But it is not clear why the federal government should be risk averse rather than risk neutral given its unique ability to pool resources across generations of taxpayers, effectively self-insuring against market risk (Moss 2004). Further, a negative subsidy under fair-value accounting rules would beg the question of why the federal government is involved at all. In fact, CBO estimates negative subsidy rates using fair-value accounting for home purchase loans endorsed in FY2014 with loan-to-value (LTV) ratios of 95 percent or more and credit scores of at least 680. "Those savings imply that private investors in an orderly market could guarantee such loans profitably under FHA's 2014 fee schedule" (Castelli et al. 2014).

IV. The FHA in the Twenty-First Century

Although its market presence is likely to retreat from its heights during the housing crisis, the FHA will remain an integral part of the American housing finance system in the twenty-first century. In the near term, the FHA must balance the need to rebuild the MMI Fund with the need to ensure continued access to sustainable mortgage credit. In the long term, the FHA is in a position to help address two demographic trends that will likely shape America's housing markets for the next century: the aging and the "browning" of America.

A. Balancing Risk and Access

According to the National Affordable Housing Act, the operational goals of the FHA's mortgage insurance program include minimizing the risk to the MMI Fund and to homeowners from default, maintaining an adequate capital ratio, avoiding adverse selection, and meeting the needs of homebuyers with low down payments and first-time homebuyers by providing access to mortgage credit. Obviously, these goals are sometimes in conflict.

For the past several years, the focus has been on tightening underwriting standards and raising premiums to reduce defaults and improve the financial health of the MMI Fund. A minimum credit score of 500 was necessary to be eligible for FHA insurance after 2010 (FHA 2010d). FHA also began evaluating lender performance using "compare ratios." If a lender has a two-year default rate 50 percent higher than the equivalent rate for the state in which the lender is active, then the FHA may terminate their direct endorsement authority (FHA 2010b; FHA 2013b). In response, lenders have been using credit overlays to tighten underwriting standards beyond the steps the FHA has already taken.

The single most important underwriting change was the banning of seller-funded down payment assistance programs. Popular at the height of the housing bubble, these programs skirted HUD rules against inducements to purchase by inflating sales prices and laundering funds through a non-profit agency, essentially financing the down payment and increasing the effective LTV ratio (Concentrance 2005; Government Accountability Office 2005; Foote 2009). HUD attempted to prohibit seller-funded down payment programs as far back as 1998, but the practice was not banned until the passage of the Housing and Economic Recovery Act in 2008. Appraisal standards were also strengthened to ensure independence and accuracy (FHA 2008c; FHA 2009). However, the damage was already done. The most recent actuarial review finds that loans with down payment assistance from non-profit organizations accounted for 32.1 percent of the negative present value of cash flows from endorsements between FY2001 and FY2008 compared to just 13.5 percent of origination volume. In total, these loans are projected to ultimately cost the MMI Fund roughly $16 billion (IFE 2014a). That is, the MMI Fund may have remained solvent if not for seller-funded down payment assistance programs that the FHA did not have the flexibility to ban without Congressional action.

These underwriting revisions and a lack of competition from conventional mortgage lenders have led to a dramatic change in the credit risk composition of recent FHA books of business. The average borrower credit score has increased from as low as 626 in 2007Q4 to over 700 in early 2011. In fact, the average credit score on a *denied* application for an FHA-insured home purchase mortgage was 669 in 2013 (Ellie Mae 2014). The result has been a reduction in default rates. Early payment delinquencies, defined as a 90-day delinquency in the first six months, was 2.5 percent for loans origination in 2007Q3 but has been less than 0.5 percent since 2010. Overall, the serious delinquency rate on FHA-insured loans has fallen from 9.6 percent at the end of 2009 to 6.2 percent in mid-2014.

What is the right default rate? Pinto (2012) argues that the FHA should not insure with a projected claim rate greater than 10 percent, assuming no house price appreciation or depreciation, and should target an average claims rate of 5 percent. However, the FHA has not had a book of business with a cumulative default rate less than 5 percent since 1977 (Figure 5.4). That includes all loans endorsed in the 1990s, when the economic value of the MMI Fund grew over $28 billion after adjusting for inflation. The average across all books of business is over 11 percent. Whether that risk of default is a

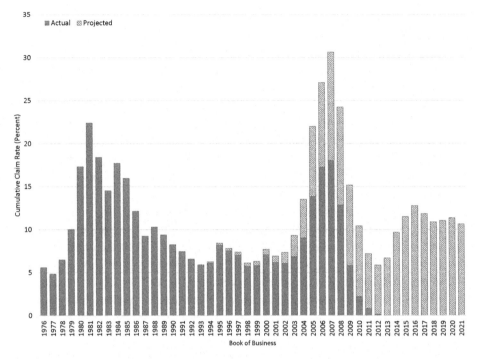

Figure 5.4. Actual and projected cumulative claim rates by book of business.
Independent actuarial reviews.

benefit to borrowers and housing markets involves a complex weighing of
the social and financial benefits of homeownership against the social and
financial costs of foreclosure.

One important underwriting criterion that the FHA has been reluctant
to tighten is the down payment requirement or, equivalently, the maximum
LTV ratio. Low or negative levels of home equity are seen as the primary de-
terminant of default risk in economic theory (Quercia and Stegman 1992;
Foote, Gerardi, and Willen 2008). At the same time, the amount of household
wealth necessary for a substantial down payment is an exceptionally binding constraint on homeownership (Linneman and Wachter 1989; Linneman
et al. 1997; Gyourko, Linneman, and Wachter 1999; Quercia, McCarthy, and
Wachter 2003; Barakova, Calem, and Wachter 2014). For example, in analyzing proposed down payment requirements for the Qualified Residential
Mortgage standard, Quercia, Ding, and Reid (2012) find that a maximum
97 percent LTV ratio excludes six performing loans for every prevented loan

default, but this "exclusion ratio" rises to nine and ten performing loans excluded for down payment requirements of 10 and 20 percent, respectively. Nevertheless, the Housing and Economic Recovery Act increased the minimum down payment from 3.0 to 3.5 percent, and borrowers with credit scores under 580 have not been eligible for LTV ratios greater than 90 percent after 2010 (FHA 2008b; FHA 2010d).

In addition to improving the credit quality of recent books of business, FHA mortgage insurance premiums have also been raised repeatedly (FHA 2008a; FHA 2010a; FHA 2010c; FHA 2011; FHA 2012; FHA 2013a). In 1983, the FHA replaced its 0.5 percent annual premium with a 3.8 percent up-front fee, which could be financed in the loan amount. Since 1990, the FHA has levied both up-front and annual premiums. In 2014, the premium for a thirty-year fixed-rate home purchase mortgage under $625,500 with an LTV ratio over 95 percent included a 1.75 percent charge up front and a 1.35 percent annual fee.

The FHA has also revised when or if insurance premiums could be cancelled or refunded. Originally, borrowers could be reimbursed upon prepayment for excess premium contributions, but the National Affordable Housing Act ended the practice of paying distributive shares as a means to rebuild the MMI Fund. More recently, the FHA implemented a policy in 2001 of cancelling mortgage insurance premiums when the amortized balance fell to less than 78 percent of the original house value, as required of private mortgage insurance companies under the Homeowner Protection Act of 1998. But they rescinded the policy in 2013, again to improve the financial health of the Fund. Instead, premiums will be assessed for the life of the loan, or up to eleven years if the origination LTV ratio is 90 percent or less (FHA 2013a).

The stronger credit quality, premium increases, and improved loss mitigation procedures have all contributed to a rebound in the economic value of the MMI Fund. The actuarial review finds the 2007 to 2009 books of business will cost the MMI Fund $26.6 billion. In contrast, the 2010 to 2013 books of business will contribute $34.0 billion and the 2014 book alone will add $11.1 billion. Consequently, the actuarial review projects the economic value to increase to over $15 billion in another year, with the capital ratio improving to 1.3 percent and exceeding the 2 percent threshold by FY2017.

What is the right capital ratio? Private mortgage insurers are seeing their regulatory capital ratios increase to 5.6 percent in light of the inadequacy of the previous 4.0 percent requirement.[4] In its most recent annual report to Congress, the FHA appears to be following suit, pointing out that the net present value of losses at its trough is expected to be roughly 8.5 percent.[5] Although the FHA assumes that another Great Recession or crisis of similar magnitude is unlikely over the next twenty years, given a portfolio of $1 trillion insurance in force and stream of mortgage insurance premium revenue of about $40 billion, "this suggests that FHA should continue to build a reserve that reaches $45 billion."

However, a goal to build the MMI Fund sufficient to weather another collapse in housing may be self-defeating. The premiums needed to increase the capital resources of the MMI Fund would make the FHA less competitive. The problem of adverse selection is particularly acute for the MMI Fund given the lack of variation in mortgage insurance premiums. Private mortgage insurers and conventional mortgage lenders can often underprice the FHA for the lowest-risk borrowers. However, as with regionally uniform pricing, the lack of risk-based pricing acts as a stabilizing influence in the mortgage market. Rather than increase the debt burden on higher-risk borrowers, the FHA can cross-subsidize borrowers by pooling risk across its entire portfolio. This is only possible by leveraging the lower cost of capital criticized by proponents of fair-value accounting. The CBO notes, "Although FHA could raise the fees it charges to reduce those fair-value subsidies, raising fees to achieve a substantial negative fair-value subsidy would be difficult due to competition from the private sector. Thus, fair-value accounting could hinder setting fees to accumulate a positive capital reserve ratio, as FHA is required to do under current law" (Castelli et al. 2014).

More importantly, the goal to be entirely self-financing is at odds with the social purpose of the MMI Fund. Twenty-five years ago, the first actuarial review of the MMI Fund noted, "Finding the right size of the cushion given the MMI Fund's implicit public purpose presents a particular challenge. Too little equity risks making MMI reliant on the Treasury (and ultimately the taxpayer) in even moderately adverse conditions. . . . If the equity target is set too high, the resulting high premiums may make ownership unaffordable and potentially exclude those individuals most in need of the services FHA was meant to provide." The actuarial review concluded, "We do not believe it is possible to build MMI's equity to a level needed to cover catastrophic risk. To do so would require premiums at levels that would impair MMI's social purposes. Catastrophic risk is implicitly covered through the backing of the U.S. Treasury" (Price Waterhouse 1990). Consequently, the credit subsidies associated with FHA's books of business during the housing crisis can be compared to other automatic economic stabilizers like unemployment insurance or countercyclical legislation such as the Emergency Economic Stabilization Act of 2008 and the American Recovery and Reinvestment Act of 2009.

The importance of ensuring access to mortgage credit is why President Obama announced a 50–basis point reduction in the annual mortgage insurance premium in 2015 that will save borrowers an estimated $900 per year. Moody's Analytics estimates that this reduction could increase single-family housing starts by twenty thousand and home sales by forty-five thousand in 2015, with only a modest delay in recapitalizing the MMI Fund by curbing adverse selection and stabilizing the FHA's market share (Zandi and deRitis 2015). Over time, the independent actuary expects the FHA's market share to revert to its long-term average of 8–10 percent, but with a "prolonged impairment of the role of other mortgage market institutions," including the uncertain future of the GSEs, the share could remain elevated at 15 percent (IFE 2014a).

Even aside from its countercyclical role, FHA is in position to play a larger part in the American housing finance system in the long term. FHA's reverse mortgage product will help the aging Baby Boom generation be financially secure in retirement. Meanwhile, the next generation of homeowners is likely to come from minority households and other populations traditionally served by FHA.

V. Aging in Place—Reverse Mortgages

Almost all reverse mortgages in the United States are insured by the FHA under the Home Equity Conversion Mortgage (HECM) program created by the Housing and Community Development Act of 1987 "to meet the special needs of elderly homeowners[6] by reducing the effect of the economic hardship caused by the increasing costs of meeting health, housing, and subsistence needs at a time of reduced income, through the insurance of home equity conversion mortgages to permit the conversion of a portion of accumulated home equity into liquid assets." In contrast to refinancing or obtaining a home equity line of credit, the borrower receives rather than makes payments in a reverse mortgage. The loan amount grows over time through the accumulation of mortgage interest, insurance premiums, and servicing fees, and is paid off when the borrower dies, moves out of the home, or the loan is refinanced. Starting as a demonstration program, the number of endorsements has grown steadily, peaking in 2009 at nearly 115,000. Since 1989, FHA has insured more than 879,000 reverse mortgages.

The need that the HECM program addresses is likely to grow with the aging of the Baby Boom generation. The Joint Center for Housing Studies (JCHS) projects that the number of households aged seventy years and older will increase over 8 million between 2015 and 2025 and account for more than two-thirds of all household growth (JCHS 2014). Unfortunately, many older households are not financially prepared for retirement. Over half of working-age households will not be able to maintain their current standard of living after retirement, including 44 percent of fifty-year-olds (Munnell, Rutledge, and Webb 2014). Home equity is and will remain an important source of funds for retirement. Four out of every five householders sixty-five years old or older own their own home, down less than 2 percentage points from its peak in 2004. And older households have benefited from more years of house price appreciation and the forced savings that accompanies fully amortizing mortgage payments. Taking out a reverse mortgage can improve the financial position of retirees and protect against house price declines (Munnell, Orlova, and Webb 2012; Haurin et al. 2014). The proceeds of about one-fifth of reverse mortgages are used for medical expenses, allowing borrowers to age in place (Nakajima and Telyukova 2013).

Households can receive funds in fixed monthly payments as long as the borrower is in the home (tenure plan), fixed monthly payments for a specified number of years (term plan), as a line of credit, or some combination. The most popular plan has been lump sum disbursements at closing or early in the loan. In part, this is because lenders encourage such withdrawals in order to limit interest rate risk (IFE 2014b). Unscrupulous brokers have also packaged reverse mortgages with other financial investments that were not in the best interest of borrowers (Duhigg 2008). Large early draws reduce the amount of equity available to the borrower to meet future necessary expenses. Although freed from monthly mortgage payments, borrowers are still liable for property taxes, homeowner's insurance, and other assessments. As of 2014, 12 percent of loans were in default due to failure to pay these housing expenses (IFE 2014b). In addition, homeowners are still responsible for home maintenance, not to mention expenses like utilities, food, and health care that proceeds from the reverse mortgage were intended to cover.

The financial health of the HECM program has suffered from the decline in property values, tax and insurance delinquencies, and other factors. Since it was transferred from the General and Special Risk Fund to the MMI Fund in FY2009, every book of business has required a subsidy, ranging between 4.3 and 6.3 percent based on the most recent re-estimates by the Office of Management and Budget (OMB 2014).

In response, FHA has tightened underwriting standards. Annual mortgage insurance premiums were increased from 0.5 percent to 1.25 percent (FHA 2010e). The Housing and Economic Recovery Act specifically prohibited lenders from conditioning HECMs on purchase of unrelated insurance, annuities, or other financial products. Principal limit factors, comparable to LTV ratios that vary by borrower age and mortgage interest rate, have been repeatedly reduced, limiting how much equity borrowers can extract. For example, the principal limit factor for a sixty-five-year-old borrower under a 7 percent interest rate decreased from 48.9 percent prior to FY2010 to 33.2 percent in mid-2014 (FHA 2014). Restrictions were enacted on the ability for borrower's to draw more than 60 percent of the principal limit[7] in the first twelve months (FHA 2013c). Borrowers may be denied or required to set aside funds in escrow to cover taxes and insurance based on a financial assessment including credit history and debt burden (FHA 2013d). Moulton, Haurin, and Shi (2014) simulate that restrictions on the initial draw will reduce HECM volume by 20 percent and reduce the probability of default by 21 percent. Credit history standards are found to have a greater impact on the likelihood of default, with a smaller impact on take-up rates. For example, requiring a life expectancy set-aside for borrowers with credit scores below 580 reduces HECM volumes by 4 percent but reduces the predicted default rate by over 44 percent.

The HECM program is currently only a small portion of FHA's insurance portfolio, constituting just 8 percent of insurance in-force. Further, just 2 percent of eligible borrowers have a reverse mortgage when the potential market may be up to three times higher (Nakajima and Telyukova 2013). Nevertheless, the HECM program had been considered a successful demonstration prior to the housing bubble (Rodda, Herbert, and Lam 2000). Further proof of the viability of reverse mortgages post-crisis will increase its popularity and likely spawn conventional alternatives. The competition may reduce the FHA's market presence and create more potential for adverse selection, but would be fitting with the FHA's history in not only showing the feasibility of mortgage insurance but also popularizing the long-term fixed-rate prepayable mortgage that dominates the American mortgage market.

VI. The New Face of Homeownership

The early history of FHA with respect to race relations is regrettable. The first FHA underwriting manuals warn about the "ingress of undesirable racial or nationality groups" and systematically favored financing suburban developments rather than houses in urban, minority areas (Stearns n.d.). The lack of equal access to FHA insurance is one factor that contributed to a lack of wealth building among minority households in postwar America (Coates 2014).

The situation has been reversed for the past several decades, with minorities more likely to rely on FHA insurance than non-Hispanic white households. Much of the difference can be explained by the lower income, lower wealth, and worse credit histories of many minority borrowers. For example, Bhutta and Ringo (2014) find that controlling for credit score can reduce the unexplained difference in the incidence of higher-priced lending between Hispanic and non-Hispanic Whites from 24 percentage points to 16 and the difference between whites and blacks from 32 to 14. Minority households also have less wealth for a down payment. The median net wealth of white households in 2013 was thirteen times the median wealth of black households, the largest gap since 1989. White households also had ten times the wealth of Hispanic households, the largest since 2001 (Kochhar and Fry 2014). Conventional lenders and private mortgage insurance companies typically require higher premiums for lower credit scores and higher LTV ratios, increasing the cost of servicing a given loan amount. Finally, the median household income of white, non-Hispanic households is $17,000 more than that of Hispanic households and nearly $24,000 more than that of black households, making any debt burden easier to bear for white households.

During the housing bubble, minority borrowers were steered into subprime mortgages (Apgar, Bendimerad, and Essene 2007; Bocian, Ernst, and Li 2008; Karikari, Voicu, and Fang 2011). These loans often included exotic loan features such as interest-only or negative amortization schedules, adjustable interest rates with teaser introductory periods, and low or no documentation of income and assets and therefore the ability to repay. In contrast, the FHA has always relied on full documentation and overwhelmingly favors thirty-year fixed-rate loans. The FHA lost market share and was criticized for a lack of product "innovation" before the housing crisis (e.g., Government Accountability Office 2007; Jaffee and Quigley 2007). However, these loan products are associated with an increased risk of default regardless of borrower characteristics (Ding et al. 2011). Consequently, although the serious delinquency rate on subprime loans topped 30 percent in late 2009, only 9 percent of FHA-insured loans were seriously delinquent.

The rash of foreclosures during the housing crisis disproportionately affected minority households, leading to a growing homeownership gap (Bocian, Li, and Ernst 2010). The difference in homeownership rates between white and black households has increased to roughly 30 percentage points since hitting a low of 26 in 2000. The difference between white and Hispanic homeownership rates bottomed in 2007 at 25 percentage points and has since increased to 27. Yet these populations will be the source of new household formation in the twenty-first century. Harvard's Joint Center for Housing Studies (2014) projects minorities will be responsible for 76 percent of net household growth over the next ten years.

The decline in economic mobility suggests that these populations will continue to rely disproportionately on the FHA to achieve homeownership. Even record low mortgage interest rates have not been able to offset low wealth and stagnating wages in reducing housing affordability. According to the Census Bureau, only 50.3 percent of families had sufficient income and wealth to afford to purchase a modestly priced home in 2009, down from 60.4 percent in 1984 (Wilson and Callis 2013). Moreover, credit conditions, including FHA's own underwriting standards, remain tight. Consequently, the next generation of homeowners has been handicapped from entering the market. First-time homebuyers accounted for just 29 percent of existing home purchases in 2014, down from 45 percent in 2008 (the first year the National Association of Realtors began tracking) (Davidson 2015). First-time homebuyers typically account for roughly four out of every five FHA-insured home purchase loan originations, and the FHA accounted for as much as 56 percent of all first-time home purchase originations in 2010 and 2011 (HUD 2011).

At the same time, the American housing finance system should not tolerate steering qualified borrowers away from the conventional mortgage market. Even after controlling for credit risk, minorities have still typically been found to disproportionately use FHA insurance (Fullerton and MacRae 1978; Canner, Gabriel, and Woolley 1991; Gabriel and Rosenthal 1991;

Holmes and Horvitz 1994). Additional housing policies such as the afford-able housing goals of the GSEs and the Community Reinvestment Act, which was explicitly designed to combat red-lining, are also integral to ensuring that lower-income, minority, and other underserved households have access to the best available loan products.

On the other hand, the FHA is more clearly focused on promoting specifically middle-class homeownership rather than excessive housing consumption among higher-income homeowners compared to some other federal housing policies. The home mortgage interest tax deduction, at a cost of roughly $80 billion a year—greater than the entire budget of the U.S. Department of Housing and Urban Development—is the country's largest housing program. Yet over 82 percent of the tax expenditure goes to filers earning over $100,000 a year (Joint Committee on Taxation 2014). The implicit subsidy enjoyed by the GSEs in the early 2000s was estimated at over $20 billion a year, or a net present value of $73 billion. But Fannie Mae and Freddie Mac are more likely to serve existing homeowners and higher-income borrowers. Moreover, the Enterprises retained, and thereby passed onto shareholders, between a third and half of the value of this subsidy (Lucas and Torregrosa 2004; Passmore 2005). Unfortunately, these costs are more hidden than the $1.7 billion "bailout" the FHA received in 2013.

FHA's mortgage insurance program targets a relatively narrow segment of borrowers most in need of assistance but still capable of sustaining homeownership. And because these borrowers will constitute an increasing share of new homeowners, the FHA is likely to play a larger role in the American housing finance market in the twenty-first century.

VII. Conclusion

The FHA insures safe and affordable mortgage loans and thereby ensures mortgage credit is continuously available through housing cycles and to underserved borrowers. Most recently, the FHA has focused on stabilizing the mortgage market in the aftermath of the Great Recession, effectively responding to conditions similar to those that gave rise to its creation in 1934. This countercyclical role has proven costly to the MMI Fund but indispensable to the American housing finance system. The tension between public purpose and financial solvency has been debated throughout the agency's eighty-year history and will continue to exist, but as former FHA

Commissioner John Weicher (1995) argued, "The fact that FHA does not lose money on its home mortgage insurance is not a justification for its existence; the justification is that it serves a public purpose. Serving that purpose without losing money is an indication that FHA home mortgage insurance works reasonably well—not perfectly, but reasonably well."

Over time, the FHA is likely to play an important role in addressing demographic challenges that face America's housing finance system. The development of a financially viable reverse mortgage program with appropriate consumer protections will be important to aiding the retirement of the Baby Boom generation. And ensuring access to mortgage credit for first-time and low-wealth borrowers will be crucial for making the American Dream a reality for a new generation of homeowners.

CHAPTER 6

The Federal Home Loan Bank System
and U.S. Housing Finance

W. Scott Frame

The Federal Home Loan Bank (FHLB) System is a government-sponsored enterprise (GSE) comprised of twelve regional wholesale FHLBs and an Office of Finance that acts as their portal to the capital markets.[1] Each of the twelve FHLBs is cooperatively owned, and together they serve over seventy-five hundred member financial institutions, about two-thirds of which are commercial banks. The FHLB System's consolidated balance sheet at the end of 2013 was $834 billion.

The mission of the FHLB System is to provide member financial institutions with financial products and services that assist and enhance the financing of housing and community lending. Since its creation in 1932, the principal way in which FHLBs achieved this mission was by making collateralized loans, known as "advances," that are secured by members' residential mortgage loans and securities. Advances, in turn, are largely funded by consolidated debt obligations that benefit from a market perception of an implied federal guarantee owing to the FHLB System's government sponsored enterprise (GSE) status. (FHLB System–consolidated debt obligations are considered Agency securities, like those issued by Fannie Mae and Freddie Mac.) This market perception also allows the FHLBs to profitably maintain large investment portfolios comprised of mortgage-backed securities (MBS) and mortgage pools sold to them by members.

Despite its name, size, and principal activities, the FHLB System today actually provides little targeted support to the U.S. housing finance system.

For more than fifty years, the FHLB membership was limited to mortgage-oriented institutions, particularly thrifts and insurance companies. By limiting FHLB membership and acceptable collateral, the Congress was largely able to direct FHLB System benefits to the housing finance sector. But following the 1980s thrift crisis, the Financial Institutions Reform, Recovery, and Enforcement Act of 1989 (FIRREA) expanded FHLB membership to include more diversified depository institutions (commercial banks and credit unions).[2] Today, for example, commercial bank members can pledge eligible mortgage-related collateral to obtain an advance that, in turn, may fund virtually any type of financial asset. Hence, FHLB membership liberalization broke the relatively tight link between FHLB advances and member collateral that historically ensured that much of the GSE benefits flowed, as intended, to support residential mortgage finance. (Note that since 2000, FHLB advances made to "community financial institutions" can be used to finance small businesses, small farms, and small agribusinesses.) Below, we summarize research that is consistent with the FHLB System acting as a general source of liquidity to commercial banks of all sizes.

The FHLBs' investment in MBS and whole mortgages are more directly tied to housing finance. However, most of these assets are widely traded in global capital markets, and the FHLBs are no more special investors than their large commercial bank members or the other two housing GSEs (Fannie Mae and Freddie Mac). Put differently, if FHLB investment portfolios did not exist, there would not likely be a noticeable impact on residential mortgage markets. Moreover, these investment portfolios have also caused material risk management problems at some FHLBs in recent years. The FHLBs affordable housing programs do provide targeted support for housing, although funding is modest (the greater of $100 million or 10 percent of FHLB net income annually) relative to the size of the FHLB System.

Today, the FHLB System acts as a subsidized source of wholesale liquidity for members. Although Congress has expressly authorized such activity for community financial institutions, the reality is that the vast majority of FHLB lending (and associated benefits) flows to the very largest U.S. banking organizations. Such institutions do not need FHLB access as they can issue in public debt markets and, in times of turmoil, borrow from the Federal Reserve's Discount Window.

This chapter begins by describing the structure and governance of the FHLB System. We then outline the FHLB business model and identify its key business risks. Next, we discuss the FHLB System as a GSE. This is followed by a summary of recent research that is consistent with the FHLB System acting as a general source of liquidity to commercial banks—both before and during the financial crisis. A conclusion follows.

I. FHLB System: Structure and Governance

Each FHLB is cooperatively owned by its financial institution members. By law, membership is limited to commercial banks, credit unions, thrifts, insurance companies, and community development financial institutions that are chartered within each FHLB's legally defined service area.[3] FHLB members must either maintain at least 10 percent of their asset portfolios in residential mortgage-related assets (at the time of application) or else be designated as "community financial institutions."[4]

A stock purchase is required for FHLB membership based on two permissible classes of stock: Class A stock is redeemable on six months' written notice from the member, and class B stock on five years' notice.[5] FHLB stock is not traded, is valued at par, and pays a dividend. Members resigning their membership are subject to a five-year lockout from the FHLB System.

As discussed in Flannery and Frame (2006), most FHLB capital plans share some general characteristics. First, almost all of the FHLBs rely exclusively on the more permanent class B shares. Second, the stock purchase requirements contain both "membership" and "activities" components. (The membership component is generally tied to a measure of member size, whereas the activity-based component tends to depend on activities that directly affect the size of an FHLB's balance sheets, like advances.) Finally, each stock purchase requirement is specified with ranges to allow individual FHLBs to adjust their requirements without having to seek regulatory approval.

Table 6.1 shows that the twelve FHLBs differ substantially in both asset size and number of members. The New York FHLB is the largest in terms of total assets ($128.3 billion), but it has the third-fewest number of members (333). Conversely, the Dallas FHLB has the smallest balance sheet ($30.2 billion) but the third largest membership (875). Perhaps more importantly, each FHLB balance sheet is dedicated to a few large members. The five largest members account for between 27 percent and 78 percent of individual FHLB advance portfolios (Dallas and Cincinnati, respectively); and the five largest equity holders are similarly prominent.

Table 6.1. Federal Home Loan Bank Size and Membership by District
(Data as of December 31, 2013)

FHLB	Total Assets $Billion	Number of Members	Membership Concentration (Five Largest Members) Share of Capital	Share of Advances
Atlanta	$122.32	996	46.70%	55.50%
Boston	$44.64	443	47.40%	34.30%
Chicago	$68.80	759	35.70%	56.10%
Cincinnati	$103.18	727	59.60%	77.70%
Dallas	$30.22	875	18.10%	26.90%
Des Moines	$73.00	1183	41.10%	58.80%
Indianapolis	$37.79	404	35.00%	42.30%
New York	$128.33	333	56.90%	62.50%
Pittsburgh	$70.67	297	64.80%	77.40%
San Francisco	$85.77	354	54.60%	62.20%
Seattle	$35.87	329	61.30%	75.60%
Topeka	$33.95	804	32.40%	46.30%

Federal Home Loan Banks Office of Finance (2014).

An elected board of directors controls the operations of each FHLB. Despite the concentration of equity holdings illustrated in Table 6.1, two important voting limitations make effective control much more diffuse than the equity ownership data would suggest. First, no member may vote more than the average number of shares owned by members in its state as of the prior year's end. This rule limits concentration of voting rights because every state has large numbers of small institutions. Second, voting occurs on a state-by-state basis, and each state must have at least one director. To the extent that large members are not equally distributed among the states, therefore, concentrated control is even more limited. See 12 CFR § 1261, Subpart B, for a complete set of regulations pertaining to FHLB directors and voting rights.

II. FHLB System: Consolidated Balance Sheets and Associated Risks

Table 6.2 presents the consolidated balance sheet for the FHLB System as of December 31, 2013. The largest asset category is member advances ($498.6 billion, or 59.8 percent of total assets). Advances are available in various

Table 6.2. Federal Home Loan Bank System Combined Balance Sheet
(Data as of December 31, 2013)

	($ Millions)	(% of Assets)
Assets		
Advances	$498,599	59.8%
Short-term investments	$62,324	7.5%
Long-term investments	$180,539	21.6%
Agency debt	$22,589	2.7%
Agency MBS	$104,943	12.6%
Private-label MBS	$20,839	2.5%
Other	$32,168	3.9%
Mortgage loans (net)	$44,442	5.3%
Other assets	$48,296	5.8%
Total Assets	$834,200	100.0%
Liabilities		
Consolidated obligations	$767,141	92.0%
Discount notes	$293,296	35.2%
Bonds	$473,845	56.8%
Deposits	$10,555	1.3%
Mandatorily redeemable capital stock	$4,998	0.6%
Other liabilities	$6,436	0.8%
Total liabilities	$789,130	94.6%
Capital		
Capital stock	$33,375	4.0%
Retained earnings	$12,206	1.5%
Accumulated other comprehensive income	$(511)	−0.1%
Total capital	$45,070	5.4%

Federal Home Loan Banks Office of Finance (2014).

maturities, carry fixed or variable rates of interest, sometimes contain embedded options, and are fully collateralized. In terms of maturities, as of December 31, 2013, 42.1 percent of advances were due in less than one year, 46.4 percent were due in one to five years, and 11.4 percent were due thereafter. The most common forms of advance collateral are single-family mortgage loans, home equity loans, and commercial real estate loans.[6] Collateral may be posted through a blanket lien, specific listing, or physical delivery.[7] Discounts, or haircuts, are applied to advance collateral by the individual FHLBs, based on type, listing method, and borrower health. This means that

Table 6.3. Top 10 FHLB Advance Holders by Holding Company
(Data as of December 31, 2013)

Holding Company	Par Value of Advances ($ Millions)	Percent of Total Advances
JP Morgan Chase & Co.	$61,831	12.60%
Bank of America Co.	$28,938	5.90%
Citigroup Inc.	$25,202	5.10%
Wells Fargo & Co.	$19,141	3.90%
Capital One Financial Corp.	$16,314	3.30%
MetLife, Inc.	$15,000	3.00%
PNC Financial Services Group, Inc.	$12,907	2.60%
New York Community Bancorp, Inc.	$11,084	2.30%
Banco Santander, S.A.	$8,965	1.80%
BB&T Corporation	$8,182	1.70%
Total	$207,564	42.20%

Federal Home Loan Banks Office of Finance (2014).

FHLB advances are actually "overcollateralized" in the sense that the book value of collateral exceeds the advance amount. (In many ways, FHLB advances are akin to "covered bonds," which are a popular method of financing mortgages in Europe.) Beyond their explicit collateral, the FHLBs also have priority over the claims of depositors and almost all other creditors in the event of a member's default—including the Federal Deposit Insurance Corporation.[8] No FHLB has ever suffered a credit loss on an advance.

FHLB members generally view advances as an attractive source of wholesale funds. Advance interest rates are set by the individual FHLBs and generally reflect a markup to the cost of comparable debt funding secured by the Office of Finance. However, in order to receive an advance, a member must also purchase FHLB stock in an amount dictated by the individual FHLB's capital plan.[9] Hence, the all-in cost of advance borrowing includes the note rate, the opportunity cost of tying up collateral, and the net benefit/cost of holding FHLB stock versus an alternative investment.[10] The terms are presumably attractive: five of the six largest FHLB advance users are considered to be systemically important financial institutions (JP Morgan Chase, Bank of America, Citigroup, Wells Fargo, and MetLife) and accounted for 30.5 percent of total FHLB advances as of year end 2013. Table 6.3 lists the ten largest FHLB advance holders at that time.

Table 6.4. FHLB Asset Composition (Data as of December 31, 2013)

	Advances (% Assets)	Investments (% Assets)	Mortgages (% Assets)	Total (% Assets)
Boston	62%	29%	8%	98%
New York	71%	16%	2%	88%
Pittsburgh	71%	20%	5%	95%
Atlanta	73%	22%	1%	96%
Cincinnati	63%	22%	7%	92%
Indianapolis	46%	29%	16%	91%
Chicago	34%	53%	11%	98%
Des Moines	63%	28%	9%	99%
Dallas	53%	43%	0%	97%
Topeka	51%	26%	18%	94%
San Francisco	52%	41%	1%	94%
Seattle	30%	63%	2%	96%

Federal Home Loan Banks Office of Finance (2014).

Each FHLB also maintains a portfolio of highly rated investments, which on a combined basis, totaled $242.9 billion at the end of 2013. For liquidity, the FHLBs hold about one-quarter of this portfolio ($62.3 billion) in short-term investments, such as federal funds. The FHLBs also hold longer-term investments to enhance interest income ($180.5 billion)—primarily Agency debt and MBS.[11] DeMarco (2010) argues that such a large portfolio is inconsistent with the purposes of the FHLB System and represents a misuse of the GSE's preferential access to capital markets.

The FHLB System's combined balance sheet also includes residential mortgages acquired from participating member institutions under either the Chicago FHLBs Mortgage Partnership Finance Program or the other FHLBs' self-branded Mortgage Purchase Programs. Generally speaking, under these programs the member-seller guarantees most of the mortgage's credit risk, and the interest rate risk is borne by the FHLBs (see Frame 2003 for a detailed discussion). As of year end 2013, the FHLB System held $44.4 billion in mortgage loans (net of loan loss allowances)—an amount that has been gradually declining over the past decade.

Table 6.4 presents the asset composition shares for the twelve FHLBs as of year end 2013. The Chicago and Seattle FHLBs have remarkably small shares of their balance sheets devoted to advances (34 percent and 30 percent, respectively) and large shares devoted to investments. This has been a long-run phenomenon for the Chicago FHLB, but a more recent (post-crisis) development for the Seattle FHLB. (Both institutions have been subject to various regulatory orders over the years.) It is not clear whether such balance sheet structures are consistent with the FHLBs mission and the long-run viability of the individual institutions.[12] Indeed, the Chicago FHLB previously considered a merger with the Dallas FHLB; and the Seattle FHLB has recently agreed to be absorbed by the Des Moines FHLB.

The FHLB asset portfolios are largely funded with debt, almost all of which takes the form of "consolidated obligations" issued by the Office of Finance and for which the twelve banks are jointly and severally liable (i.e., cross-guarantee). As of December 31, 2013, the FHLB System had $767.1 billion in consolidated obligations outstanding. Discount notes (maturities up to one year) represented 38.2 percent of consolidated obligations at that time.[13] Consolidated bonds, which have maturities almost exclusively between one and ten years, comprise the remaining 61.8 percent. Of the $473.2 billion in FHLB System consolidated bonds, 73.8 percent carried fixed rates and 25.9 percent included call options.

The FHLB System also maintained $45.1 billion in equity capital at that time (4.5 percent of total assets). Member stock subscriptions are the dominant form of equity ($33.4 billion), with the remainder in retained earnings ($12.2 billion) and accumulated other comprehensive income (-$0.5 billion). Retained earnings has been a growing share of FHLB System equity since its 2011 Joint Capital Enhancement Agreement entered into following the completion of their RefCorp obligation.[14]

The Federal Housing Finance Agency (FHFA) enforces minimum leverage and risk-based capital requirements for the twelve FHLBs. The minimum leverage requirement is 5 percent of total assets, although this is computed as 1.5 times permanent capital (Class B stock and retained earnings) plus all other capital. Under this measure, as of year end 2013, FHLB leverage ratios ranged from 5.0 percent (Seattle) to 11.2 percent (New York). The FHFA also computes a risk-based capital requirement based on each bank's credit, market, and operational risks.[15] As of December 31, 2013, required risk-based capital for the individual FHLBs ranged widely from 0.5 percent of total assets (New York) to 4.6 percent of total assets (San Francisco).

FHLBs long faced very little credit risk in their asset portfolios, which were largely comprised of advances and Agency MBS. However, this changed during the recent financial crisis as initially AAA-rated private-label mortgage securities held by the FHLB lost significant value. Indeed, the Boston,

Chicago, and Seattle FHLBs posted significant net losses for 2008 and 2009, due in large part to write-downs on these securities.

Prior to the financial crisis, FHLB risk management concerns centered on their significant exposure to interest rate risk associated with long-term advances and fixed-rate prepayable mortgages (whole loans and MBS).[16] FHLBs principally manage their mortgage-related interest rate risk by issuing callable bonds, of which they had $86.9 billion outstanding as of year end 2013. FHLBs also regularly use interest rate derivatives to transform their liability maturities and to hedge some of the negative convexity associated with fixed-rate mortgages. As of December 31, 2013, the FHLB System had $539.3 billion in total (notional amount) interest rate exchange agreements outstanding—mostly interest rate swaps. Nonetheless, it is very difficult to discern how much interest rate risk the FHLB System actually retains.

III. The FHLB System as a GSE

Like Fannie Mae and Freddie Mac, the FHLB System is considered a GSE since it has been expressly created by an Act of Congress (the Federal Home Loan Bank Act of 1932) that includes several institutional benefits designed to reduce its operating and funding costs. In terms of operating costs, GSEs are exempt from federal corporate income taxes and Securities and Exchange Commission registration requirements for their debt securities. As with Fannie Mae and Freddie Mac, market participants have to come to view FHLB System consolidated debt obligations to be implicitly guaranteed by the U.S. government despite explicit, legally prescribed denials in offering materials. This perception allows GSEs to borrow at favorable interest rates in the hopes that most of these savings are passed on to customers.[17] The U.S. Congressional Budget Office (CBO) (2001, 2004) provides estimates of annual implicit subsidies to each of the housing GSEs. Hence, by chartering a GSE, the federal government seeks to direct benefits toward a specific sector of the economy without recognizing the attendant opportunity costs in the federal budget.[18]

In the case of the FHLB System, the idea is that reduced FHLB borrowing costs will accrue to members via lower advance rates and higher dividend rates than would otherwise be the case. Prior to the passage of FIRREA, this meant that the implicit subsidy flowed to members that were principally engaged in home mortgage lending, with some portion flowing through to borrowers. However, following the liberalization of FHLB membership, the subsidy is diffused among the variety of member business activities (CBO 2001).

Three provisions in the FHLB Act are especially important for creating the perception of an implicit government guarantee of FHLB consolidated obligations. First, the U.S. Treasury is authorized to purchase up to $4 billion of FHLB System debt securities. Second, FHLB debt securities are considered government securities under the Securities and Exchange Act of 1934. (This status means that the securities can be used as collateral for public deposits, can be bought and sold by the Federal Reserve in open-market operations, and may be held in unlimited amounts by federally insured depository institutions.) Third, FHLB debt securities are eligible for issuance and transfer through the Federal Reserve System's book-entry system, which is also used by the U.S. Treasury.

The market perception of an implied guarantee of GSE obligations distorts the institutions' risk-taking incentives in a way that may increase the probability of financial distress. (A similar situation is well understood in the context of federally insured depository institutions.) To protect against potential moral hazard, the federal government supervises the FHLB System for safety and soundness to limit potential taxpayer exposure.[19] The FHFA is an independent agency within the executive branch that supervises Fannie Mae, Freddie Mac, and the FHLB System.[20] The supervisor is authorized to set capital standards, conduct examinations, and take certain enforcement actions if unsafe or unsound practices are identified.

An important cost associated with financial institutions operating with government guarantees (implicit or explicit) is the aforementioned moral hazard incentive for such institutions to increase their risk exposure in order to maximize shareholder returns. However, the FHLBs are cooperatively owned, and the incentives created by such an ownership arrangement are less well understood. Flannery and Frame (2006) discuss some unique features of the FHLB System and how they may act to enhance or subdue FHLB risk-taking incentives relative to Fannie Mae and Freddie Mac.

IV. FHLB Membership, Collateral, and Liquidity Provision

As discussed above, between 1932 and 1989 the FHLB System long acted as a reliable supplier of long-term funding via advances for the thrift industry.

These institutions faced statutory asset limitations that resulted in balance sheets almost entirely comprised of residential mortgage-related assets. Moreover, all depository institutions were subject to limitations on the interest rates that they paid depositors (since 1933 under Regulation Q), which periodically resulted in liquidity pinches. Specifically, deposits would decline when the regulation was binding, making FHLB advances an important source of substitute funding to maintain the flow of mortgage credit.

A series of legislative changes since 1980 significantly altered the role of the FHLB System within the U.S. mortgage finance system. First, the Depository Institutions Deregulation and Monetary Control Act of 1980 and the Garn-St. Germain Depository Institutions Act of 1982 terminated the Regulation Q ceiling on savings account interest rates and gave thrifts expanded investment powers. Second, the Financial Institutions Recovery and Reform Act of 1989 opened FHLB membership to all depository institutions with more than 10 percent of their portfolios in residential mortgage-related assets (i.e., whole mortgages and MBS). Third, the Financial Services Modernization Act of 1999 expanded the mission of the FHLB System to act as a general source of liquidity to "community financial institutions" and lifted the requirement that federally chartered thrifts be FHLB members.[21]

All three pieces of legislation served to erode the link between FHLB advances and residential mortgage funding. Indeed, given the modest constraint on FHLB membership related to residential mortgage activity, the portfolio composition of most FHLB members (especially the largest members that dominate advance activity), and the simple fact that money is fungible, FHLB advances could fund virtually any type of asset.

Frame, Hancock, and Passmore (2012) show that eligible collateral has not been a binding constraint for commercial bank borrowing from the FHLB System. Looking at commercial banking organizations of various sizes and over time, the authors find that the ratio of FHLB advances to eligible collateral is very low. This represents a necessary condition for banking organizations to use advances as a general source of liquidity.

Frame et al. (2012) also estimate panel vector autoregressions that include bank portfolio composition and macroeconomic variables for three banking organization size categories and three distinct time periods between 1996 and 2009. The authors find three key results. First, bank portfolio responses to FHLB advance shocks are of similar magnitude for residential mortgages, commercial and industrial loans, and other real estate loans (i.e., loans for construction and development, agriculture, and commercial real estate). Second, unexpected changes in various types of bank lending are accommodated using FHLB advances, although specific results depend on banking organization size and the time period studied. Third, small and medium-sized banking organizations appear to use FHLB advances to reduce the variability in residential mortgage lending resulting from either federal funds rate shocks or gross domestic product (GDP) shocks. Overall, the authors conclude that FHLB advances are being used to fund all types of banking assets, not just residential mortgages.

FHLB outstanding advances jumped during the onset of the financial crisis—from $641 billion to $875 billion during 2007 and then rose to $929 billion by the end of 2008. (Advance volume then slid back to pre-crisis levels in 2009, to $631 billion.) Ashcraft, Bech, and Frame (2010) show that during the second half of 2007, the ten most active FHLB members accounted for almost $150 billion of this new lending. (Washington Mutual, Bank of America, and Countrywide borrowed the largest amounts from the FHLB System during this period.) Notably, four of the ten institutions subsequently failed or were acquired, and two others required "exceptional assistance" from the U.S. government during the financial crisis. The authors also present statistical evidence suggesting that large banks and thrifts (those with greater than $5 billion in assets) principally used FHLB advances as a substitute for short-term borrowing via the federal funds and repo markets.

Ashcraft et al. (2010) note that as liquidity pressures developed during the fall of 2007, FHLB advances became an attractive source of funding in terms of pricing. FHLB funding costs moved well below other benchmarks, like LIBOR and AA-rated asset-backed commercial paper, whereas the average spread between a thirty-day advance from the FHLB New York and four-week FHLB System discount notes remained unchanged at about 25 basis points. FHLB advances were also cheaper than borrowing from the Federal Reserve's Discount Window during this time, despite a 50–basis point reduction in the central banks' primary credit rate.[22] FHLB advances were also attractive in terms of available maturities—with many members electing to borrow long term.

According to Ashcraft et al. (2010), the reduction of the discount rate to 25 basis points over the federal funds target in March 2008 almost established parity in terms of the all-in cost of Discount Window loans and FHLB advances. During the following months, the Discount Window became more attractive from a pricing perspective. An important reason for this was a negative change in investor attitudes toward Agency debt issues that started during the summer of 2008 as a result of financial distress at Fannie Mae and Freddie Mac.[23] Later that year, following the Lehman Brothers bankruptcy, the Federal Deposit Insurance Corporation expanded deposit insurance coverage limits and established the Temporary Liquidity Guarantee Program of bank debt. These developments likely contributed to stagnant advance growth in late 2008 and 2009.

Ashcraft et al. (2010) point out that the FHLB System's experience during the financial crisis demonstrates the limitations of relying on a government-sponsored emergency liquidity provider with only implicit government backing. Hence, the authors describe the FHLB System as being the "lender of next-to-last resort."

V. Conclusion

For over fifty years, the twelve FHLBs provided low-cost liquidity to the mortgage market via collateralized advances to specialized mortgage lenders. However, legislative changes in the 1980s and 1990s broke the link between FHLB advances and mortgage lending. Today, the FHLB System acts as a general source of subsidized liquidity to its members—not only "community financial institutions" but also systemically important banking organizations. Hence, despite its name and size, the FHLB System today actually provides little targeted support to the U.S. housing finance system. Indeed, if today's FHLB System was to provide such targeted support, it would likely require limiting membership to the small handful of financial institutions with very large concentrations of home mortgages. This would likely mean a much smaller FHLB System (in terms of size and the number of institutions) that may not be economical.

Two recent proposals have emerged to improve the alignment of FHLB System activities with their statutory mission. A white paper issued by the U.S. Treasury and U.S. Department of Housing and Urban Development (2011) suggested limiting borrower advances in an effort to better target FHLB System benefits toward small and medium-sized financial institution members. The document also proposed reducing FHLB investment portfolios, which have limited mission benefits and have caused risk management problems. The FHFA has also considered tying ongoing FHLB membership to member asset composition (FHFA 2014b), specifically, that FHLB members maintain 10 percent of their portfolios in residential mortgage assets, with an exception for community financial institutions (1 percent of their portfolios in residential mortgage assets). Perhaps not surprisingly, even these modest changes aimed at better aligning the FHLB's activities to their statutory mission have met strong political opposition.

PART III

Housing Finance Infrastructure

CHAPTER 7

The TBA Market: Effects and Prerequisites

Akash Kanojia and Meghan Grant

I. Introduction

The to-be-announced (TBA) market for agency mortgage-backed securities (MBS) plays a critical role in the provision of low-cost capital to homeowners in the United States. This piece reviews how the TBA market works today, and specifically how it transforms a heterogeneous group of risky mortgage loans into a homogeneous group of risk-free liquid securities through the combination of the cheapest-to-deliver framework and the credit wrap provided by Fannie Mae, Freddie Mac, and Ginnie Mae. We also review how current legislative and administrative reform efforts may affect the TBA market in the future. Finally, we offer a set of principles for policy makers to consider when contemplating changes to the TBA market.

Mortgage finance in the United States differs substantially from that in the rest of the world (Green and Wachter 2005) due to the prevalence of fixed-rate mortgages (FRMs) and substantial government involvement in the sector. The most common mortgage product in the country is a thirty-year fixed-rate, prepayable, amortizing loan that is guaranteed by one of the so-called "Agencies." The borrower is therefore protected against a rate increase over the loan's life and has the option to refinance the loan, without a penalty, should interest rates decline. The Agencies include both the government-sponsored enterprises (GSEs) Fannie Mae and Freddie Mac, and the government-owned corporation Ginnie Mae.

Academic research suggests that the prepayment penalty-free FRM is a more economically viable loan product than the adjustable-rate mortgage, as it allows households to more closely match assets and liabilities and encourages labor force mobility (Svenstrup 2002). This "penalty-free" refinance option is largely unique to U.S. FRMs, as unscheduled prepayments in most other developed countries generally require a fee to be paid to the lender in order to compensate for the early termination of the payment stream.[1]

In the post–financial crisis world, the Dodd-Frank Wall Street Reform and Consumer Protection Act (Dodd-Frank) (U.S. House of Representatives 2010) has greatly restricted the scope of mortgage product offerings—for example, interest-only loans and balloon mortgage structures are no longer widely available in the U.S. Adjustable-rate mortgages (ARMs) are still available but have also declined substantially. ARM origination has declined from $1.490 trillion a year at the peak in 2005 to $196 billion in 2013 (Inside Mortgage Finance 2014b).

II. Background of Agency MBS Securitization

Home mortgage credit is the second largest source of non-financial debt in the United States, with single-family mortgage credit at $9.9 trillion outstanding as of Q4 2014.[2] For context, the U.S. Treasury market is $12.3 trillion and corporate debt is $7.7 trillion. Of this $9.9 trillion in mortgage credit, more than half is securitized into MBS and traded in the secondary market.[3] The remainder is generally held as whole loans on bank balance sheets. Of the portion that is securitized (roughly $6.3 trillion), the lion's share ($5.6 trillion as of 2014) consists of what is known as Agency MBS. The remaining roughly $700 billion[4] is known as private-label or non-agency MBS, which simply refers to MBS issued by any entity other than one of the three Agencies.

Agency MBS is any MBS that is guaranteed by the government-sponsored enterprises—the Federal National Mortgage Association, known as Fannie Mae (FNMA), and the Federal Home Loan Mortgage Corporation, known as Freddie Mac (FHLMC)[5]—or the Government National Mortgage Association (GNMA), a fully government-owned corporation known as Ginnie Mae. The Agency share of new MBS production has grown dramatically since the financial crisis, with 98 percent of the roughly $1 trillion of MBS issued in 2014[6] being Agency MBS.

The defining characteristic that sets Agency MBS apart from other mortgage-related securitized products is that principal and interest payments are guaranteed to the investor, regardless of the delinquency status of the borrower underlying the mortgage. These cash flow guarantees are provided by Fannie Mae, Freddie Mac, and Ginnie Mae,[7] and largely free investors from considering credit risk when investing in these securities.

Under the current housing finance framework, Ginnie Mae MBS have an *explicit* government guarantee. The U.S. government's explicit guarantee of GNMA MBS means that these securities are backed by the full faith and credit of the U.S. government. On the other hand, Fannie Mae and Freddie Mac MBS are considered to have an *implicit* guarantee, as they do not enjoy the formal support of a "full faith and credit" guarantee. Instead, investors consider these MBS to be partially supported by the U.S. government. The nature of the implicit support was demonstrated by the government's investment in the GSEs during the financial crisis.

The credit guarantees, whether implicit or explicit, essentially serve to make the investor whole in the event of a default on the part of the borrower. When a borrower goes delinquent on a GSE mortgage for a certain amount of time, the guaranteeing enterprise will purchase the mortgage out of the MBS pool. The Agencies fund this purchase through an insurance premium called a "guarantee fee," or g-fee for short. The g-fee can be paid up front or as a monthly fee. As of 2013, g-fees for FNMA and FHLMC MBS were roughly 58 basis points.[8] Ginnie Mae g-fees are typically far lower, with single-family g-fees a mere 6 basis points annualized. The Ginnie Mae g-fee is lower than the g-fee for conventional loans because the Federal Housing Authority (FHA) and Veterans Administration (VA), whose loans back most Ginnie Mae MBS, charge their own mortgage insurance premiums, separate from the g-fee. Further, Ginnie Mae does not buy loans out of pools like Fannie Mae and Freddie Mac do.

Once a lender obtains a credit guarantee from one of the Agencies, groups of mortgages with similar characteristics can be pooled and securitized. The securities themselves are typically structured as "pass-throughs." Pass-throughs are untranched securities in which investors receive a pro rata share of principal and interest payments, with no levels of seniority within the capital structure. The lack of different tranches simplifies the security selection process, as investors only need to understand the prepayment characteristics of the mortgage pool as a whole rather than analyzing multiple tranches simultaneously.

The GSEs and Ginnie Mae also impose strict guidelines on which mortgages are eligible for their credit wraps. These guidelines serve an important purpose in maintaining relative homogeneity among the mortgages securitized into Agency MBS. Mortgages not eligible for GSE or government guarantees are either held as whole loans on the balance sheets of their originators or are securitized separately into the private-label or non-agency securitization market (PLS). PLS may be issued by banks, real estate investment trusts (REITs), or other market participants.

Private-label MBS grew rapidly prior to the financial crisis but are not a major part of new issuance today. Total PLS MBS issuance began to decline from its peak of $1.2 trillion in 2005, falling to $1.1 trillion in 2006 and $700 billion in 2007. By 2008, the market had virtually vanished, with total issuance falling to $60 billion. In 2013, only $30 billion of private-label securities were issued.[9] Of this amount, roughly two-thirds was comprised of resecuritizations of previously nonperforming loans. Only one-third was newly originated loans. By comparison, gross issuance of fixed-rate agency MBS was $1.5 trillion in 2013 and $900 billion in 2007.[10]

III. What Is the TBA Market?

Roughly 68 percent of MBS trading volume[11] takes place in what is known as the "to-be-announced," or TBA, market.[12] Essentially, the TBA market functions like a forward market in which the trade counterparties must specify six parameters of the trade—the price and par amount, plus the agency, coupon, term, and settlement date. Moreover, counterparties to a trade do not have to specify exactly which mortgage pools will be delivered in satisfaction of the contract. The exact securities the seller will deliver to the buyer are announced two days prior to the settlement date. Like most fixed-income markets in the United States, the TBA market is an over-the-counter market in which customers transact with a market maker rather than with each other over an electronic exchange.

Market participants can take long or short positions in TBA contracts up to three months into the future. Because there are only three issuers whose securities currently trade in the TBA market, the total number of TBA securities that can be traded is relatively small. Typically, this will be six coupons each for thirty-year and fifteen-year Fannie Mae and Freddie Mac MBS, and six coupons each for the Ginnie Mae I and II programs, for a total of thirty-six securities. With three settlement dates available per security, the total number of fixed-rate TBA contracts that are available to trade is around 108.

Of these 108, the most liquid tend to be the front-month contracts for the coupons that are currently being produced by mortgage originators, typically no more than three per agency and term. Given Ginnie Mae's gradual wind-down of the Ginnie Mae I program, much of the new production and trading activity in the Ginnie Mae market has flowed into the Ginnie Mae II market. This means that the lion's share of TBA trading activity takes place in ten or fifteen contracts, and these contracts offer excellent liquidity.

Settlement dates for TBA trades are determined in advance. There are four settlement days each month, with securities divided into classes denoted by letters. MBS securitized by thirty-year GSE mortgages settle on Class A settlement day; fifteen-year MBS, on Class B; Ginnie Mae MBS, on Class C; and adjustable-rate mortgages, on Class D settlement day. For example, all thirty-year Fannie Mae MBS trades for the January 2015 TBA contract settled on January 12, 2015 (Class A settlement day). Sellers notify buyers of the securities that will be delivered into a TBA trade two business days prior to the settlement day—this day is known colloquially as "forty-eight-hour" day because it occurs forty-eight hours prior to settlement.

When determining which securities to deliver into a trade, sellers examine the entire inventory of securities that will satisfy the parameters of the trade, and choose the least valuable bonds. These bonds are called the "cheapest to deliver" (CTD). The ability to determine which securities to deliver into a trade two days prior to the settlement date (which could be months after the trade date) is a defining feature of the TBA market. Because all rational investors will deliver the cheapest securities (usually those with the least favorable prepayment characteristics), the entire TBA market prices to the level of the cheapest securities. Securities with more advantageous prepayment characteristics are typically priced at a premium over TBA contract prices. This premium is called a "pay-up." Securities with significant pay-ups usually trade in what is known as the "specified pool" market, even though they may be eligible for delivery into TBA trades.

In the same way that the government guarantee allows an investor to participate in the MBS market without spending much energy on credit analysis, the CTD convention allows an investor to participate without understanding the prepayment characteristics of every mortgage loan in the market. Investors only have to understand the prepayment characteristics of the securities with the worst characteristics in the market in order to have a good perspective on the level of interest rate risk they are taking with a position in a TBA contract.

It is this combination of the CTD convention and the implicit/explicit government guarantee that takes a heterogeneous market for credit, with millions of borrowers taking out trillions of dollars of loans, and turns it into a fungible, homogeneous, liquid market for securitized mortgages. From the investor's standpoint, participating in the U.S. Agency MBS market absolves the investor from allocating resources to credit analysis. Instead, the investor only has to manage the (admittedly complex) interest rate risk of one group of securities in the market—those that are the CTD. Effectively, the CTD and the government guarantee together turn a credit market into a rates market similar to that of U.S. Treasuries.

IV. What Does the TBA Market Do?

The TBA market dominates Agency MBS trading because of the advantages it delivers to market participants. These can be organized into three categories: liquidity, risk management, and the ability to trade without taking physical delivery.

A. Liquidity

The MBS market is highly liquid. A wide variety of investor types transact in the market, with varying goals, time horizons, and trading strategies, all of which contribute to the market's depth and liquidity. Active participants include the Federal Reserve, foreign central banks, commercial banks, mortgage originators, servicers, hedge funds, money managers, and REITs. To measure the liquidity advantage conferred by the TBA market, one can compare the trading volumes and costs of Agency MBS versus other types of fixed-income products. Comparisons to the corporate and municipal markets are particularly useful as these markets are also composed of highly heterogeneous underlying collateral. According to the Securities Industry and Financial Markets Association (SIFMA) (n.d.), the corporate bond, municipal bond, and U.S. Treasury markets were $7.7, $3.6, and $12.2 trillion in size, respectively, as of the third quarter of 2013.[13] The total outstanding amount of fixed-rate Agency MBS as measured by Mortgage-Backed Securities Online (eMBS) (2015) was roughly $5.3 trillion.[14] SIFMA data show that the average daily trading volume in 2014 was $505 billion for Treasuries, $178 billion for Agency MBS, $20 billion for corporate debt, and $10 billion for municipal debt.[15] Comparing the numbers above, it appears that the relationship between the total outstanding amount and daily trading volume of Agency MBS is of a similar proportion to that of the Treasury market. However, Agency MBS daily trading volume dwarfs that of both the municipal and corporate bond markets, both of which are similar in size to the MBS market.

Looking beyond sheer trading volume, multiple studies have used bid-ask spreads as a means to measure liquidity in the TBA market in comparison to other fixed-income markets. Campbell, Li, and Im (2014) found that bid-ask spreads—defined as the "round trip transaction cost of buying and selling an asset"—for Agency MBS (5–10 basis points) were significantly lower than the bid-ask spreads of 100–150 basis points on a typical investment-grade corporate bond, and slightly higher than the 2–basis point bid-ask spread on a Treasury bond. Bessembinder, Maxwell, and Venkataraman (2013) and Friewald, Jankowitsch, and Subrahmanyam (2012) also found that TBA trades offered the lowest trading costs among securitized products, with trading costs[16] of 1–5 basis points for TBA trades versus an average of 24–66 basis points for the securitized product markets as a whole, depending on the study.

Analysis by Bessembinder et al. (2013) has shown that nearly two-thirds of trading activity in the TBA market consists of interdealer trades, with nearly 95 percent of interdealer and 81 percent of customer-to-dealer trades being larger than $1 million in size. Based on this evidence, Bessembinder et al. call the TBA market an "institutional" market, compared to other structured product markets, which have much smaller trade sizes and relatively lower dealer-to-dealer trading activity. The analysis of trade volumes, bid-ask spreads, and trade sizes in the TBA market underscores its liquidity advantages compared to other fixed-income markets and is likely a reason that so many different investor classes can readily participate in large size.

It is important to note that not all Agency MBS trade through the TBA market. Trades that are done outside of the TBA market are normally called specified pool trades, because the exact pool of mortgage securities to be delivered into the trade is specified at the time of the trade rather than announced forty-eight hours before trade settlement. Agency MBS specified pool trades generally fall into one of two categories: MBS that are Agency guaranteed, but not eligible for delivery into a TBA trade; and MBS that are TBA eligible but exhibit underlying features that give them superior prepayment characteristics (and therefore greater value). In the current rate environment, examples of TBA-eligible MBS that will typically trade as specified pools include pools with low loan balances, impaired credit, high loan-to-value ratios, and mortgage pools that have gone through government-assisted refinancing programs such as the Home Affordable Refinance Program. All of these pool types consist of mortgages that are less likely to respond to refinancing incentives than the CTD cohort and are thus more desirable.

As discussed above, specified pool trades that are TBA eligible usually trade at a premium to TBA contract prices. The securities themselves are quoted at a spread over the corresponding TBA contract. Non-TBA-eligible specified pools may also be quoted as spreads to TBA trades, although the non-eligible pools often trade at discounts to the corresponding TBA contract due in part to their worse liquidity.

B. Risk Management

The TBA market also serves as a useful risk management tool for banks. There are two ways in which banks use the TBA market as a risk management tool: offloading interest rate risk from the bank's balance sheet, and hedging interest rate risk during the mortgage origination process.

Issuing a thirty-year FRM—which is the dominant mortgage product in the United States—creates three major risks for a mortgage lender. These risk factors are advantageous to the borrower and risky to the lender—the thirty-year term (which exposes the lender to credit risk), the fixed rate on the loan (which together with the thirty-year term exposes the lender to interest rate risk), and the embedded prepayment option (which exposes the lender to prepayment risk, which is largely another aspect of interest rate risk). The government guarantee alleviates a large degree of the credit risk faced by the lender, but the two elements of interest rate risk remain and can be expensive to hedge. The amalgamation of these factors creates a strong incentive to offload these risks from the lender's balance sheet to the capital markets through securitizing and selling the MBS, which can be readily done through the TBA market.

TBA buyers absorbing the interest rate risk seek duration exposure and are comfortable with the volatility-related risks of the MBS's prepayment option. However, these investors are not necessarily capable of evaluating the credit risk of the mortgages that the banks originated. The TBA market together with the government's implicit or explicit guarantee puts the interest rate risk where it is least costly to fund. The result is, presumably, a lower required rate of return for a long-term FRM than if banks needed to manage this risk. Perhaps as a result, the thirty-year fixed rate identified by Green and Wachter (2005) as the "American mortgage" is not offered in countries without secondary markets because its costs to borrowers would be far higher than the ARMs that are offered.

Moreover, Fuster and Vickery (2014) have found that the fixed-rate share of mortgage origination is sharply lower when mortgages are difficult to securitize (defined as periods when there is a lack of access to liquid securitization), which implies that banks are less willing to provide FRMs to borrowers when they cannot offload their duration exposure to the capital markets.

Mortgage originators also use the TBA market for risk management purposes when hedging their so-called "pipelines." When borrowers visit a local bank branch on a given day and obtain one- to two-month rate locks from the bank, so that they know the rate they will be obligated to pay when the loan closes, the bank becomes exposed to interest rate risk because it is committed to honoring the quoted interest rate to the borrowers for the length of the rate lock regardless of where interest rates go in the financial markets (this is the period when the loan underwriting process takes place). In other words, the bank is now short an option to the borrower with a term of up to two months. In order to hedge that risk, the bank's trading desk will sell TBA contracts forward based on the number of borrowers that the bank's loan officers expect to ultimately accept the bank's mortgage offer. Because the loan officers do not know exactly which borrowers will close, the ability to sell the security forward at current market prices without specifying the exact collateral is a great advantage in managing the "pipeline" aspect of interest rate risk. In the absence of this function, borrowers would not know their mortgage costs and perhaps would not even be able to close on their home given interest rate volatility and the need to be within debt-to-income ratio guidelines mandated by the QM loan criteria.[17]

C. Avoidance of Physical Settlement

Finally, because the TBA market is essentially a futures market, market participants can easily take risk in the market without worrying about the physical management of collateral. If an investor is long TBA contracts as the settlement day approaches, the requirement to eventually take delivery of the MBS can be avoided by entering an offsetting short position in the same TBA contract or through the use of a specialized financing transaction called a "dollar roll."[18]

A dollar roll is a pair of offsetting TBA trades that functions in some ways like a one-month repo transaction. In a dollar roll, the "roll seller" sells TBAs in one month and simultaneously buys TBAs in the following month. This way, the seller essentially "rolls" the TBA position forward by one month, thereby postponing settlement. Unlike a repo, in a dollar roll the securities sold in the front month only have to be substantially similar to the securities bought in the back month—and in many cases there are no actual securities involved because the trade is simply a set of offsetting positions in TBA futures contracts. Many market participants use the dollar roll to express views in the mortgage market and may rarely take delivery of securities. Absent a TBA trading convention, dollar roll trades would not be possible, and without a dollar roll market, fewer investors would participate in MBS trading.

V. Scope of Current Reforms

In general, most legislators, policy analysts, and market participants recognize the cost advantages the TBA market provides to both the borrower and the lender. Thanks to the TBA market's facilitation of trades that can settle up to three months in the future and do not require collateral to be specified, borrowers are able to obtain rate locks for an extended period of time. The TBA market also permits lenders whose funding is short term to obtain capital from long-term investors who are not in a position to evaluate credit risk.

Since the financial crisis, several groups of legislators have put forward pieces of housing finance reform legislation in Congress. According to market participants, many of the reform proposals face high hurdles to becoming law, although several of the bills contain components that are relatively noncontroversial. One of the proposals that analysts believe is more likely to be the basis for a future effort is the bipartisan Johnson-Crapo bill. Furthermore, although it may be unlikely that Congress will pass major housing finance reform legislation in the near term, that does not mean that changes cannot be made through the administrative rule-making process. The Federal Housing Finance Agency (FHFA) in particular has significant authority to mandate changes to the housing finance system through its role as conservator of the GSEs. In this section, we discuss two existing reform initiatives that would make modifications to the TBA market: the Johnson-Crapo legislation introduced in Congress and the FHFA's single-security proposal.

Most bipartisan and nonpartisan reform proposals explicitly call for preserving the TBA market as a source of capital for mortgage borrowing, and the bipartisan Johnson-Crapo bill is no exception. Johnson-Crapo would create a new TBA contract, with Fannie and Freddie MBS deliverable into the new contract. The new contract would be backed by a new Federal Mortgage Insurance Corporation (FMIC), which would replace Fannie and Freddie. Johnson-Crapo would also extend the explicit guarantee to legacy GSE MBS (relevant in the case of specified pools or non-TBA deliverable securities).

Essentially, the creation of a new, explicitly guaranteed FMIC contract into which Fannie and Freddie MBS can be delivered would lead to the collapse of price differentials between Fannie and Freddie securities, assuming no major differences in prepayment speeds. Because the FMIC securities would enjoy an explicit government guarantee, they would likely receive the favorable risk-weight and liquidity coverage ratio treatment of Ginnie Mae securities under the Basel III framework.[19] This would lead to shrinkage in the price differential between Ginnie Mae securities and GSE securities, although some differences would likely persist due to differences in liquidity and the underlying differences in the characteristics of Ginnie Mae borrowers. Because both Fannie and Freddie securities would be deliverable into an FMIC TBA trade, this would likely lead to compression in the Fannie Mae/Freddie Mac price spread unless significant prepayment differences materialize between the two Agencies' mortgage collateral.

The FHFA's single security proposal could have an effect similar to Johnson-Crapo's creation of the FMIC TBA contract. Under the current proposal, the FHFA envisions the creation of a single type of GSE mortgage-backed security that would be eligible for a credit wrap from either Fannie Mae or Freddie Mac. Further, a single security wrapped by Fannie Mae could effectively be "rewrapped" into a Freddie Mac–guaranteed security or vice-versa. The FHFA hopes that this second-level securitization option will, for example, allow a Freddie Mac security to obtain a second-level guarantee from Fannie Mae and therefore be eligible for delivery into a Fannie Mae TBA contract. This would effectively merge the tradable floats of GSE MBS and should improve the liquidity for both securities. Because either security could be delivered into a trade, price differences between the two would quickly be arbitraged away. Whether Fannie Mae prices would decline to Freddie Mac levels or whether Freddie Mac prices would rise to Fannie Mae levels remains an open question and would probably depend on market participants' assessment of the relative prepayment risk of the two securities.

If successful, the proposal could substantially increase liquidity by merging the tradable floats of Fannie Mae and Freddie Mac MBS. However, Fannie Mae and Freddie Mac securities do currently have some structural differences, and the FHFA has proposed steps to harmonize the structural differences between the issuers. Specifically, the FHFA intends for the single security to use Fannie Mae's design structure and Freddie Mac's disclosure requirements. One important design change is the modification of Freddie Mac's standard forty-five-day payment delay[20] to the fifty-five-day delay used by Fannie Mae.

In general, market participants' reaction to the proposal has been mostly positive. However, some investors have identified some risks presented by the proposal. First, some investors believe that significant differences in the creditworthiness of the two GSEs could lead to the securities of the less creditworthy GSE becoming the cheapest to deliver. This view has some merit as the GSEs do not technically have explicit, unlimited backing from the U.S. government and have a cap on how much capital they can draw from the Treasury in an emergency. This means liquidity and pricing differences could re-emerge in the Agency MBS market even after the introduction of a single security. The FHFA's idea of allowing investors to obtain second-level credit guarantees could alleviate this potential problem during normal times. In times of distress, however, one can imagine that the resecuritization option would not alleviate investors' concerns about GSE creditworthiness. For example, consider this entirely hypothetical scenario: during an economic downturn, Fannie Mae finds that its underwriting standards were insufficient and blows through its loan-loss reserves and its capital draw from the Treasury. Investors, afraid that Fannie Mae will not be able to make them whole in the event of defaults in their mortgage pools, rush to Freddie Mac to obtain a second-level guarantee. How should Freddie Mac price its second-level resecuritization? In this hypothetical example, Freddie Mac would only have reserved enough capital to meet its guarantees on its own mortgage book, not its own book *and* Fannie Mae's book. If Freddie Mac charged more than a nominal sum for its second-level guarantee, meaningful valuation differences would arise between Freddie Mac securities and Fannie Mae securities in this scenario, likely leading to a schism in the TBA floats of the two GSEs.

The second concern highlighted by observers, investor overconcentration, is also related to the creditworthiness of the GSEs. Currently, some investors have portfolio-level limits on their allocation to the securities of a single GSE. These limits exist in part to mimic benchmark exposures and in part to limit counterparty credit risk. Under a single security regime, investors buying agency MBS on a TBA basis would have no idea whether they will ultimately be delivered Fannie or Freddie bonds. This means that over time an investor's balance of Fannie and Freddie bonds could deviate significantly from a target level. Market participants have suggested that this problem could potentially be overcome through the use of the FHFA's proposed resecuritization mechanism. Analysts have also suggested that over time the benchmark weightings themselves and the corresponding investor targets could change or be abolished altogether as the market adapts to the new single security.

VI. Principles for Reform

Given the impact of the government backstop and the TBA market—transforming heterogeneous assets with significant credit risk into homogeneous assets with effectively no credit risk—most GSE reform proposals include preserving the TBA market as a goal.

But the simple requirement in legislation that TBA be maintained does not in itself accomplish this result. In this section, we outline six major principles that ideally should be kept in place in order to preserve the TBA market. These include preserving the credit risk protection provided by the government guarantee, ensuring reasonably similar prepayment speeds among the deliverable cohort, harmonizing security characteristics, harmonizing underwriting standards, minimizing information acquisition costs by restricting loan-level data, and continuing to allow MBS exemptions from security registration laws. Many of these principles relate to maintaining the homogeneity of the underlying collateral and thereby maximizing the size of the CTD cohort. Although these principles may seem simple to list, they are each rather complex and will not simply appear through a mandate to do so—the market and the underlying securities must be designed in a way that facilitates the TBA function.

A. Provide a Credit Guarantee

In our view, in order to preserve depth and liquidity, the MBS market needs to be kept as a rates market that does not require significant credit analysis.

Ultimately, the liquidity of the TBA market is bolstered by the homogeneous and implicitly risk-free nature of the underlying assets. Without the explicit and implicit government backstops, investors would be forced to allocate significant resources to pricing the default risk they face. This would be through estimating the capital adequacy of any private mortgage insurers who guarantee the loans, in addition to conducting loan-level credit analysis to determine the default risk of various pools—both of which could raise the costs of MBS trading and mortgage financing.

Furthermore, the concept of the CTD security in the TBA market increases the homogeneity of what is a very heterogeneous area of credit formation. Because MBS investors currently do not need to evaluate credit risk, agency MBS prices to the level of the underlying mortgage pools with the least beneficial *prepayment* characteristics. If the TBA market contained securities with appreciable levels of credit risk, the determination of the CTD cohort could shift from evaluating prepayment risk to evaluating credit risk. Some market participants believe that the TBA market would not survive if investors had to consider credit losses in addition to prepayments when determining the CTD cohort—hence the inclusion of an explicit government credit guarantee in most proposals.

Even without a TBA market, of course, there are other disadvantages to the absence of government guarantees. As discussed earlier in this volume, this market would suffer from the procyclicality inherent in the mortgage market. During a period of financial market stress, investors would be even more reluctant to supply capital to the mortgage market absent a reliable government guarantee.

B. Manage Prepayment Differences

We have discussed above that the TBA market rests on the assumption of homogeneity. However, MBS are not homogeneous, as evidenced by the specified pool market, which offers investors prepayment protection by carefully selecting mortgage pools with characteristics that are linked to lower refinancing propensity (in the current rate environment). In the past, market participants have observed significant differences in prepayment speeds between Fannie Mae and Freddie Mac bonds, which in turn have affected their pricing. Critics of the FHFA's single security proposal have highlighted the divergence in prepayments between the two GSEs in the past and have suggested that if prepayment differences materialize in the future, the expected gain in liquidity from merging the Fannie Mae and Freddie Mac floats would be lost or actually worsened. Under this logic, if Freddie Mac prepayment speeds rise above Fannie Mae levels (as they did in the past), the Freddie Mac float would become the CTD, and the Fannie Mae float would trade at a pay-up.

The same logic applies in a multiple-guarantor world. Under a multiple-guarantor model, it stands to reason that the guarantors would attempt to compete in different ways. Some guarantors may seek to gain market share by aligning their systems with specific originators or through a different geographic focus. If the originators themselves have different servicing practices, or tend to attract different types of borrowers as customers, these differences could produce prepayment differences in the securities. Even today, mortgage pools guaranteed by the same Agency, with the same coupon, and with similar average loan balances and times to maturity can exhibit drastically different prepayment speeds based on the operational practices of the servicer. Historically, Fannie Mae and Freddie Mac have had preferential relationships with certain lenders that may have contributed to the aforementioned differences in prepayment speeds. These differences may have arisen from geographic discrepancies or a lender's operational practices.

The risk of having prepayment differences between the securities is that it could compromise the TBA float. Consider a scenario in which the total volume of government-guaranteed "agency" MBS is $5 trillion, evenly divided between ten guarantors. If one of the guarantors has significantly different selling guidelines from the others, or if one of the guarantors works closely with lenders that are more aggressive in soliciting refinancing, that guarantor's MBS could exhibit markedly different prepayment characteristics from its peers. This could lead to a fracturing of the TBA market. The guarantor with the different practices would see its securities become the CTD, and the remainder of the market ($4.5 trillion) would all trade as specified pools. This outcome, though extreme, would be substantially worse for market liquidity than the present structure.

C. Harmonize Underwriting Standards

Another element critical to preserving homogeneity in the market is to ensure that originators that create mortgages for securitization into TBA-deliverable MBS use similar underwriting standards. Currently, Fannie and Freddie carefully specify the criteria for their securitization programs in their selling guides. Without reasonably similar underwriting standards, mortgage investors will need to invest resources into understanding the discrepancies between different originators' underwriting practices in order to determine the CTD cohort if divergence in underwriting standards leads to differences in prepayment speeds or default rates (because a default is treated as a prepayment from the standpoint of the investor in the case of agency-guaranteed MBS).

In a multiple-guarantor world, some sort of higher-level regulatory body would need to mandate and enforce compliance with a harmonized set of underwriting standards. Under Johnson-Crapo, the FMIC could perform this function, perhaps requiring the underwriting standards to be met on a pool or individual loan basis in order to receive government re-insurance. A reinsurer that is not a government-owned corporation—such as a cooperatively owned utility (Dechario et al. 2010)—could also perform this function. Under the FHFA's current Common Securitization Platform (CSP) initiative, the CSP could perform this function even though it does not provide a backup credit guarantee. The CSP could simply mandate compliance with certain underwriting standards in order for a mortgage originator or guarantor to use the securitization infrastructure. Other reform proposals that do not envision an explicit government backstop for the mortgage market will still need some sort of mechanism to enforce harmonized underwriting standards.

D. Harmonize Security Characteristics

Any reform effort that seeks to replace the Fannie Mae-Freddie Mac duopoly with a new set of mortgage guarantors will also need to consider the underlying characteristics of the securities produced by these guarantors. If policy makers envision the future state of secondary market trading as revolving around a single TBA contract, each guarantor's TBA-eligible securities will need to have similar designs in order to avoid fragmentation of the CTD cohort. The FHFA has already considered this factor in its single security proposal, as the current ten-day difference between Fannie Mae and Freddie Mac's payment delays results in a concrete difference in the economic value of the securities. In theory, if the prepayment characteristics of the two securities are the same, the privilege of receiving principal and interest payments ten days earlier should lead to Freddie Mac securities being more valuable than Fannie Mae bonds in a merged TBA market. This would mean that Fannie Mae securities become the CTD cohort, and Freddie Mac bonds would all trade at a pay-up equal to the value of receiving principal and interest ten days earlier.

In a multiple-guarantor world, some overarching entity would have to ensure that each guarantor's security design does not meaningfully differ from its peers. The FHFA has not only identified a need to harmonize design differences like the payment delay but also disclosure standards. Harmonizing disclosure standards among guarantors would likely also involve some top-down guidance about technology infrastructure, along with data-gathering and reporting procedures.

E. Restrict Availability of Loan-Level Data

If loan-level data becomes increasingly available and models that predict borrower prepayment behavior become more sophisticated, market participants will be able to better analyze pockets of under- or overvalued prepayment risk in sectors of the mortgage market. Availability of this information could be detrimental to TBA market liquidity. Vickery and Wright (2010) have posited that the limits on information disclosure inherent in the TBA market improve the market's liquidity by making the securities fungible and reducing investors' information acquisition costs.

For example, pools with high loan-to-value ratios and low loan balances typically trade at a price premium over the TBA contract price. As loan-level analysis improves, investors may identify further pockets of prepayment protection in heretofore unknown areas, reducing the total float of securities that investors are willing to trade at the TBA contract price. Float reduction could hurt TBA trading volumes and liquidity, ultimately leading to higher liquidity premia on MBS.

F. Exempt Guarantors from Securities Registration Laws

The TBA market is able to function as currently structured because of the GSEs' exemption from the Securities Act of 1933 (the Securities Act). The Securities Act mandates that securities to be sold in the United States must be registered with the Securities and Exchange Commission (SEC). Thanks to the exemption, however, the GSEs are allowed to produce and sell MBS without registration, including through the TBA market. This exception is particularly significant, as in many cases TBA trades are allowed to take place before the underlying securities that will eventually be delivered into the trade even exist.

From a reform standpoint, any guarantor wishing to participate in the MBS market would most likely need a similar exemption from the Securities Act, especially if the guarantor creates a loan delivery window similar to the GSEs' current system. Under the GSEs' current loan delivery system, participating banks can deliver loans to the GSEs in exchange for cash or MBS, per the participating bank's choice. The securitization window typically turns loans around within five days, a period that would likely be longer if the new MBS required SEC registration.

VII. Conclusion

Market participants generally agree on the advantages that the TBA market brings to the market. This includes most obviously the liquidity provided by the second-largest (by volume of trades) fixed-income market in the United States after Treasuries. In addition, lenders are able to hedge the interest rate risk at low cost that they are exposed to during the warehousing period and not shift this risk to borrowers, who otherwise would not know the cost of their mortgage until the day of closing. Most importantly, the TBA market allows rate investors who are best able to manage interest rate risk take on this function while only requiring them to understand the prepayment characteristics of a specific subset of the market. With respect to credit risk, although any credit risk at all would make such investments more costly from the perspective of investors, even the provision of guarantees by the federal government does not in itself deliver the liquidity which drives low warehousing costs, low costs for the borrower rate lock option, and low interest rate risk management costs.

In its current form, the TBA market's liquidity and depth rest on a combination of the risk-free nature of Agency MBS and the concept of the CTD security. This combination transforms the market from one that would otherwise be heterogeneous from both a credit and prepayment perspective into one that is largely homogeneous along both lines. The prepayment homogeneity derives from the TBA market itself, and not a government guarantee.

Most reform proposals do not explore the impact that any changes to the current housing finance system would have on the TBA market and the functions it provides. Although the benefits and risks from providing a government backstop to the Agency MBS market have been widely debated, there has been little discussion thus far of the factors that could potentially impair the homogeneity of the underlying collateral or the size of the CTD cohort and therefore cause the TBA market to fracture to the point that it would no longer deliver its liquidity. These factors include underwriting standards, security design features, fundamental differences in prepayment speeds, and the availability of loan-level data. Another factor that policy makers should consider is the unique exemption that the Agencies enjoy from SEC registration requirements, and how that exemption should be carried over to future entities that replace the role of Fannie Mae and Freddie Mac.

Without a TBA market, in ordinary times the costs of long-term securitized mortgages would be higher to borrowers, and warehousing costs and lock-in costs would be higher for lenders. In times of distress, the absence of the homogenizing impact of the TBA market would likely lead to even more volatility and worse liquidity than the market would otherwise experience.

Fundamentally, the TBA market is governed by a set of rules outside those that define the roles of the government, banks, and GSEs in the housing finance system. However, the TBA market is also an outcome of an institutional framework that can be changed by decisions that those actors make. In order to provide liquidity to investors and the option of long-term fixed rate capital to homeowners, policy makers should consider the effects that reforms will have for the TBA market, and for borrowers more directly.

CHAPTER 8

The Significance and Design of a National Mortgage Note Registry

Stephanie Heller and Dale A. Whitman

The Great Recession of the late 2000s exposed the fact that the entire mortgage market was fraught with fragility. So long as real estate values continued to grow and mortgage defaults were relatively rare, none of this mattered. But when the price bubble burst and defaults began to grow to alarming proportions, the weaknesses of the mortgage market structure quickly became apparent. The most obvious deficiencies were in the processes for originating and servicing loans. More subtle, and becoming clear only over a longer period, were weaknesses in the legal regime under which mortgage loans are transferred and enforced, and servicers act.[1] These weaknesses led to an avalanche of litigation and unresolved controversy that remain with us to this day.

Critical to the workings of the mortgage market is the right to enforce the mortgage, that is, to have recourse to the legal system in the event of default, to foreclose on the property. Without this right, there would be no mortgage market, only consumer debt, which of course is orders of magnitude more expensive to the borrower and would not allow for the affordable financing of home ownership. Prior to the crisis in the residential mortgage industry, it would have been uncommon to see significant debate in the legal community as to who was entitled to enforce a residential mortgage note, and even more surprising to see debate as to whether the party initiating foreclosure had the right to do so. No one really worried about whether residential mortgage notes or mortgage themselves were "enforceable" or whether the holder of such note had the special status of a "holder in due course."[2]

With the growth of securitization through the private-label mortgage market expansion, there came a need to transfer mortgage notes quickly. To do so, the Mortgage Electronic Registration System (MERS) was created in the mid-1990s to hold mortgages on behalf of their investors, but no one paused to worry that identifying MERS on the mortgage might somehow separate the mortgage from the mortgage note, compromising the ability to enforce.[3] And no one would have lost a moment of sleep concerned that the use of custodians to store physical notes would threaten the lender's status as the possessor of that note.

And yet, since the beginning of the financial crisis these issues have been routinely litigated, and the weaknesses in the legal framework supporting the ancient paper-based legal infrastructure governing residential mortgage notes have become visible everywhere. Reading the popular press, it would be easy to dismiss the litigation tsunami as the result of questionable practices by the lawyers bringing these cases and the lenders and servicers that originated and serviced the loans.[4] Indeed, there are a multitude of cases that can be characterized as demonstrating at best sloppy practices on the part of lawyers, lenders, and servicers, and at worst outright fraud.

Although it is not our intention to downplay the importance of these factors, the reality is that, regardless of the reasons for the litigation, the cases have shed light on uncertainties in the framework of the law itself. The legal uncertainties exist largely because (1) modern practice has not sufficiently accounted for the legal formalities required by the arcane law of negotiable instruments and may have placed too high a reliance on the application of the common law of agency to real property transactions;[5] and (2) commercial law and real property law both address the same fundamental transaction (a loan secured by real property), but in ways that are not consistent.

In this chapter, we describe a proposal for the creation of a national registry for the maintenance and transfer of mortgage notes and the associated mortgages (the "National Registry") as a means of bringing legal certainty to this market while supporting modern practice and protecting the interest of all stakeholders.[6]

In order to put forth a solution, it is important to explore how the current legal design of the residential mortgage note market has contributed to legal problems, particularly with the growth of securitization. Secondary market trades of mortgage notes are extremely common in the modern American economy. As of the beginning of 2015, there were nearly $10 trillion in outstanding residential (one-to-four-family) mortgages, about another $1 trillion in multifamily mortgages, and more than $2.5 trillion in commercial and farm property mortgages. The great majority of the residential loans, and a substantial number of all other mortgages, are sold on the secondary market, and it is not unusual for a loan to be the subject of multiple transfers over its lifetime.

Current judicial and legal systems are not equipped to handle the securitization-based housing finance system that has developed in the United States. The mechanics by which this market operates are driven by Articles 3 and 9 of the Uniform Commercial Code (the UCC). However, judges and lawyers in the field have been slow to understand the Code's requirements or indeed its overall paradigm for transferring mortgage notes. That understanding was greatly assisted by the publication in 2011 of a white paper on the topic by the Permanent Editorial Board (PEB) of the Uniform Commercial Code.[7] As that paper points out, one who buys mortgage loans on the secondary market ordinarily wants to acquire two distinct sets of rights: ownership and the right to enforce. Ownership means the economic benefits of the loan—the right to the monthly payments and the proceeds of a payoff or a foreclosure. The right to enforce, on the other hand, means the right to sue on the note or take other actions against the borrower or the property, such as instigating foreclosure of the mortgage. These two sets of rights are distinct and need not necessarily reside in the same person, but buyers of mortgages in the secondary market want them both.

The issues are made more complex by the fact that multiple sources of law apply, depending on the nature of the mortgage note. The right to enforce the note is governed by UCC Article 3 if the note is negotiable and by the common law if it is not. Transfers of ownership are governed by UCC Article 9, whether the note is negotiable or not. (Negotiability is a highly technical concept that depends on the precise wording of the note. It requires satisfaction of a number of technical requirements, which may or may not be present in a particular promissory note.)[8]

First, we consider transfer of the right to enforce a note. Under the law of negotiable instruments, the original inked, signed mortgage note has special legal significance. It is treated as the reification of the payment obligation;

the debt owed merges into the paper, and the paper becomes one and the same as the debt. It follows, then, that to be able to enforce the debt, one must have the piece of paper. In this way, the ability to produce the inked, signed note becomes of paramount importance if enforcement of a negotiable instrument is challenged. If the note is a negotiable instrument and the party trying to enforce the note does not have possession of the original inked signature note, it does not have the claim.

Thus, under Article 3, the right to enforce a negotiable note can be transferred only by delivery of possession of the original document to the transferee.[9] Moreover, although not absolutely essential, it is wise for the note to be signed over to the transferee (otherwise referred to as indorsed); without indorsement, the transferee may be required to offer proof that the delivery was made for the purpose of transferring the right of enforcement,[10] while no such proof is necessary if the note is properly indorsed.[11] There is greater flexibility with respect to nonnegotiable notes, and by the prevailing view they can be transferred either by indorsement and delivery or by a separate document of assignment.[12] However, it is not always clear in advance of litigation whether a note is negotiable.[13]

Transfers of ownership, governed by UCC Article 9, likewise can be accomplished either by delivery of possession or by a separate document of assignment.[14] But Article 9 attributes a special type of "perfection" to transfers by delivery of possession, and one who takes ownership by this method will prevail over any competing claimant who perfected by another method, such as filing a financing statement or merely completing the transfer.[15] Purchasers of mortgage notes generally want the enhanced form of perfection that is conferred by possession, because otherwise the purchaser would be at risk of having its rights cut off by a wrongful second sale to a party who did get possession of the note. This principle, as we have mentioned, applies whether the note is negotiable or not.

We can summarize the effect of these rules by saying that knowledgeable mortgage note purchasers will always insist on having the promissory note delivered to consummate the sale. They also will prefer to have the note indorsed (i.e., signed) in the name of the purchaser, if the note has not previously been indorsed in blank, so that any party in possession has the benefit of the indorsement. But delivery and indorsement add significantly to the costs of the securitization process, even if custodians are used to hold possession of the mortgage notes.[16]

Originating loans for sale in the secondary mortgage market involves the bulk transfer of hundreds of mortgage notes multiple times before a final transfer to a securitization trust. In a typical securitization, there are at least three steps: the originating lender sells its loans first to the "sponsor," which in turn sells the loans to the "depositor," which in turn sells the loans to the special-purpose vehicle (SPV) that is the securitization trust. The originator, sponsor, depositor, and SPV are each separate legal entities, and the transaction flow from originator to SPV is structured to try to ensure that the securitization trust is, among other things, bankruptcy remote. This means that if the originator or sponsor enters bankruptcy, the securitization trust will be unaffected. In order for the securitization trust to have obtained a right of enforcement in each of the mortgage notes that form the corpus of the securitization trust, physical possession of the note must have passed from originator to sponsor, from sponsor to depositor, and from depositor to SPV.

The system requires moving tangible pieces of paper around the country and keeping track of them. It is all too easy for notes to be lost or mislaid. Most investors use independent custodians to hold their notes, but this necessitates contracting with, establishing standards for, and compensating the custodians. If the note is sold and the buyer wishes to continue to use the same custodian, records must be kept to show that authority to direct the custodian has been transferred. An actual note needs to be produced for purposes of borrower examination or litigation on only relatively rare occasions, such as foreclosure proceedings in some states, but there must be an established procedure for doing so.

Indorsements add a further layer of complexity. Each indorsement must be individually written, signed, and (ideally) dated. It is mechanically difficult to write indorsements on the original notes, so they are often placed on separate pieces of paper, called "allonges," that are attached to the notes. But it is easy for an allonge to become detached from its parent note, thus calling its legal sufficiency into doubt. Foreclosure defense lawyers have repeatedly "flyspecked" the transfer process, looking for instances of notes that were undelivered or unindorsed. In the transactions that characterized the frenzied mortgage market before the collapse of 2007, they found plenty of evidence of carelessness and error.

In addition to the legal formalities that surround the right to enforce and the ownership of mortgage notes, questions have also arisen concerning the legal right to enforce a mortgage note and the associated mortgage simply because a mortgage note is a separate document from the related mortgage.[17] Of course, notwithstanding the technical separation of the note from the mortgage, these two documents are intrinsically connected—the mortgage is extremely important consideration offered to the lender to induce the making of the loan. If the note's relationship to the mortgage were severed, the note would represent only an unsecured loan and would be far less attractive and valuable in the market. It is not surprising, therefore, that the law developed so that, absent extraordinary circumstances, the transfer of an interest in a mortgage note results in the transfer of an interest in the associated mortgage.

This principle has existed in the law since at least 1872, when the United States Supreme Court held that "the note and the mortgage are inseparable. . . . An assignment of the note carries the mortgage with it, while an assignment of the latter alone is a nullity." And yet, since the crisis a plethora of cases have discussed whether the note and the mortgage can be separated so that the note holder as such is unable to foreclose. To aid the courts in resolving this question, the PEB Report called attention to Article 9 of the UCC, which provides that any transfer of a mortgage note for value transfers the interest in the mortgage securing the note.[18] Despite the fact that these legal principles are quite clear, a good deal of litigation during the mortgage crisis was spawned by the argument that if the note and the mortgage were not both transferred to the same party, they should be regarded as "separated," and the mortgage could become unenforceable.[19]

For many commercial lawyers unfamiliar with mortgage notes, the Uniform Commercial Code is the beginning and end of the discussion. Unfortunately for the residential mortgage market, commercial law and the law of real property do not always align. In about a dozen states, the right to enforce the mortgage note, although perhaps necessary, is not sufficient to authorize foreclosure of the mortgage. In these states, a third level of complication is added by the need to record a chain of mortgage assignments in the local real estate records as a precondition of the right to foreclose. For the most part, these requirements apply only when the holder of the mortgage wishes to foreclose nonjudicially, but because nonjudicial foreclosures tend to be relatively quick and cheap, the need for a chain of assignments often applies.

Recording adds considerable cost and complexity; the lender needs to determine which of the roughly 3,600 recording offices in the United States is the appropriate filing place, prepare and execute assignments in the specific form accepted by that specific recording office, and calculate the necessary fees. The recording of assignments has other advantages to the buyer of a mortgage loan,[20] beyond qualifying it for foreclosure in the states mentioned above, but the point to be made here is that it is a labor-intensive, error-prone, and burdensome process.

The burden of this process at least in part led to the advent of MERS in the 1990s.[21] To remove the need to record assignments, MERS was established to serve as the mortgagee of record, but merely as a nominee for the note holder and its successors and assigns, meaning MERS is acting on behalf of the note holder and not on its own behalf. Hence, in theory no recordation of a mortgage assignment is necessary when a note that has MERS as the mortgagee of record is transferred from one holder to another, because the recording office already identifies MERS as the mortgagee of record for the note holder's successors and assigns. MERS tracks who the note holder is at any point in time so as to be able to identify the party that it serves as nominee (i.e., the actual mortgagee). This was a seemingly ingenious solution to the burdens of recording successive assignments.

But ultimately the use of the MERS system gave rise to all sorts of litigation, including claims questioning foreclosure proceedings initiated by MERS as nominee for the note holder and claims that the note and the mortgage were separated through the use of MERS. (Other problems concerning the governance and operation of MERS also arose, leading to a loss in confidence by some and general skepticism by the public as to the use of the MERS system.)

Moreover, although MERS could be viewed as a type of national registry, it serves a very limited function; it keeps track of information about the identity of note holders. The existence of MERS does not eliminate the need for and the complexities resulting from the paper requirements discussed above other, than recording interim mortgage assignments. The current paper-based process used to deliver and indorse notes and to assign mortgages required by current law is outdated, even archaic, when one realizes that today nearly all other financial instruments are tracked and transferred electronically. The current system for transferring interests in mortgage notes is costly, prone to human error, and productive of litigation. It also fails to provide borrowers a quick, simple,[22] and accurate way of determining who holds and who services their mortgages notes at any given moment in time. This information, along with information concerning a servicer's authority to modify a loan, is critical to the success of a borrower in resolving a mortgage note default.[23]

So what is the answer? At least part of the answer may be to establish through new legislation a National Registry that is subject to public oversight, whether run by the private sector or by the government. A National Registry as described in this chapter would establish the person entitled to enforce the mortgage note and foreclose on the associated mortgage, would permit borrowers free access to this and other core information about the mortgage note and the servicer in real time), and would provide the means to transfer such legal rights. Significantly, the proposed legal framework would make the acts of the National Registry in response to directions from mortgage holders have legal consequence. It would be these acts, as opposed to the acts of physical delivery, note indorsement, and mortgage assignment, that would result in the creation of legal rights. This transformation is similar to the transformation in the securities market, where the use of bond powers to transfer interests in paper certificates has given way to instructions to transfer agents to reflect movements of uncertificated/dematerialized (nonpaper) securities on their books.

Contrast this with a system like MERS today. The MERS system itself does not create legal rights; it is merely a source of information about actions taken externally to the system that have a legal effect.[24] To illustrate this difference, consider the following example. Lender A originates a residential mortgage loan. MERS is the mortgagee, and the note associated with the loan indicates that homeowner promises to pay Lender A and its successors and assigns. Lender A wishes to sell the note to Bank B, and Bank B is willing to pay Lender A an agreed amount. Lender A instructs MERS to update its records to identify Bank B. Five years later, the loan is in default, and Bank B brings an action to enforce the note. The fact that the MERS system records show Bank B as the owner of the note has no legal effect. Instead, in order to enforce the note, Bank B will have to prove that the note was sold to it. If the note is a negotiable instrument, as discussed above, Bank B would generally have to have possession of the note indorsed in blank or to it. The fact that MERS has updated its records, even if it has correctly done so, does not mean that Bank B has possession of the note indorsed in blank or to it. With the National Registry, all that would be necessary to enforce the mortgage note would be a certification from the Registry operator, indicating that Bank B is the person associated with the note, a person we refer to as the registrant.

In the remainder of this chapter, we outline the main features we believe should be addressed in the design of legislation establishing a National Registry.

I. Federal or State Law?

A fundamental issue in structuring a National Registry is whether it should be created by federal or state law. An underlying premise of this question is that *some* form of statutory support for the proposed National Registry is needed. We believe it is, if for no other reason, because it is necessary to override the combination of UCC § 1-201(21)'s definition of "holder" and UCC § 3-301's explanation of how one becomes entitled to enforce a negotiable note. The present effect of these two provisions of law is that unless a mortgage note has been lost, one must have physical possession of it in order to enforce it. But it is this very mandate of possession that a National Registry must shake off; notes for registered mortgage loans must be enforceable by the registrant without possession, but with registration deemed the legal equivalent of possession.[25]

In principle, a uniform national registry could be fashioned by state statutes, but the prospect is daunting. Every state legislature would need to act, and the resulting statutes would need to be identical or nearly so in order to create a single well-functioning registry. Even if this could be accomplished, it would not likely be a quick process. Although our initial draft was agnostic on the federal/state law issue, we expect subsequent drafts to reflect a choice of federal law in recognition of the interstate nature of the secondary market for mortgage notes and the resulting need for a fifty-state solution that comes into effect at the same moment in time.

To minimize the impact of the choice of federal law, and in recognition of the strong interest of the states in laws affecting rights in real property located within their states, the federal legislation should be drafted to minimize the impact on state law. We believe this is best achieved by treating a mortgage note deposited in the National Registry as though it still was a mortgage note under state law, even though it has changed from physical to electronic form. If the deposited notes are treated as having the same legal characteristics as prior to deposit, there should be greater certainty to all parties with an interest in the note, because the rich state statutory and case law governing these transactions will largely be preserved.

In order to make this approach work, it will be necessary in certain instances for the federal law to tell us how to apply state law after the deposit and dematerialization of a mortgage note. In a few instances it may be necessary to go one step further and change state law in a more substantive way. Despite the interstate nature of the National Registry, we expect that Congress will be very reluctant to preempt state laws absent a strong public policy to do so. We would suggest that where the issue is one of the integrity of the National Registry system, there may be strong public policy reasons to consider preemption. This is especially true if use of the National Registry is voluntary, as contemplated by the initial draft. We describe in more detail below where we would suggest the need for interpretive laws and where we see a potential need for preemption.

Of course the proposed federal legislation could include provisions that permit state law to supersede those specific provisions of the federal law directly affecting the application of state law where, for example, the state law is substantially similar to the federal law as determined by the regulator. Another option for the federal law would be to have a sunrise provision that provides that the specific provisions addressing state law are only effective if, at the time the National Registry begins operations, all fifty states (and the District of Columbia) have failed to uniformly adopt laws that are substantially similar to those in the federal law.

There are many other legislative design issues that might lead one to favor federal law over state law, including questions as to whether the National Registry should be operated by a government entity. If it is a private sector entity, there would be a need for a "regulator" with both supervisory and regulatory authority to ensure that the National Registry is operated in a safe and sound manner, in the interests of the various stakeholders and with appropriate recognition of its likely systemic importance. The present draft leaves these matters open for further discussion.

II. Who Could Register Mortgage Notes?

A person or entity entitled to place a mortgage note in the National Registry is known as a "depositor." Once the mortgage note is placed in the system, the person or entity shown in the National Registry system's records as holding the mortgage note is a "registrant." Thus, the depositor would be the initial registrant. Depositors would be required to meet standards established by the regulator (or the Registry itself, if it is a public agency) with respect to data quality, information security, and capital. If a party wished to deposit a mortgage note but did not meet the standards, it could employ the services of a "third-party service provider" (which might be a bank or other financial institution, a local recording office, or a closing agent such as a title insurer) that met them.

III. What Data Would the Registry Maintain?

Registration would require the depositor to provide both structured data on the note and mortgage, submitted in an acceptable format, and electronic representations of both documents as well as any preregistration modifications or amendments to either. Post-registration modifications or amendments would also have to be submitted to the National Registry. Information on the loan's servicer would also be carried. The National Registry would maintain a history of the actions taken on the Registry with respect to the mortgage loan.

IV. Relationship to Local Recording Offices

At present, local (typically county or town) recording offices receive original mortgages for recordation. Recording establishes the priority of the mortgage vis-à-vis the rights of the owner/borrower and all other interests in the land, such as other liens, easements, restrictive covenants, and the like. Subsequent assignments of the mortgage may also be recorded, although many secondary market purchasers forgo recording an assignment unless and until it becomes necessary, typically immediately before a foreclosure is instituted. If a foreclosure occurs, various notices so indicating may be recorded, and ultimately a foreclosure deed will be recorded to the successful purchaser of the property. If there is no foreclosure and the mortgage loan is paid off in due course, a release (sometimes called a discharge or satisfaction) will be recorded, confirming that the mortgage no longer encumbers the real estate.

How would these roles of local recorders change if a National Registry were instituted? The answer to that question as a general matter is that the role of the local recorders would not change at all—the National Registry contemplated by the authors is not a recording system and the deposit of a mortgage note and the related mortgage with the registry would not have the legal benefits afforded a mortgagee as a result of recording. Thus, the initial recording of the mortgage would continue to be essential in establishing the mortgage's priority. Because liens on real property other than mortgages are recorded in the land records (e.g., tax liens, construction liens), if mortgages in the National Registry were in essence "deemed" to be recorded, title searchers would be forced to consult both the local records and the national registry to identify all possible encumbrances on the property—a highly inconvenient result. Likewise, at the other end of the mortgage's life, its foreclosure deed or its release upon payoff would need to be recorded locally, just as at present.

In fact, the registry's statute or rules might impose an absolute requirement that only locally recorded mortgages could be deposited, establishing a legal mandate of recording that does not currently exist under state law.[26] Although the initial draft did not include such a requirement, the inclusion of a recording requirement prior to deposit in the National Registry could help to ensure the integrity of the National Registry and would be largely consistent with current practice.[27] The federal legislation might go one step further and require that all assignments of the mortgage prior to the deposit of the mortgage note in the National Registry be recorded prior to deposit. As discussed above, such a requirement does not exist in current law in a majority of states, and where it does exist, recording of assignments is only required prior to enforcement. Nevertheless, making this a requirement for use of the National Registry could provide greater certainty as to the enforceability of mortgages associated with mortgage notes in the National Registry, and would likely incent lenders to deposit mortgage loans with the National Registry upon origination (a desirable outcome as it makes the likelihood of various types of fraud far less likely). Such a rule would make it a lot less likely, however, that mortgage loans originated prior to the enactment of the federal law would be deposited in the National Registry.

Regardless of whether any recording is mandatory before use of the National Registry, once the mortgage loan is deposited in the National Registry and until it is discharged, all transfers would be shown only on the records of the National Registry. This approach would establish once and for all that the transfer of a mortgage note indeed transfers the rights in the mortgage. At least two legal provisions in the National Registry's enabling legislation would be needed to make this change functional. One would be an authorization for local recorders to accept into the public record a brief notation that the mortgage had been registered and given an identifying number in the National Registry. This would allow any title examiner, upon discovering the mortgage's existence in the local records, to then track its progress in the secondary market through the National Registry's records. The duty to place this notation in the local records might be imposed on the depositor as a condition of registration. In effect, the notation would provide a connecting link between the local and national systems.

A second essential legal feature would be a provision that if the mortgage is recorded, the registrant identified in the National Registry's records as associated with that mortgage be treated as a legal matter as the mortgagee of record. This will ensure that anyone holding a mortgage as shown in the National Registry will be entitled to service of process in any litigation or other proceeding affecting the real property or the mortgage. Such proceedings are diverse; examples include an eminent domain action, a zoning enforcement proceeding, an environmental cleanup order, or a contest over the mortgage's priority. Whoever currently holds the mortgage has a strong interest in learning of, and perhaps intervening in, such proceedings, but unless the National Registry's records are deemed to give public notice of the holder's identity, litigants will have no obligation to give the holder service of process.[28]

The combination of a notation in the records of the recording office that a note related to a recorded mortgage is in the National Registry, and making the registrant the equivalent of the mortgagee of record, will also give the current holder of the mortgage note protection against fraud by mortgage note sellers. For example, suppose an originating mortgage lender records a mortgage and subsequently sells the related mortgage note on the secondary market. If the secondary market sale is not reflected in any public record, the originating lender appears in the land records to still be the mortgage's holder. It may then connive with the borrower to fraudulently release the mortgage without receiving a payoff, thus giving the borrower the appearance of owning the property free and clear. The borrower may then sell the property to a bona fide purchaser, who will take title free of the mortgage.[29] However, if the registry's records are deemed to be a matter of public notice, this scheme cannot succeed because anyone buying the property will be held to know that the release of the mortgage was executed by a party who had no right to do so, and hence was fraudulent.

These two functions—ensuring that the holder of the mortgage will be given notice of any pending litigation and preventing a prior holder of the mortgage from fraudulently releasing it—are currently served by recording an assignment of the mortgage in the local recording office. But as we have already indicated, local recording of mortgage assignments is highly burdensome to national secondary market investors, and many of them no longer do it routinely. Such a requirement is also in tension with the long-standing legal principle that a transfer of the rights to enforce a note also transfers the right to enforce the mortgage. By including a provision in the National Registry law that any requirement under state law to record an assignment is satisfied by the noting of such assignment in the records of National Registry, and ensuring public access to such records (more on that below), current law is harmonized, and the needs of the various stakeholders are met with little additional cost.

The impact of the approach suggested above on the local recorders will be essentially the same as with loans registered with MERS; the local recorders would continue to record (and earn revenue from) the beginning and end points of the mortgage process—initial recording and payoff—but would get no income from at least some of the intermediate transfers. Local recording officials have bitterly opposed this MERS operating model,[30] although to virtually no avail. Nevertheless, any legislation proposing a National Registry should consider requiring that local recorders be given free access to the transfer records maintained in the National Registry, with the right to provide such records to the public as a means of lessening their concerns.

V. Interaction of the Registry with the Uniform Commercial Code

One of the key goals in the design of a National Registry should be to disrupt or preempt existing rules and expectations only to the minimum extent necessary. And so, although the National Registry law could create an entirely new type of property, a deposited obligation that is created upon deposit of a mortgage note with the National Registry, we would propose that it treat such deposited note as though it were still a note governed by the Uniform Commercial Code. However, as we have indicated above, under present law possession of the promissory note is the key criterion in determining whether a party has the right of enforcement under UCC Article 3, and also whether a party is regarded as perfected in ownership of the note as against competing claimants under UCC Article 9. To preserve these existing concepts, a critical feature of the statutory support for the National Registry must be a provision that states that when applying state laws requiring possession, the registrant is deemed to be in possession of the note.

We say "deemed" because, after deposit, the paper note will no longer have any legal force or effect and may even be destroyed as part of the process of initial registration.[31] This is necessary because otherwise anyone into whose hands the physical note subsequently fell would be able to claim actual possession, potentially leading to a situation in which two different parties—the registrant and the person with the physical note—could both assert that they had possession. That situation is untenable, of course. One of the strengths of the present system is that there can be only one physical note and therefore only one possessor.[32]

What legal results are accomplished by deeming the registrant to be in possession of the note? If the note is suitably indorsed,[33] the registrant will be its holder and thereby the person entitled to enforce it (the PETE).[34] If the note is negotiable and the registrant fulfills the other applicable requirements (having no notice of claims and defenses, paying value, and so on), the registrant can be a holder in due course.[35]

Because the utility of the National Registry is significantly diminished if we cannot rely on a registrant being the PETE, it is important for the National Registry law to address indorsements. Although the act of indorsing under current law is voluntary, we believe there is little harm in having the National Registry law deem each transfer of a deposited mortgage note on the National Registry as being accompanied by an indorsement so long as the transferor can direct the National Registry to record the indorsement as nonrecourse and without warranty.

Alternatively if the current law applies and indorsement is optional (based on instructions to the National Registry), the possessor can still be the PETE if it has the status of a "nonholder in possession of the instrument who has the rights of a holder."[36] To acquire PETE status in this way, the possessor must show that the note was delivered "for the purpose of giving to the person receiving delivery the right to enforce the instrument."[37] This requirement can be supplied by the registry statute itself, and to do so it should provide that a transfer of registration is deemed to be a delivery of the note for the purpose of transferring the right to enforce it. Under either approach, however, the National Registry would not permit the transfer of a deposited mortgage note unless such transfer results in the new registrant being the PETE.[38]

The foregoing illustrations are based on UCC Article 3, and therefore apply only to negotiable notes. If the note in question is nonnegotiable and is appropriately indorsed, it is clear that the "deemed in possession" language of the registry statute will constitute the registrant a PETE (Whitman forthcoming). However, it is not certain whether the courts, when faced with a nonnegotiable note that is not properly indorsed, would apply the "nonholder in possession who has the rights of a holder" concept of Article 3. As we will see below, however, that problem can be solved simply by treating nonnegotiable notes as if they were negotiable for purposes of Article 3.

At least for negotiable notes, can we say on the basis of the rules laid out above that the registrant will always be the PETE? Not quite. But the only situations in which a registrant would not be the PETE would be a case in which the initial registrant stole a note indorsed in blank[39] or the initial registrant had possession (as would be required to register the loan), but was not a holder of the note (because of the lack of the appropriate indorsements) and could not show that it received delivery for the purpose of transferring the right of possession. These situations are conceivable, but highly remote. Moreover, the introduction of the National Registry does nothing to increase the likelihood of these situations arising. The limited nature of the problem, as well as a desire to preserve current state law, may lead some to accept an approach to the National Registry law that allows for the possibility that on occasion the person identified by the National Registry as the registrant will not be the PETE.

However, a key purpose for establishing a National Registry is to provide greater transparency and certainty to borrowers and loan purchasers concerning the party with the right to enforce or sell a specific mortgage note or initiate foreclosure of the mortgage associated with the note. To achieve this purpose the National Registry law may need to go further in assuring that a registrant has PETE status. At a minimum, the law should provide that only a PETE may deposit a mortgage note in the National Registry and create new deposit warranties as to depositor PETE status (see discussion below on warranties). But this may not be enough to accomplish the public policy goals, and it may be that the National Registry law should establish a clear and objective rule that the registrant is always the PETE. In those rare instances where the "true" PETE was not the depositor, the National Registry law could provide remedies against the falsifying depositor, but importantly the law would ensure that parties that relied on the records of the National Registry to identify the PETE would be protected.

The fact that the registrant is deemed to be in possession of the note also has implications for ownership of notes under UCC Article 9. If an outright sale of the note is made, "attachment" (i.e., the taking effect) of the sale may be accomplished either by delivery of possession pursuant to an agreement of sale, or by a separate written document of assignment.[40] Since the registry statute will treat the registrant as having received a delivery of the note, every registrant will have ownership if there is an agreement of sale. If there are competing purported transfers of ownership, their priority is determined by their perfection. Perfection of an outright sale is automatic,[41] but can also be accomplished by filing a financing statement[42] or by transfer of possession of the note.[43] However, a transferee who perfects by taking possession of the note, has no knowledge of any competing claim, and buys in good faith will take ownership free of the claims of other parties who perfected by any other method.[44] This is an extremely desirable status, and the "deemed in possession" provision of the registry statute will ensure that the registrant will have it.

If there is a transfer of ownership of the note for collateral security purposes, rather than an outright sale, perfection is not automatic (as it is with outright sales),[45] but can only be accomplished by filing or the taking of possession of the note. But here as well, possession trumps filing if the party in possession has no knowledge of any competing claim and takes in good faith.[46] Registration will not definitively indicate who is the holder of a security interest in a mortgage note, since that determination will depend on the existence (or absence) of a security agreement that will not necessarily appear in the registry. But by virtue of the "deemed in possession" provisions of the registration statute, registration will greatly simplify and facilitate the creation of security interests in mortgage notes.

In sum, the National Registry system described here can be accomplished with little or no violence to the existing expectations of parties to mortgage transfers. Current concepts under the UCC would continue to operate, except that instead of a physical note with written indorsements, the parties

would use an electronic transfer and indorsement process. The only significant changes to present law that must be made are (1) to make registration
the legal equivalent of possession, and (2) to provide that when the registered
party is changed, the change of the "deemed" possession will be regarded as
made for the purpose of transferring the right of enforcement. For the National Registry law to fully advance its public policy objectives, however, the
law should confer PETE status on the registrant—a change to current law
that would be significant in a small number of cases.

VI. Servicer Identity and Other Information

It is very desirable for the National Registry to disclose the identity of the servicer of each mortgage. Indeed, information about servicing is perhaps the
item of information that is of greatest importance to borrowers. As envisioned, either the statute establishing the National Registry or the regulations implementing the National Registry would require each registrant to
indicate if it is a servicer, and if it is, to indicate for whom it is servicing. If
the registrant is not a servicer, it would need to identify its servicer. The
registrant would be required to keep this information current and the
National Registry system would be required to make the information available to the borrower. Consideration could also be given to allowing (or
obligating) the registrant to state the servicer's scope of authority, perhaps
including authority (if applicable) to enter into loan modifications. While
current law requires that borrowers be provided notice as to the identity of
the servicer of their loans, there is no current requirement to disclose the
scope of the servicer's authority to enter into loan modifications. Having
some insight into a servicer's authority to modify a loan, coupled with the
identification of the owner of the loan, will better enable borrowers to determine if a modification or workout of a defaulted loan is possible. Of course,
servicers change from time to time, and the scope of their authority may
change as well. Hence, the Registry would need to keep this information
current as changes occur.

    The National Registry could serve as a repository for all of the documents
that are ordinarily part of the loan file, and that would otherwise be transferred along with the note and mortgage when the loan is sold. If properly
implemented, this could be a great boon to the mortgage industry, entirely

eliminating the need to transfer custody of separate files when mortgage notes are sold. It is not clear whether the marginal benefit of including loan files in the National Registry would outweigh the additional operational risk to the National Registry. Nonetheless, this functionality is not needed for the National Registry to achieve its goals, thus the initial focus of any legislative effort might be on the necessary core functionality.

VII. Foreclosure and Discharge

Existing law varies considerably from state to state with respect to a party's ability to establish standing to foreclose a mortgage or deed of trust. The registry statute would not change any state's foreclosure process, but it would establish that, from the time of deposit of the mortgage into the registry forward, transfers shown in the records of the registry would be conclusively sufficient to transfer standing to foreclose the mortgage. This means that if any transfers occurred before the mortgage was deposited, those transfers would have to conform to existing state law. Thus, for purposes of discharging the mortgage, existing state law would need to be satisfied with respect to any transfers that occurred before deposit in the registry. Of course if the National Registry law were to require that all such assignments to be recorded prior to the deposit of a mortgage note in the National Registry, there could be no issue under state law. The National Registry would provide certificates as needed to record in the local land records or to produce in court in order to facilitate foreclosures or discharges.

VIII. Warranties

A party who deposits a mortgage with the registry would be required to warrant that it was in rightful possession of the original note and had the right to enforce it. It would also warrant that the instrument was genuine and had not been altered, and that the depositor had no knowledge of any adverse claims to it. Perhaps of equal importance, the law will need to include warranties that address the conversion of information in paper form to electronic form, including warranties of compliance with technical standards, accuracy and completeness, and destruction or invalidation of the paper. Warranties will also need to address the possibility of duplicate deposits, especially if deposits can be made solely in electronic form.

Some small lenders or individuals who wish to deposit a mortgage loan in the registry may not qualify, or may not be willing to make the infrastructure investment necessary, to do business with the registry. To accommodate such parties, the draft allows them to make use of a "third party servicer provider" that is qualified under the registry's rules. If this approach is used, the service provider would be required to make the deposit warranties indicated above.

IX. Electronic Notes and Nonnegotiable Notes

While most residential mortgage notes are probably negotiable and hence subject to UCC Article 3, there are two categories of notes that do not fit this description. The first is the electronic note, or as it is termed in the Uniform Electronic Transactions Act (UETA) and E-SIGN (the federal law analog of UETA), the "transferable record." These statutes modify the concepts of delivery and possession for electronic notes. Because an electronic note can be reproduced as many times as desired, and each copy is indistinguishable from the original, UETA and E-SIGN create the concept of the note as a "transferrable record."[47] Such records must be held within a system in which "a single authoritative copy of the record (the note) exists, which is unique, identifiable, and unalterable." To have the equivalent of possession of such a note, if it has been transferred, a person must have "control" in the sense that the system for tracking such notes must reliably establish that the person enforcing the note is the one to whom the record was transferred. Finally, if the record has been transferred, the authoritative copy of the record itself must indicate the identity of the person who whom it was most recently transferred.

It would be reasonable to include electronic notes within the scope of the proposed National Registry's operations. The registry can readily accept such notes, and can require the person depositing the note to provide evidence, and to warrant, that it is party with "control" of the note. However, we believe that the National Registry statute should provide that, once registered, the note is treated like any other negotiable note within the National Registry. It was clearly the intent of UETA and E-SIGN to apply UCC Article 3 to transferable records[48] and it would be highly undesirable to have one set of electronic negotiable notes (paper converted to book-entry as a result of a deposit into the National Registry) governed by one set of laws (UCC Article 3) and to have another set of electronic negotiable notes (transferable records) governed by another set of laws (UETA and E-SIGN).

A different problem is posed by nonnegotiable notes, which are sometimes used in mortgage transactions. The difficulty with such notes is that there is no codified body of law governing transfers of the right to enforce them, and the existing case law is sparse, outdated, and conflicting. The solution is the same as for electronic notes: to treat them, once deposited, as subject to the same UCC Article 3 rules and principles as negotiable notes. While treating nonnegotiable notes as if they were governed by Article 3 is not essential to operate the National Registry, we believe that it will provide additional certainty in the market place, especially since it is sometimes difficult to know with certainty at the time of a transaction whether a court will view an instrument as negotiable or nonnegotiable. There is one caveat, however, that should be included in the statute: the holder in due course doctrine cannot be applied to nonnegotiable notes.

X. Data Security and Access

The information the National Registry keeps on each loan would be available online to various parties, depending on their credentials. In simplified form, one might imagine three tiers of persons who could query the system: (1) the general public, (2) the borrower, and (3) the current registrant (and its servicer) as well as anyone to whom the current registrant might confer access (typically, for the purpose of demonstrating the quality of a portfolio of loans that the registrant might intend to sell or to use as collateral). For group 1, access would be limited to the image of the mortgage, general data concerning it (including transfer history on the registry), and the identity of the current registrant and its servicer. This would be essentially the same data available through the local recording system or that would have been available if a chain of mortgage assignments had been recorded. All persons affected by this information would be, as a matter of law, held to have notice of it. Groups 2 and 3, consisting of borrowers and registrants, would have access to all data and images concerning each loan to which they were parties, but only group 3 would be permitted to extend access to prospective buyers or lenders on the security of a loan or pool of loans. Access rules would probably best be issued by the regulator or system operator, rather than hardwired into the statute, so that they could be easily adjusted as the need arose.

In addition to rules concerning access rights to view information, technology and security standards will have to be set for communications with the National Registry that affect its information. Finally, it is obvious that the registry must maintain state-of-the-art security and anti-hacking measures to protect its data from corruption or theft. The law will also need to consider an appropriate liability scheme that protects users of the National Registry system from such risks.

Although these changes are complex and would require federal legislation, a National Registry could bring several notable benefits, which we summarize as follows:

1. The complex and error-prone, present-day processes of physically delivering promissory notes, making indorsements, and recording mortgage assignments would be supplanted by a simple online electronic transfer procedure.

2. Every borrower and every litigant filing an action affecting the mortgaged property or the mortgage would be able to determine by means of a simple web search the identity of the holder and servicer of every mortgage loan.

3. The lack of clarity in the distinction between negotiable and nonnegotiable notes that exists today would become irrelevant for purposes of loan transfer. Negotiable and nonnegotiable notes would be treated exactly alike and would be transferred in the same manner. Eliminating these distinctions could help to reduce ongoing litigation by creating greater legal clarity.

4. Any confusion and litigation about separation of notes from their mortgages would be brought to an end. All foreclosures, both judicial and nonjudicial, could be conducted with assurance that the correct party was foreclosing. The registry would treat the note and mortgage in a unitary manner, and its records would confirm that the same party had the right to enforce both documents. Again, this should reduce the number of disputes, thereby reducing future litigation.

5. Borrowers would be protected against competing claims to the right of enforcement by purported mortgage holders. Whether in cases of loan modification, payoff and discharge, approval of a short sale, or foreclosure, a borrower would know with virtual certainty whether a

purported holder's claim to the right to enforce the loan was authentic and whether its servicer was authorized to act.

XI. Conclusion

In this paper, we identify key weaknesses in the current legal framework governing the transfer and enforcement of mortgage notes, as evidenced by intense litigation in the aftermath of the housing finance crisis, and describe how a National Registry could help to alleviate these weaknesses and also provide greater transparency to borrowers.

Overall, the system that is described here is neutral—providing greater certainty to all parties with an interest in a mortgage note, favoring neither borrower nor lender/investor. Both groups should find at least certain aspects of the system advantageous.

From the homeowner perspective, the system provides a definitive answer to who is entitled to enforce the mortgage note and foreclose on a mortgage and does so in a manner that will not require the borrower to be a lawyer in order to understand—the only person that could enforce the note or foreclose the mortgage would be the registrant. Lenders may realize cost savings with respect to transferring mortgage notes on the National Registry, and with the increased certainty on a transferee's ability to enforce a mortgage note that could result from the National Registry, investors may be more willing to support the private securitization market, thereby providing additional demand for loan originators. These improvements in the secondary mortgage market may ultimately lead to greater credit availability to borrowers and lower interest rates.

We believe that over the long run the cost savings of an electronic registry system will be significant; nevertheless, it is hard to quantify many of the benefits noted above and the short-term costs of implementing a new system such as the National Registry (both the creation of the registry itself and the needed technology for the various parties that will need to interface with the system). Moreover, as with any law reform effort, changes to the law inevitably have some unintended, unforeseeable consequences.

Ultimately, if the status quo is kept, many of the problems we have discussed could be resolved in the long run through a series of costly court cases that establish precedents—albeit not uniformly throughout the nation and not necessarily in a manner that creates efficiency in the mortgage note market.

CHAPTER 9

Informed Securitization

Susan M. Wachter

I. Introduction

The housing finance system began to unravel nearly a decade ago, but the ghosts of its demise continue to haunt us to this day. The housing finance system remains on government life support with no clear plans as of this writing on when or how to resuscitate it despite a substantial recovery in the overall economy. The placement in conservatorship of Fannie Mae and Freddie Mac on September 6, 2008, in the aftermath of the global financial crisis (GFC) has created a de facto government-funded housing finance system in the United States. More than seven years since the federal government placed these institutions in conservatorship, they continue to remain in that status, with no established exit plans. As of the beginning of 2016, Fannie Mae, Freddie Mac, and Ginnie Mae are virtually the only issuers of mortgage-backed securities (MBS). The public actions taken to support Fannie Mae and Freddie Mac were successful in their short-term aims of supporting the housing market and removing the two firms as an immediate source of systemic risk to the financial system. The conservatorship, however, does not achieve the goal of reforming securitization markets.

The Achilles heel of the pre-crisis securitization market, inherent in its structure, was the potential for systemic instability due to credit or default risk.[1] As lending standards declined, surging housing prices veiled growing credit risk. Securitization markets shrouded rather than revealed information on the mounting system-wide leverage. The bursting of the housing bubble led to massive defaults, the collapse of securitization, systemic failure, and, in response, unprecedented public interventions to support the financial sector and the overall economy (Frame et al. 2015).

Episodes of systemic risk linked to real estate and housing finance markets are endemic across countries and history. This time securitization markets were at the center of the crisis. As a financial instrument, MBS markets can provide information on developing market risks. However, the structure of securitization markets precluded this in the GFC.

This chapter presents principles for stable securitization. The focus is on the role of market information and the potential for securitization to inform and complete rather than destabilize markets. The incomplete nature of real estate markets, due to high transaction costs and lack of short selling mechanisms, is well established. This chapter proposes solutions to information issues that otherwise make it difficult for market actors and regulators to properly assess and monitor risk.

Section II, which follows, examines long-standing information issues that characterize real estate and housing finance markets. Section III describes how nontransparent securitization and structural shifts worsened financial instability in the run-up to the crisis. Section IV discusses a specific reform to monitor mortgage debt at the property level. Section V lays out what is needed to monitor mortgage debt on an economy-wide basis. Section VI concludes.

II. Real Estate Bubbles

Systems that do not account for interdependencies between asset prices and lending conditions are vulnerable to overborrowing and overlending. This is particularly the case for lending based on real estate assets. Like other assets, real estate is subject to waves of optimism (Shiller 2006); unlike other assets, pessimists cannot easily exert downward pressure on real estate prices.

In efficient markets, asset prices follow a random walk. When prices get out of line with fundamentals, they are subject to downward pressure through short selling, thus incorporating all available information on market pricing. Investors sell the asset (that they do not own at the time of the sale) at the inflated market price and buy back the same asset at a deflated price to return to the seller at a future time, profiting from the difference. Real estate is heterogeneous, and because of this, even if investors are confident that market prices are too high, they cannot sell a property they do not own and buy back that specific asset at a lower price.[2] As a property owner, you can sell your own property. But selling your own property is also subject to the heterogeneity problem. You are not likely to be able to buy it back; you will need to purchase another house, perhaps not as satisfactory as your own home, and incur large transaction costs in the process.

Again because real estate is heterogeneous, buyers are likely to have different views on the pricing of real estate. However, it is the pricing of optimists, whose reservation prices exceed fundamental value[3] that is likely to prevail in the absence of short selling, when prices are rising. Real estate markets are incomplete, and they are also highly correlated across space, and heavily influenced by expectations. When demand slows and prices stall, price declines may follow, as the premium for expected appreciation disappears. Because prices are serially correlated (Case and Shiller 1989), their decline will not happen all at once, and declines will be predictable, which will have consequences for the private supply of capital into real estate markets and potential policy interventions. Price declines may be widespread if major financing channels become illiquid, which is likely if national credit markets are implicated.

Housing bubbles are not likely to persist or become systemically important without an expansion of mortgage credit. Optimist buyers are typically allowed to use more leverage as markets heat up because recent losses to lenders have been negligible. This additional leverage allows optimistic buyers to bid on a larger share of housing transactions (Haughwout et al. 2012). Consequently, optimistic buyers, instead of being wiped out by their investment decisions, may be supported by increases in lending that is underpriced for the risk. Mortgage markets ratify optimist set prices because lenders use appraisals, which are based on market prices, when deciding on how much to lend (Herring and Wachter 1999).

The implication of mortgage markets in real estate asset bubbles goes beyond the ratification of optimist set prices through appraisal-based lending. Financial accelerators propagate increases in the price of real estate (Bernanke, Gertler, and Gilchrist 1999). Rising prices may lower the perceived risk of lending to real estate with the result that lenders increase the supply of credit to borrowers, ease lending terms, and accelerate price increases in a positive feedback loop. In long periods of rising prices, lenders and investors may underestimate the risks of heavy concentrations of real estate lending due to the infrequency of price shocks and resulting disaster myopia. Competition reinforces this dynamic, leading to erosion in underwriting standards. There may then be a sharp repricing of credit when risk becomes apparent, which in itself will cause prices to fall and raise the risk of future price declines.

Misaligned managerial incentives that reward short-term loan production rather than long-term performance may play a role in the propagation of asset bubbles. Managers may accelerate efforts to close risky loans in the presence of a bubble because, not in spite of, their awareness of growing risk to "make hay while the sun shines." Investors may find it difficult to detect increased credit risk due to the opacity of bank holdings or may themselves have short-term horizons. Forbearance on the part of regulators may allow failing institutions to continue lending into a bubble, and the resulting moral hazard may encourage managers to "gamble for resurrection."

The accelerated provision of cheap credit due to misaligned incentives magnifies asset bubbles. Nonetheless, asset bubbles and mispriced credit may arise even without misaligned incentives, given incomplete markets and competition for market share. Some lenders may be aware of market interdependencies of asset prices and lending conditions and of growing market risk; but others may not be aware of these interdependencies and may misprice credit accordingly. These disaster-myopic lenders gain market share. Competitive markets may make it impossible for lenders and investors who are not disaster myopic to price transactions as if there were a finite probability of a major shock, or tail risk, when those who are disaster myopic price them as if that probability were essentially zero (Herring and Wachter 1999, 2003). As underpriced tail risk grows, short-term players or those who misjudge risk increase their market share. Systemic risk worsens because, in order to lend more, myopic financial institutions increase their own leverage as well, worsening liquidity shocks when prices decline.[4]

The macroliterature has developed models (Jeanne and Korinek 2010) that explain the inefficiency of overborrowing and overlending. Easing borrowing terms initially makes loans more affordable, but this inhibits the ability of house price rises to ration demand, and upward price pressures continue. As underwriting standards continue to ease, this leads to increases in the likelihood of future defaults when demand growth stalls and prices decline, which they will as expectations of further price increases are eliminated. The ability to pledge collateral and raise collateralized funds is then debased, which leads to a decline in the real economy. Models of default behavior can be used to predict increases in credit risk that result from embedded mortgage lending terms that are easing, given scenarios of future price paths, but they can only do so if lending terms are known and interdependencies are recognized.

III. Securitization in the Crisis

In this crisis, securitization markets propagated the real estate asset bubble and veiled increases in leverage and risk. Securitization markets thus had two fault lines: a structure that encouraged a race to the bottom in underwriting standards and information gaps that shrouded the resulting increases in leverage and credit risk. While high house price rises relative to rents (and to income and to other fundamentals that determine demand, including expectations on price rises) were identified in many markets, especially in the so-called "sand" states, changes in the pricing of and characteristics of credit expansion were not well measured. This was in part due to structural changes in securitization markets (Wachter 2014) and regulatory shifts (McCoy, Pavlov, and Wachter 2009) that enabled the growth of "shadow lending."

Much of the increased funding for mortgages prior to 2007 came from private-label securitization (PLS). Although characteristics of mortgages backed by PLS were available in loan tapes, these were not readily available to investors or regulators, and the data fields often contained missing or inaccurate information. Investment prospectus summary documents lacked critical data; and the data that were provided were not standardized, making it difficult to aggregate credit flows and track lending terms over time. In particular, the complexity of mortgage instruments and MBS made it difficult to identify the pricing of risk along with mortgage volume and characteristics. Moreover, it was not feasible to track credit (along with characteristics) extended to specific regional markets over time, thus precluding linking credit supply characteristics to property market outcomes.

PLS were backed by nontraditional mortgages (NTMs) and subprime loans. These loans included complicated features such as the use of teaser rates or balloon payments as well as reduced documentation, as in the so-called liar loans. But information on the share of these loans by combinations of features, fees, lending rate and origination fees, in the aggregate and by region, was not available. Although HMDA data, albeit with more than a year delay, provided information on the origination of subprime loans by region, other than this, characteristics of loans were not readily available. In particular, information on a key predictor of loan default, the combined loan-to-value ratio (CLTV) was not available (Moulton and Quercia 2013). Loans with high CLTV ratios grew sharply in the years immediate to the crisis, funded by an increase in second liens, that is, piggy back loans (Levitin and Wachter 2015), but the extent to which this occurred was not known at the time, as discussed below. In the aggregate, we know now that NTMs, subprime loans, and second liens grew in market share from less than 10 percent in 2000 to almost 50 percent of mortgage origination in 2006, funded mostly through PLS, and then shut down in 2007 (Levitin and Wachter 2012).

Changes in the structure of securitization markets contributed to the expansion of leverage through NTMs, subprime loans, and second liens, as did regulatory shifts. From the early 1980s to 2000, most mortgage securitization had occurred through government-regulated entities that precluded significant competition on rates or terms. With deregulation, there was a change in the structure of securitization markets, which contributed to the expansion of non-agency credit. Private-label securitization firms and the GSEs competed for market share, moving away from a traditional de facto regulated securitization mechanism in which the GSEs held market power and dictated origination terms (Wachter 2014).

For chartered institutions, like GSEs or banks, which benefit from market power, the value of the option to survive and remain in business can limit the level of risk taking as a strategy to maximize value. Increases in competition that reduce the value of surviving can result in a change in strategy in which actors increase their level of risk taking as a way to extract value through underpriced options. The introduction of non-agency securitization may have led to additional risk taking by Fannie Mae and Freddie Mac (Lai and Van Order 2014). Between 2003 and 2007, the share of nonstandard and risky loans guaranteed by Fannie Mae and Freddie Mac increased. At Fannie Mae, the percentage of newly purchased loans where the loan amount was 90 percent or more of the appraised property value increased significantly, from 7 percent in 2003 to 16 percent by 2007, while at Freddie Mac the percentage increased from 5 percent in 2003 to 11 percent in 2007 (Frame et al. 2015).

Nonetheless, the major expansion of mortgage funding in this period came through securitization markets and mostly from private-label securitization (Levitin and Wachter 2012). The rapid increase in private-label securitization occurred in large part through the expansion of CDOs, which are derivatives of PLS. Funded through CDOs, credit expanded rapidly in the commercial sector as well. Duca and Ling (2015) provide evidence of the resulting declines in the cost of credit and rise in rent-to-price ratios, or cap rates, in the commercial property sector. Levitin and Wachter (2012) record how the structure of securitized lending shifted in the commercial market, which had relied on equity owners of the riskiest tranche of CDOs but increasingly shifted to securitization of all tranches.

After the fact, we know that the pricing of credit risk decreased in this period for PLS, CDOs, and for agency and non-agency debt (Davidson, Levin, and Wachter 2014). As the prevalence of high CLTV mortgages increased, the overall cost (combined opportunity cost of the down payment and the mortgage interest rate) of prime credit decreased (Davidson et al. 2014). Pricing of NTMs funded by PLS decreased relative to that of prime loans, funded by GSEs, lowering the cost of lending through both channels. These declines in the price of credit to the real estate market set up a flight from housing finance when risk became apparent.

Declines in credit risk premia that are correlated with rising prices ex ante predict the severity of price declines in the downturn (Pavlov and Wachter 2009a, 2009b; Levitin, Pavlov, and Wachter 2012). In the Asian Financial Crisis (AFC), countries that shored up their capital reserves and decreased their underpricing of credit through raising lending rates relative to deposit rates experienced lower price declines. In the aftermath of the AFC, they were able to continue to lend, and their financial sector was not as vulnerable to the Asia-wide tightening of credit conditions (Green et al. 2009). In the United States, in the run-up to the crisis, bank capital requirements were lowered, enabling the expansion of lending to residential and commercial real estate (McCoy, Pavlov, and Wachter 2009).

The resulting excessive leverage and the subsequent inability to pledge collateral and raise collateralized funds led to a decline in the real economy. In response to the crisis, the Dodd-Frank Wall Street Reform and Consumer Protection Act of 2010 (DFA) restricted the use of NTMs by establishing Qualified Mortgage (QM) loan standards that provide liability protection to issuers. As of now, non-QM loans remain a small share of the market, thus eliminating from the current market most nonstandardized mortgage products. In addition, as noted above, almost all of the securitized mortgage debt is currently being issued by the GSEs, which now do provide information on mortgage pools, as discussed below. The standardization of mortgage product in the QM and GSE space provides information on loan characteristics of mortgage pools. Nonetheless, important information on market leverage is still not readily available.

IV. Information on Property Level Leverage

The most important indicator of default risk is the overall level of leverage associated with an individual property. Overall leverage is measured by the CLTV, summing up all the liens against a given property.

Information on the evolution of this for originated loans and for the housing stock in the aggregate has important implications for the level of risk in the housing finance system. To track CLTVs requires data on origination and pay downs of both first and additional liens, as well as information on property values, linked in time to default.

In the U.S. context, borrowers are currently able to add a second lien on their property without the agreement of the first-lien holder. First-lien holders cannot call due a mortgage or change its terms upon the addition of a second lien, even if the second lien increases the CLTV beyond the original LTV from the first lien. This means that all mortgage products have embedded a leverage option that is priced ex ante for the possibility that borrowers can increase their CLTV beyond the original LTV.

Levitin and Wachter (2015) show that this embedded option may contribute to increased mortgage costs and make it difficult to obtain information about the overall leverage associated with a specific first-lien loan in a security in particular and market-wide leverage in general. They show that when graphing LTV at origination and estimated CLTV over the recent cycle (Figure 9.1), the increased leverage in the system came entirely from the increase in the CLTV at origination that reached almost 90 percent at the top of the boom due to the extensive use of simultaneous second (piggyback) loans. Levitin and Wachter (2015) show that this increase in overall leverage could not be measured by market participants or regulators due to the lack of information about second liens at the individual loan and aggregate levels. There is no requirement for lenders to report second liens in a way in which they would be automatically matched with the first lien. Second liens are recorded on property title, but there is no comprehensive dataset that matches all first-lien mortgages with eventual second liens, although that information exists for segments of the market (Levitin and Wachter 2015).

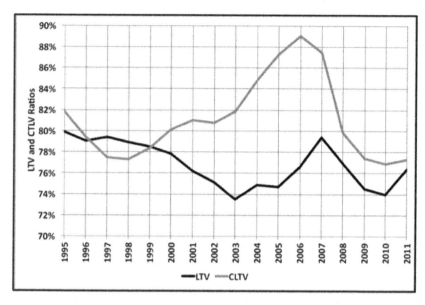

Figure 9.1. LTV and CLTV ratios over time. Levitin and Wachter (2015).

The continued unavailability of CLTV data limits the ability of investors and regulators to accurately measure the level of risk in the system and therefore to properly price this risk. In addition to credit agency notations, investors in MBS during the boom largely limited their analysis to credit scores and LTV information in order to price risk (Rajan, Seru, and Vig 2010). LTV on first liens is well documented as an important predictor of credit risk and loss given default, but the existence of a second lien has important implications for the risk associated with that loan, and the prevalence of second liens in the market also contributes to overall risk.

Lee, Mayer, and Tracy (2012) find that during the boom, over 40 percent of home purchases in a number of bubble markets (Phoenix, Las Vegas, Miami) were using simultaneous piggyback loans. In addition, they find that two-thirds of purchases with a piggyback had CLTV above 95 percent, meaning that a 5 percent decline in house value was enough for the borrower to be underwater. The issuer of the mortgage might have known about the presence of simultaneous seconds, sometimes originating both and keeping the second lien on portfolio while securitizing the first lien, but that information was unlikely to be reported to investors.

In addition to giving first-lien holders control over the amount of leverage on the collateral they are lending against, un-embedding the leverage option in the way proposed by Levitin and Wachter (2015) would facilitate the gathering of real-time market-wide leverage information. As second liens have to be reported to first-lien holders, a system would be in place to facilitate the exchange of the information, and it would become possible to capture all liens being issued on one property in a single national repository.

V. Structure and Data for an Informed Market

Distinguishing between credit booms that are sustainable and those that will lead to systemic risk remains a challenge (Bakker et al. 2012). The data requirements for this include information on volume of mortgage supply, mortgage terms, and borrower characteristics and mortgage rates (Hunt, Stanton, and Wallace 2012). Importantly, these data must be linked to property market data. An issue is what entities are responsible for the development and collection of standardized data and to what end. The structure of securitization markets can incentivize the development and use of data to monitor risk if the structure internalizes the risks of individual lender decisions.

The proposal put forth by Dechario et al. (2010) (chapter 2, this volume) is designed to accomplish this. Dechario et al. (2010) propose a cooperative structure controlled by financial institution member/owners to carry out securitization so that default risk is borne by all members, thus rewarding the enforcement of origination standards that promote market stability.[5]

Such a structure, however, does not preclude races to the bottom by nonmembers. To deal with this, Hancock and Passmore (chapter 3, this volume) propose requiring catastrophe insurance. This neutralizes an advantage of new entrants who might enter and grow in markets in good times and exit markets quickly in bad times, outcompeting in good times those entities who are required to pay for catastrophe insurance. Thus, effectively, Hancock and Passmore propose that alongside a substantial private capital loss position, the government would require all mortgages, regardless of whether they are government-sponsored or not, to be insured against catastrophic outcomes. This government-provided catastrophic reinsurance would be implemented through an explicit guarantee fee (g-fee) for securitizations paid by issuers to contain externalities otherwise imposed by underpricing lenders.

To carry this out, regulators need to determine the appropriate level of the g-fee. In order to do this and to set capital requirements for entities holding and securitizing mortgages, regulators must be informed on credit risk, requiring linked mortgage and property data.

Under the DFA, the CFPB has issued new Home Mortgage Data Act requirements, and the FHFA and the CFPB are in process of developing the National Mortgage Database, the first fully representative national sample of the flow of U.S. mortgage supply. These will enable the ongoing collection of data on the characteristics of individual mortgages, including those eligible for purchase by Fannie Mae and Freddie Mac and those that are not, and including subprime and nontraditional mortgages. The NMDB data are merged with HMDA data to identify borrower characteristics and property value.

In addition, Nakamura (2010) describes a proposal to track financial institution credit risk exposure, through a macro-micro database using the Federal Reserve's Flow of Funds framework to link to the financial assets and liabilities of all U.S. parties (including households, nonprofits, firms, governments, and the rest of the world). The macro side of the database would summarize aggregate data on nominal quantities of financial instruments and the identities of debtors and current asset holders, using individual firm entity identifiers through a Legal Entity Identifier. This could be connected to micro-database satellite accounts that could be linked to individual mortgages through unique loan identifiers. The database could be linked to the National Registry proposal suggested by Heller and Whitman (chapter 8, this volume). With a reporting requirement on information on all first and additional liens and also with loan characteristics and property values, this database could be used to produce a "national scorecard" combining bank and securitized lending, as well as measures of credit exposure for financial entities, which is necessary for regulatory oversight.

Combined with data from servicers on loan performance, these data could support studies of the changing risks of instruments. With information on interest and fees charged, the data could support pricing analysis that would bring financial, economic, and econometric theory to bear on the determination of potential systemic risk and enable regulators to observe counterparty risk and to undertake regular systemic stress testing informed by property sector risk. These databases could be used to increase transparency of institutional portfolios as well as to detect buildups of systemic risk outside the regulated financial system, given mandatory reporting requirements.

Eventually, public versions of the datasets could be made available to engage the broader academic and industry research community in systemic risk analysis. However, the ability to use such data to monitor securitization markets will be constrained by the underlying complexity of mortgage instruments, securities, and derivatives themselves; thus attention must be paid to the underlying securitization standards as well.

Beyond the data, might there be the potential to structure markets so that market risk could be traded? When prices are out of line, macroprudential policy to contain credit has recently been instituted in several countries, and in the United States and elsewhere, stress tests that consider house price vulnerability are in place. Beyond these new regulatory stances, are there market-based mechanisms that could be brought to bear in the mispricing episodes? If the problem at base is a lack of financial derivatives or other market-based instruments to sell short overpriced real estate, is there a potential role for derivatives to signal mispricing and weigh against the market? The common fundamental of mispriced real estate and the absence of a short sell instrument suggest that securitization or derivatives could be structured to trade credit risk (Shiller 2012).

Current efforts to do this include an innovative credit risk transfer mechanism, which can reveal current market pricing of risk, as well as several initiatives to gather data, to better inform markets. GSEs are now reporting the characteristics of their insured loans, and in a new development, they are each offering credit linked notes (CLNs) in a form of credit risk transfer. The CLNs are structured to hedge the GSEs against the loss arising from default, and the price of the note is linked to the expected performance of insured mortgages, thus providing information on the market perception of the risk of the GSEs pool of loans and the appropriate level of the g-fee as well.

At the heart of the housing boom and bust was a lack of transparency. In the buildup to the crisis, market participants did not have enough information to identify the risk generated by the institutions that were most exposed to this risk. Had market participants been able to monitor the mortgages owned by these and other institutions, credit might not have flowed so amply and so cheaply—and capital markets might not have seized so abruptly when the information finally came to the surface. Nonetheless, there are two caveats to the widespread reliance on such risk transfer instruments. First, it is global risk, not just GSE risk that will determine the fragility of the system; thus GSE-insured mortgage transparency is not sufficient. Second, with a system-wide shock, private capital is likely to flee, if there is time to do so. And given the serial correlation in housing finance and real estate markets, there is likely to be both ability to predict future declines and consequences for system stability of a run from risk (see Pavlov, Wachter, and Zevelev forthcoming for a discussion). Although potentially important for price discovery, CLNs do not substitute for the provision of equity capital.

VI. Conclusion

With the demise of private-label residential securitization and the conservatorships of Fannie Mae and Freddie Mac, there is both an opportunity and a necessity to rethink principles of securitization to promote systemic stability. Establishing a means to monitor and limit credit risk is critical to the restructuring of securitization markets and the return of private capital. This chapter identifies features of the U.S. mortgage market that accentuate the information barriers across financial intermediaries, investors, and regulators, reinforcing the potential for underpricing risk and regulatory failures.

The structure of the pre-crisis securitization market led to default risk that was not discovered or properly priced. As lending standards declined and credit risk grew, surging housing prices limited current defaults, thus veiling the growing threat. Data on the overall level of leverage in the mortgage market and institutions' exposure to housing markets were not readily available. Securitization markets shrouded rather than revealed information.

The incomplete nature of real estate markets, due to high transaction costs and lack of short selling mechanisms, is well established. Securitization markets have the potential to inform and complete rather than destabilize markets. For this outcome, markets must be structured to provide incentives to market actors to monitor credit risk, and a framework for regulatory responsibilities must be in place for the development, collection, and use of data to monitor systemic risk. Expanded HMDA disclosure requirements, which are set to go into effect in January of 2018, and the new National Mortgage Database will increase transparency. Nonetheless, resolution of information issues requires attention to the structure and regulatory framework of the U.S. housing finance system.

NOTES

Chapter 1. Legislative Approaches to Housing Finance Reform

1. Thomas (2013) explores in detail the reasons for the two firms' collapse, concluding, "Fannie and Freddie's losses did not come from subprime loans made to low-income borrowers with checkered credit histories, but from [guarantees on] loans made in overheated housing markets to borrowers with better-than-average credit scores" (p. 37). Thomas also notes, "Had these institutions simply been required to hold equity capital in roughly the same proportion that banks are, shareholders would have absorbed all of the losses, and the taxpayer bailout would have been unnecessary" (p. 51).

2. Under the conservatorship, the firms' regulator, the FHFA, has the authority to operate the two companies with all the powers that would normally be exercised by shareholders, the board of directors, and company officers. At the same time, the Treasury struck bilateral agreements with Fannie and Freddie to ensure that each firm maintained a positive net worth and could therefore meet their outstanding obligations, with taxpayers receiving 79.9 percent ownership and a 10 percent dividend on any capital injections. Under the two Senior Preferred Share Agreements, the Treasury, through the middle of 2015, had put $189.5 billion of capital into the firms by purchases of senior preferred shares.

3. Over the years, well before the crisis, there had been calls for the privatization of Fannie Mae and Freddie Mac. See, for example, Wallison, Stanton, and Ely (2004); and White (2004).

4. These studies include Congressional Budget Office (2001); Ambrose, LaCour-Little, and Sanders (2004); McKenzie (2002); Passmore, Sherlund, and Burgess (2005); and Sherlund (2008).

5. As suggested by Hermalin and Jaffee (1996), the spread may be low in part because mortgage origination and securitization are imperfectly competitive markets, enabling mortgage originators and the GSEs to capture much of the benefits of the guarantee. Consistent with this view, Scharfstein and Sunderam (2014) show that when MBS yields decline, only a fraction of the reduction is passed through to borrowers in the form of lower mortgage rates. This is particularly true in more concentrated markets for mortgage origination.

6. The size of the benefit of securitization for the availability of the thirty-year FRM is far from clear. Banks are large holders of MBS backed by Fannie and Freddie and have expertise in managing the associated interest rate and prepayment risk. They are also large holders of jumbo FRMs, which have a combination of interest rate risk, prepayment risk, and credit risk.

7. For a fuller discussion of the rationale behind this approach, see Scharfstein and Sunderam (2011).

8. See Baker and Wurgler (2013), who examine the relationship between risk and return in the banking sector.

9. A challenge with risk weights is that they often depend on the discretion of the regulator, and it is difficult to incorporate precise risk weights into legislation. Concern with regulatory manipulation of risk weights is one of the rationales that has been stated for the bank leverage ratio requirement because it does not depend on risk weights.

10. Hanson, Scharfstein, and Sunderam (2014) formalize these arguments in a theoretical model of the socially optimal pricing of risk by the government.

11. The existence of such securities also makes it easier for the Federal Reserve to conduct quantitative easing through its large-scale asset purchase program.

Chapter 2. The Capital and Governance of a Mortgage Securitization Utility

The views expressed in this chapter are those of the authors and not those of the Federal Reserve Bank of New York or the Federal Reserve System. We thank Adam Ashcraft, Scott Chastain, Andy Davidson, Toni Dechario, Hamid Mehran, David Scharfstein, Grace Sone, Susan Wachter, James Vickery and participants in the NBER securitization working group, TCH-NYU Housing Finance Reform Roundtable, and the Federal Reserve Bank of Chicago's Bank Structure and Competition Conference for their comments.

1. See Dechario et al. (2011).

2. Some proponents of the fully private approach would retain the FHA/VA for lending to low and moderate income households. See Jaffee (2010a).

3. The charters of Fannie Mae and Freddie Mac restrict the types of loans that may be securitized; these limits include a set of loan size restrictions known as "conforming loan limits." For a discussion of how these limits have been adjusted in recent years, see Vickery and Wright (2013).

4. Note that the same argument does not apply to other credit markets, where boom and bust cycles also occur but where government intervention is not typical, likely because the impact of credit "busts" in other markets is not systemic with respect to the rest of the financial system and the macroeconomy.

5. See, for example, Lucas and McDonald (2007). For other discussions of mispricing government insurance, see Dwight Jaffee (2010a) and Acharya et al. (2011). Note

that in the case of the National Flood Insurance Program, the mispricing took the form of grandfathering existing properties. This would not be relevant for the government reinsurance of new mortgage originations as long as the legacy agency guarantees were not covered by the new utility.

6. See Acharya et al. (2011).

7. Similarly, Seidman et al. (2013) provide a government wrap for MBS securities. The government guarantee would pay investors only in the event that the lender's capital is fully depleted. That is, the guarantee kicks in only when the lender is a "gone" concern.

8. For example, in our baseline case to be discussed later, the government fee comprises 15 percent of the overall fee.

9. Note that, because the terms and payments of compensation for the government are laid out ex ante, there would be no need to "repay" the government by raising fees after a payout of the reinsurance.

10. It is also important to be careful in defining the alternative to the government guarantee that is being used to make this efficiency comparison. If there is no explicit government guarantee and as you move further out in the tail of the risk distribution, private firms do not completely insure against systemic shocks, then we are back to an implicit unpriced government guarantee.

11. For examples, see Scharfstein and Sunderam (2011), the Center for American Progress, Mortgage Finance Working Group (2011), and Hancock and Passmore (2010).

12. For a discussion of illiquidity of corporate bonds and associated liquidity risks, see Chen et al. (2013).

13. This puts the FHA $36 billion below the 2 percent capital level that it is required to maintain. See Integrated Financial Engineering, Inc. (IFE) (2012).

14. See Aragon et al. (2010), Gyourko (2011), and Caplin, Cororaton, and Tracy (2012). As noted earlier, changes to the overall gfee charged to borrowers over the credit cycle by the utility are market-based. This contrasts with the gfees charged by a government lender, which, as in the case of the FHA, are likely to be relatively insensitive to changes in credit risk, due to political constraints. This is exacerbated by the pressure on the government lender to define a much wider credit box than would be the case for a private utility. These factors all suggest that the risks to taxpayers may well be much higher from a backstop government lender than from an explicit and priced backstop government reinsurer for private lending.

15. For example, see Seidman et al. (2013) and the Bipartisan Policy Center Housing Commission (2013a).

16. See Demarco (2013).

17. The importance of this dynamic is underscored by recent reports that relatively subdued refinancing activity in recent years has been attributable in part to lenders' reluctance to gain exposure to other firms' underwriting over previous years.

18. One potential refinement of this model would be to allow for "representations and warranties" clauses to allow the utility to exclude some types of losses from being

mutualized. Much of the content and use of such clauses are issues that apply across proposals for institutional reform, but we discuss a few implications for a mutual structure in Section IV, on governance.

19. The utility might also issue a limited amount of debt, exclusively for the purpose of buying nonperforming loans out of securitization trusts and for funding the loss-mitigation process—although it would raise governance questions, which we highlight in Section IV.

20. That is, the losses from existing guarantees would only be offset from gfees from existing books of mortgages—not from a tax on the utility.

21. A staged transition to new platform, structures, and products is long-standing best practice for financial utilities. Such a transition path suggests that the utility will likely begin securitization activities before the existing GSEs are completely phased out. Thus as a transitional issue, the utility will likely need to begin by adopting credit and conforming loan standards consistent with current GSE securitization to guarantee continued access to mortgage credit and a smooth adjustment in market access and liquidity.

22. This is an approach that the new municipal insurer Build America Mutual seems to have successfully employed. See Chappatta (2012).

23. For examples of more formal modeling of capital and credit risk, see Smith and Weiher (2012) and the Bipartisan Policy Center Housing Commission (2013b). For a more formal modeling of mortgage rates, see Bipartisan Policy Center Housing Commission (2013b).

24. Over time, however, the characteristics of the mortgages securitized by the utility may be adjusted (with regulatory approval), but the utility should retain a focus on securitizing core, standardized mortgage products: loans to high-quality prime credit borrowers with substantial down payment requirements (for instance, 20 percent of the loan balance).

25. See Elliot (2010) and the Basel Committee on Banking Supervision (2008).

26. The GSEs were also subject to a cash flow stress test, but in practice, the minimum leverage ratio was binding.

27. The Dodd-Frank Act introduced the concept of a capital floor, which provides that the net aggregate effect of subsequent Basel standards may not produce capital requirements less than those under Basel I. However, because we are considering a monoline mortgage securitization utility, it is not possible to counterbalance adjustments to risk weightings across different asset classes (0 percent for U.S. Treasury securities, 20 percent for agency MBS, and 100 percent or more for high-yield corporate bonds).

28. That is, because 0.45 percent = capital/assets, then 0.9 percent = capital/(0.5*assets).

29. The maximum average loss severity during the financial crisis reported by Fannie Mae was 37.2 percent in 2009, according to its annual Form 10-K filings. For earlier loss severity estimates, see Qi and Yang (2009).

30. One could, of course, alternatively set an attachment point specifically to determine which vintages to cover effectively, defining the relevant tail events the government insurance will cover.

31. Weakening of underwriting standards need not take the form of lower credit scores, higher measured loan-to-value ratios, or debt-to-income ratios. Rather, it may be more subtle, showing up as appraisal or income bias.

32. Fannie Mae 2004 Annual Report describes a loss rate of the previous several years of near 0.5 basis points. This may be net of the positive effect of reinsurance so the gross rate may have been higher.

33. See Damodaran (n.d.).

34. Harrington and Niehaus (2003).

35. Data from SNL indicates that over the period 2002–2012, four mutual insurance companies (MassMutual, Northwestern, NY Life, and TIAA-CREF) provided returns of about 5 percent to 7 percent. We thank Julia Gouny for research assistance on this point.

36. This pricing differential implies that if the government gfee is inadvertently set too high, the lender cooperative would not likely lose market share (see Frame et al. 2012, p. 27). This assumes that private funding of mortgages outside of the cooperative would be required to hold adequate capital to cover the expected tail loss.

37. If the participants in the cooperative did not increase the gfee in the face of this increase in expected credit losses, then these losses would come out of their capital backing the vintage. As such, these participants have the incentive to adjust the gfee in response to changes in expected loss rates.

38. For more details, see Ashcraft and Schuermann (2009).

39. For certain institutions, demand for these securities was further supported by favorable risk weights for regulatory capital requirements.

40. As with the underwriting standards for the securitization-eligible loans themselves, standardization and simplicity of junior bonds will facilitate risk management and market discipline.

41. An 8 percent return is roughly consistent with several model projections, recent returns on Freddie Mac's STACR bond's M1 tranche, which yielded 715 basis points over Libor, as well as historical data from high-yield corporate bonds. Data from Bank of America indicate that the average option-adjusted spread on corporate bonds over 1997–2013 rated BB (the highest speculative-grade rating) has been about 400 basis points. Adding that spread to the March 2013 Blue Chip Survey's long-term predicted averaged ten-year Treasury rate of 4.7 percent produces a yield of about 8.7 percent.

42. For examples, see Feldman and Stern (2009), McCoy (2008), Bohn and Hall (1999).

43. See for example Piskorski, Seru, and Vig (2010).

44. For a description of how central counterparties and clearinghouses concentrate and manage risks, see Duffie, Li, and Lubke (2010).

45. However, recent regulatory requirements to centrally clear long-term OTC derivatives contracts such as credit default swaps and interest rate swaps may significantly extend the duration of risk taken by FMUs.

46. For examples, see Zanjani (2007), Coughenour and Deli (2002), and Damodaran, John, and Liu (1997).

47. See "Industrial Organization and Systemic Risk: an Agenda for Further Research," speech by Federal Reserve Governor Tarullo, September 15, 2011.

48. See Henehan and Anderson (2001) and Frederick (1997).

49. For the role of members' expertise in cooperative governance, see Autry and Hall (2009), pp. 42–49. See also Gould Ellen and Willis (2011), Green and Schnare (2009), and Flannery and Frame (2006). For the importance of members' proportion of exposure to a cooperative, see Hansmann (1999), 398. Note that lenders differ importantly from shareholders of large, often opaque, publicly traded companies. Most shareholders are likely to lack detailed knowledge of mortgage lending or securitization, and they typically do not face as concentrated an exposure to the company as lenders. Thus, shareholders are likely to have weaker capacity and incentives for oversight.

50. For a brief discussion of some of these dynamics, see Hansmann (1999), pp. 393–95.

51. See Cole and Mehran (1998).

52. See Esty (1997), Lamm-Tennanat and Starks (2001), and Lee et. al. (1997).

53. See Hansmann (1999), p. 398, for a discussion of members' multidimensional relationship to a cooperative.

54. Innovation could still take place by lenders for mortgages that they intend to hold on their balance sheets.

55. See Thomas and Van Order (2010) and Jaffee (2010b).

56. Tarullo, ibid., cites Anderson, Palma, and Thisse (1992) in commenting on this substitution, although he does not himself specify whether he considers mortgage lending in the previous cycle to have displayed this dynamic.

57. See Holmstrom (1999) and Hansmann (1999, p. 394).

58. In addition to realigning the incentives for lenders, mutualization of ownership would help consolidate external supervision and reduce an entire layer of profit margining by lowering the total transaction costs and displacing securitizer's focus from purely monetary profits. Of course, pass-through of these savings to individual household borrowers is not guaranteed. It is closely linked to the issues of competition and the relative market access of larger and smaller lenders.

59. Woodward and Hall (2009), p. 6. See also William B. Shear's letter to various congressional committees (Government Accountability Office 2010).

60. See Murphy (2012), p. 8, and Morgenson and Rosner (2011), p. 55.

61. Drawing on Hirschman (1970), Hansmann (1999) characterizes this dynamic as the difference between the power of "voice" and the power of "exit."

62. This is an area for further research. The Treasury white paper on housing finance reform in February 2011 implied that policy makers should focus the Federal Home Loan Bank System—a well-known lender-owned cooperative—on supporting primarily smaller financial institutions by limiting the participation of larger institutions.

63. See Holmstrom (1999) for a discussion of the influence on corporate form of shifting costs of voice and exit in various industries.

64. See Hansmann (1999), p. 397.

65. See Hansmann (1999).

66. Murphy (2012) draws on a variety of sources to describe the value of cumulative voting, notably Packel (1970).

67. See Autry and Hall (2009).

68. See Financial Stability Oversight Council (2011) and Mester (2010).

69. See Vickery and Wright (2013).

70. See Swagel (2010); Terris and Hochstein (2010); Gould Ellen and Willis (2011), pp. 323–24; and Acharya et al. (2011), p. 158. See also Woodward and Hall (2009).

71. For this reason all of the financial market utilities referenced in this chapter have been designated systemically important financial market utilities and are subject to enhanced prudential oversight under Title VIII of Dodd-Frank.

72. Vickery and Wright (2013) estimate the liquidity benefit of the TBA market, separate from any credit guarantees, is probably about 10–25 basis points under normal market conditions and significantly higher during periods of market stress.

73. See also Business Roundtable (2010), American Law Institute (2001), and Brancato and Plath (2005).

Chapter 3. Macroprudential Mortgage-Backed Securitization: Can It Work?

The views expressed are the authors' and should not be interpreted as representing the views of the FOMC, its principals, the Board of Governors of the Federal Reserve System, or any other person associated with the Federal Reserve System. We thank Shane Sherlund and Joseph Tracy as well as participants in seminars at the Board of Governors of the Federal Reserve, the Sveriges Riksbank, and the International Banking, Economic, and Finance Association (Western Economics Association meeting) for their useful comments. We thank Della Cummings, Paul Fornia, and Jay Tian for their excellent research assistance.

1. In this chapter, we focus exclusively on thirty-year fixed-rate mortgages. The thirty-year fixed-rate mortgage is a popular feature of the U.S. mortgage market because households perceive that such mortgages are affordable (because they are amortized over a long period), stable (because the payments are predictable and do not vary over the life of the loan), and flexible (because such mortgages can generally be

prepaid by the borrower at any time without penalty). As noted by Campbell (2013) and Shiller (2014), there has been little innovation in U.S. mortgage contracts since the thirty-year fixed-rate mortgage was established during the Great Depression, even though there are compelling reasons to believe a better mortgage contract could be designed for homeowners, banks, and investors alike.

2. A comprehensive review of the many nonlegislative proposals is given by Frame, Wall, and White (2013).

3. For the text of the PATH Act, see https://www.govtrack.us/congress/bills/113/hr2767/text.

4. For text of the bill co-authored by Senators Johnson and Crapo, see http://www.banking.senate.gov/public/index.cfm?FuseAction=Newsroom.PressReleases &ContentRecord_id=f8f64d97-d732-3aa9-e966-6040d7dbf169 &Region_id=&Issue _id=.

5. The government also determines that the structure of the securitization has three tranches: a highly liquid, information-insensitive tranche (guaranteed by the government); a mezzanine tranche held by the private sector; and a residual tranche that concentrates credit risk and is held by the private sector. This three-tranche structure captures the major motivations for tranching a pool of assets: the creation of a highly liquid security for uninformed investors and a risky security for well-informed investors (DeMarzo 2005). The mezzanine tranche is sometimes broken in more pieces depending on the distribution of private risk information of issuers versus purchasers.

6. The equity premium is calculated from a dynamic dividend discount model developed by Campbell and Shiller (1988).

7. The loss structure envisioned is structured to be similar to bank regulatory capital requirements. However, in the current mortgage finance system, the bank capital risk-weights are designed to set capital levels to cover the unexpected loss outcomes in a high percentage of cases (usually 98 percent, or 99 percent, or 99.9 percent of potential outcomes). In contrast, under hybrid securitization the first-loss position of the private sector is set by other means (e.g., legislation or regulation).

8. One might argue that the FHA already performs this role. During the most recent housing boom and bust, the FHA was almost unused during the boom and needed capital injections during the bust. In this sense, the government already has a backstop mortgage securitizer.

9. Supposedly, the government sees some positive externality from making government credit available alongside private sector. We don't describe the externality, but note that the U.S. government has followed such a policy with Fannie Mae and Freddie Mac for many decades.

10. The original figure presented in Zandi and deRitis (2013) was 3.7, but based on other underlying data provided in their paper, we believe this was in error.

11. For details on the calculation of the current-coupon MBS yield, see Hancock and Passmore (forthcoming).

12. Note that this liquidity/capital advantage of GSE MBS is distinct from most calculations of the GSE subsidy. This is the advantage that accrues to a holder of a GSE MBS from holding near-sovereign debt, which arises from the regulation of the holders and the structure of the secondary market. The GSE subsidy is usually a calculation of the debt advantage the GSEs have relative to private sector funders of mortgages and MBS (see Jeske, Kruger, and Mitman 2013; and Passmore, Sherlund, and Burgess 2005). Of course, the GSEs can capture more of this liquidity/capital advantage created by the government backing of GSE MBS by raising the gfee for securitization, which might increase their profitability if banks and other originators continued to sell mortgages to the GSEs.

13. These regressions are generally stationary, except during the financial crisis, as is demonstrated by unit root tests for each respective estimation window (Figure 3.7).

Chapter 4. Reforms for a System That Works: Multifamily Housing Finance

1. This chapter focuses on the multifamily businesses of Fannie Mae and Freddie Mac. It does not provide a full analysis of the FHA's multifamily insurance program, which remains a crucial source of mortgage capital for rental housing, because such an analysis is beyond the scope of this chapter.

2. This chapter is not intended to imply that if we were to start from scratch on federal housing policy, we would recreate the current system of multifamily finance. It does, however, begin with the premise that if we are going to pursue meaningful reforms of the multifamily system, we must at least ensure that any new system is more effective and efficient than the existing system.

3. According to the Urban Institute, 4 million more loans would have been made between 2009 and 2013 if credit standards had been similar to 2001 levels (Goodman, Zhu, and George 2015).

4. Multifamily construction data include units for ownership (such as condominiums) in addition to rental units.

5. According to the Joint Center for Housing Studies, there were just over 300,000 multifamily housing starts in 2013, over 90 percent of which were intended to be rentals (Joint Center For Housing Studies of Harvard University 2014, p. 23).

6. Though it should be noted that "rental housing is in generally good condition, with only 3.1 percent categorized as severely inadequate and 6.7 percent as moderately inadequate," these shares are "nearly twice those for all housing units."

7. In line with the requirement under Dodd-Frank that the Enterprises reduce the size of their portfolios, Fannie Mae's holding of multifamily MBS and mortgages has decreased steadily since 2008 as essentially all newly purchased mortgages have been securitized. Earlier in the 2000s, Fannie Mae had been increasing the percentage of its multifamily mortgages that it kept in portfolio (Fannie Mae 2015a). Freddie Mac has

also been decreasing its holding of multifamily mortgages while it has been increasing its securitization of loans through K certificates (U.S. Securities and Exchange Commission 2014, p. 85).

8. The volume of multifamily MBS that Ginnie Mae can back is essentially constrained by FHA's capacity to underwrite and endorse multifamily mortgages.

9. According to Freddie Mac, national multifamily property values fell by 40 percent from its peak in Q1 2007 to its trough in Q3 2009 (Guggenmos et al. 2012). 10.

10. The support provided by the federal government was through a line of credit with the U.S. Treasury, which has also required that the Enterprises reduce their portfolios by 15 percent per year (U.S. Department of the Treasury 2012).

11. For at least the last decade, Fannie Mae's serious delinquency rate has consistently been well below one percent of multi-family's total book (Fannie Mae 2012b, p. 26).

12. Fannie Mae has been "consistently profitable on an operating cash basis," and even though it "recorded a pre-tax GAAP loss of $1.8 billion in 2009 to boost reserves for future loan losses . . . annual pre-tax earnings for the core business have been in the range of $200 million to $500 million" (Fannie Mae 2012b, p. 23). Freddie Mac has similarly earned "$4 billion in net income" from its multifamily business since 2010 (Freddie Mac 2012, p. 11).

13. There are two common risk-sharing options for Fannie Mae DUS lenders. Most banks choose to take one-third of losses on a pari passu basis. Many nonbanks choose an alternative option in which the lender takes 100 percent of the top 5 percent of losses, with a tiered loss-sharing formula for further losses and with total losses incurred by the lender capped at 20 percent of original loan amount.

14. There are twenty-four approved Program Plus Seller/Servicers for Freddie Mac (Freddie Mac 2014).

15. The multifamily risk-sharing models adopted by both Enterprises have also helped them avoid the principle-agent problem when originators do not need to be concerned with the riskiness of the loans they sell to the Enterprises—an issue that may have been more of a problem with the originate-to-distribute approaches on their single-family side. Fannie Mae avoided it on the multifamily side by requiring DUS loan originators to absorb a share of any losses, and Freddie Mac avoided it by performing all multifamily underwriting in house.

16. In addition to the property's cash flow, the underwriter will also evaluate the condition of the property and its collateral value. The amount by which the cash flow of the property is required to exceed the debt service payments is called the debt service coverage ratio (DSCR).

17. Although a security with a single mortgage cannot, by definition, be geographically diversified, the property itself draws revenue from multiple tenants. Also, protecting the investor or guarantor from loss is the DSCR that allows for mortgage payments to be covered even if vacancies or tenant delinquencies rise.

18. It is also worth noting that both Enterprises also closely monitor the performance of loans on a quarterly basis, thus providing an opportunity to address problems early, when resolution may be more manageable.

19. The Congressional Budget Office found that the Enterprises passed on to their single-family borrowers a little more than half of the benefit they gained from having the implicit government guarantee. No estimate was made for their multifamily business (Congressional Budget Office 2001, p. 1).

20. This argument is used primarily on the single-family side. A number of studies have refuted the argument that the government push for homeownership (by President Clinton) or that the ownership society (promoted by President W. Bush) led to lower underwriting standards in the multifamily market. Nor has it been found that either the Community Reinvestment Act (requiring banks to help meet the credit needs of low- and moderate-income communities) or the Affordable Housing Goals (standards that Fannie and Freddie were expected to meet to serve traditionally underserved communities) caused the subprime crisis (e.g., see Kroszner 2009).

21. The Delaney-Carney-Himes Bill has already been reintroduced in the new Congress.

22. For an example of those that propose simply phasing out Fannie and Freddie, and with them the government guarantee for non-GNMA MBS, see White and Wilkins (2013) and Lockhart (2011, pp. 39, 46–47).

23. To provide the insurance, the Government could create a new entity or could add it to Ginnie Mae's responsibilities (Bond et al. 2013, pp. 78–79).

24. Determining the amount of the premium is also not without controversy. Some argue that the government is incapable of determining the correct level (Acharya et al. 2011, pp. 153–54). Others point to the Federal Credit Reform Act, which lays out rules for determining premium levels and, in the case of the FHA, may well have sufficient capital, including loss reserves, to ride out the most recent downturn. Although FHA was mandated to draw down $1.7 billion from the U.S. Treasury in fiscal year 2014, it still had plenty of cash reserves to cover current payments, and the latest actuarial report projects significant net earnings for the most recent cohorts of loans and a rapid rebuilding of its capital position (U.S. Department of Housing and Urban Development 2013, p. 9). No additional draw is projected as being needed for fiscal year 2015 (Swanson 2013). The challenge of setting the premium is further complicated by the debate over methodology: Should the rate be set according to the Federal Credit Reform Act (FCRA), which assumes that the government merely needs to cover its expected losses based on its borrowing costs, or on so-called "fair value" accounting, which looks to the risk-adjusted rate that the private sector would charge for providing that same level of coverage?

25. The first step of spinning off these businesses into self-contained subsidiaries could possibly be done now with the authorization of FHFA (Collins 2012). The owners

of the holders of the junior preferred stock of Fannie and Freddie have sued to clarify their ownership rights in the existing entities.

26. A bill was proposed in the last session of Congress by Senators Tim Johnson and Mike Crapo, which would provide a separate public guarantor, based in part on the model of the Federal Deposit Insurance Corporation (Hopkins and Benson 2014; Housing Finance Reform and Taxpayer Protection Act of 2014, S. 1217, 113th Cong. [2013–14]).

27. To the extent that the effective operation of these entities requires the holding of mortgages or MBS in portfolio, then a separate assessment should be made as to whether they should have access to a guarantee to lower the cost of any debt issued for that purpose. Two possible reasons for allowing these entities to maintain some portfolio capacity might be to "season" newly originated mortgages for some extended period of time before being able to sell them or to repurchase distressed loans from existing securities that they have guaranteed.

28. Currently Fannie Mae works with twenty-five DUS lenders and Freddie Mac with twenty-four so-called Program Plus Seller/Servicers, with an overlap of nineteen of those lenders on both lists. An expansion of the number of securitizers that have access to the government guarantee could also help to increase competition at the lender level.

29. Requiring that a certain share of their business serve markets that may be less profitable will also push the Enterprises to charge higher prices in other parts of the market where alternative sources of capital are also available. This pressure to raise their prices could help mitigate the danger of their crowding out other capital (see discussion below on crowding out.) However, there are limits on how much the Enterprises can charge because they need to at least be able to meet the prices their competitors are willing to charge the same borrowers.

30. More research is necessary to determine the right ratio of market rate to affordable units for such a rule, as well as the appropriate definitions for each category. As an example of how this could work, for each year since 2009 at least 74 percent of the multifamily units financed in a given year by Fannie or Freddie were affordable to low-income families (earning 80 percent of AMI or below), and at least 12 percent were affordable to very low-income families (earning 50 percent of AMI or below). In other words, for every 1 "market rate" multifamily unit financed by the Enterprises over that period, the companies financed at least 2.8 low-income units and at least 0.5 very-low-income units.

31. Author's analysis based on annual origination data from Fannie Mae, Freddie Mac, and Ginnie Mae. This total assumes that that there is roughly $6 trillion in government-insured mortgage-backed securities (including both single-family and multifamily) in any given year. As of the fourth quarter of 2014, the three entities accounted for a total of more than $6.3 trillion in outstanding mortgage debt (Federal Reserve Bank of the United States 2015b). We expect that it will take several years for the assessment to generate this level of funding because it would likely only apply to new government-backed mortgage loans, not existing loans.

32. Increases in capital requirements under Basel III may also work against banks increasing the share of commercial mortgages in their portfolios.

33. The precipitous decline of savings banks that traditionally served local mortgage markets is thought to have further limited the availability of bank mortgages. Their numbers fell from 4,000 in 1980 to 734 in 2010 (Protess 2010).

34. In 2007, outstanding ABS totaled $123.9 billion of $797.4 billion outstanding of total multifamily residential mortgages (Federal Reserve Bank of the United States 2015c, p. 123).

35. The House Financial Services Committee has already approved the Protecting American Taxpayers and Homeowners (PATH) Act (H.R. 2767, 113th Cong. [2013]), which seeks to reduce FHA's footprint, which in turn would limit the ability of Ginnie Mae to provide countercyclical support to the multifamily housing market (Enterprise Community Partners 2015).

36. This would happen because banks prefer to make shorter-term loans unless they can sell the loans on the secondary market (Min 2013, p. 482).

37. Correspondingly, interest rate risk for long-term, fixed-rate loans is higher for the lenders/investors who will, for example, see the market value of their loans fall as interest rates rise (Office of Investor Education and Advocacy 2013).

38. This was the approach taken by former FHFA Acting Director Ed DeMarco when he required Fannie and Freddie to lower their multifamily mortgage business in 2014 to a level 10 percent below what they had done in 2013.

39. For a discussion of the issues on the single-family side, see *Reforming America's Housing Finance Market: A Report to Congress* (U.S. Department of the Treasury and U.S. Department of Housing and Urban Development 2011).

Chapter 5. The Once and Future Federal Housing Administration

1. For a history of FHA's mortgage insurance program, see Vandell (1995).

2. FHA loan limits are typically set at 95 percent of the median house price, but not less than 48 percent of Freddie Mac's conforming loan limit. The Housing and Economic Recovery Act of 2008 temporarily changed the rule to 125 percent of the median house price or not less than 65 percent of Freddie Mac's loan limit. High-cost areas saw the "ceiling" increase from $312,895 to $729,750.

3. The estimated risk premium is similar to the 100–basis point increase in rates Moody's Analytics estimates would result if the FHA had ceased operation and private mortgage insurance companies continued to target a 15 percent return on capital (Zandi and deRitis 2010).

4. Differences in the degree of coverage complicate direct comparisons of capital ratios. Whereas private mortgage insurers typically only cover up to 30 percent of losses, FHA insures the entire loan amount but often recoups losses in the foreclosure process.

5. For comparison, the capital ratio of the MMI Fund fell from 7.4 percent to –1.4 percent, or roughly 8.8 percentage points.

6. Elderly is defined as a borrower at least sixty-two years old. Nonborrowing spouses may be of any age, and as a safeguard the termination of a HECM is deferred after the death of the mortgagor as long as the spouse fulfills the other eligibility requirements (FHA Mortgage Letter 2014-7).

7. The principal limit is found by multiplying the principal limit factor by the maximum claim amount, which is the lesser of the appraised value or FHA loan limit at origination.

Chapter 6. The Federal Home Loan Bank System and U.S. Housing Finance

1. The twelve FHLBs are located in Atlanta, Boston, Chicago, Cincinnati, Dallas, Des Moines, Indianapolis, New York, Pittsburgh, San Francisco, Seattle, and Topeka. The Office of Finance is located in Reston, VA. The Des Moines and Seattle FHLBs will be merged in 2015.

2. The likely rationale for this liberalization was that the FHLB System had lost a large number of members to failure during the 1980s thrift crisis but needed to thrive going forward in order to assist with paying-off the Ref Corp bonds issued to finance the crisis resolution.

3. As of year end 2013, the FHLB System had 7,504 members. Of these, 67.3 percent were commercial banks; 16.2 percent were credit unions; 12.4 percent were thrifts; 3.8 percent were insurance companies; and 0.3 percent were community development financial institutions.

4. See 12 CFR § 1263.1 for a comprehensive definition of "residential mortgage loans" for purposes of FHLB membership. Community financial institutions are federally insured depository institutions with average total assets over the preceding three-year period of less than $1.0 billion (adjusted annually for inflation). The average total asset cap for 2013 was $1.095 billion.

5. See 12 CFR § 1277, Subpart C, for a comprehensive set of requirements pertaining to FHLB capital plans.

6. See 12 USC 1430(a)(3) for a complete list of eligible collateral. See also Federal Home Loan Banks Office of Finance (2014, p. 86) for a breakdown of the types of collateral backing advances.

7. See Federal Home Loan Banks Office of Finance (2014, p. 84) for further discussion of these collateral posting methods and associated requirements.

8. See 12 USC 1430[e]. Bennett, Vaughan, and Yeager (2005) describe how FHLB advances may increase the probability of bank default and raise the FDIC's expected losses given default.

9. Such activity-based stock purchase requirements allow FHLB balance sheets to expand without disrupting the capital structure. In the event of balance sheet

contraction, such activity-based member stock becomes "excess stock" and is eligible for immediate redemption.

10. For analysis of the all-in cost of advances, see Flannery and Frame (2006) and Ashcraft, Bech, and Frame (2010). See also DeMarco (2010) for additional discussion of the benefits of FHLB membership.

11. Agency debt generally refers to debt securities issued by Fannie Mae, Freddie Mac, the FHLB System, and the Farm Credit System. Agency mortgage-backed securities are those issued and guaranteed by Fannie Mae, Freddie Mac, and Ginnie Mae.

12. See DeMarco (2010, 2011) for further elaboration on the policy demerits of FHLB investment portfolios.

13. FHLB members interact daily with the Office of Finance to discuss their short-term funding needs, which are met via direct placement with dealers (e.g., overnight discount notes) or through regular competitive auctions (e.g., term discount notes).

14. For details, see FHFA (2011). Such earnings retention is consistent with FHLB System practice prior to the enactment of FIRREA.

15. See 12 CFR § 932 for details.

16. See Flannery and Frame (2006) for a detailed discussion of FHLB System interest rate risk management.

17. See Ambrose and Warga (2002) and Nothaft, Pearce, and Stevanovic (2002) for analyses of individual housing GSE debt funding advantages relative to other highly rated financial institutions. Such studies find that housing GSE debt carries yields about 30–40 basis points below those of similar firms (holding various factors constant) and that this advantage is similar for Fannie Mae, Freddie Mac, and the FHLB System.

18. Of course, large actual costs can be incurred in the event that the Government provides support to an insolvent GSE, as was evidenced by the rescue of Fannie Mae and Freddie Mac in 2008. See Frame et al. (2015) for a discussion.

19. Ironically, federal supervision of the GSEs may encourage investors' faith in a federal guarantee despite the government's and the GSEs' explicit disavowals. Hence, as a theoretical matter, it is unclear whether the presence of a safety-and-soundness supervisor for GSEs actually increases or decreases expected taxpayer exposure (Frame and White 2004).

20. The FHFA was created by the Housing and Economic Recovery Act of 2008 and effectively consolidated prior GSE mission and safety-and-soundness oversight responsibilities of the Office of Federal Housing Enterprise Oversight, the Federal Housing Finance Board, and the U.S. Department of Housing and Urban Development.

21. The Housing and Economic Recovery Act of 2008 expanded the definition of a "community financial institution" from $500 million to $1 billion in total assets (with each figure adjusted over time to account for inflation).

22. The authors estimate that the rate on a thirty-day advance from the New York FHLB was 20–40 basis points cheaper than a similar Discount Window loan in late 2007 following the Federal Reserve's reduction in the primary credit rate.

23. See Frame et al. (2015) for a detailed discussion of financial distress at Fannie Mae and Freddie Mac during this time.

Chapter 7. The TBA Market: Effects and Prerequisites

The authors would like to acknowledge the help of Brett Rose, Christian Cabanilla, and Gregory Powell from the New York Fed in the preparation of this chapter.

1. For a discussion of mortgage finance in other parts of the world, see Lea (2010) and Svenstrup (2002).

2. From Federal Reserve Bank of the United States (2015a).

3. From Securities Industry and Financial Markets Association (SIFMA) (n.d.).

4. From Inside Mortgage Finance (2015).

5. Freddie Mac refers to their securities as participation certificates, or PCs.

6. From Inside Mortgage Finance (2015).

7. In the case of Ginnie Mae-guaranteed MBS, the federal government also provides insurance to the lender through the Federal Housing Administration (FHA), the Veterans' Administration (VA), the Rural Housing Service (RHS), and the Office of Public and Indian Housing (PIH).

8. For more information on gfees, see FHFA (2015).

9. From Inside Mortgage Finance (2013).

10. From Mortgage-Backed Securities Online (eMBS) (2015).

11. TRACE (2014), Tables S20 and S21.

12. For a more detailed discussion of the TBA market, see Vickery and Wright (2010) and (2013).

13. From SIFMA (n.d.).

14. eMBS (2015).

15. SIFMA (n.d.).

16. Bessembinder et al. use one-way trading costs, whereas Friewald et al. use two-way trading costs. Both measures are based on bid-ask spreads.

17. The Qualified Mortgage Rule of the Dodd-Frank Act (2010), which was adopted in 2014.

18. For a more in-depth discussion of dollar rolls, see Zhaogang Song and Haoxiang Zhu (2014).

19. U.S. Department of the Treasury, Federal Reserve System, and Federal Deposit Insurance Corporation (2012).

20. The payment delay refers to the difference in time between when borrowers make their monthly payments and when MBS investors receive their payments of prin-

cipal and interest. For example, if a borrower makes a payment on June 1, the MBS investor will not receive that payment until July 15 for Freddie Mac securities, and July 25 for Fannie Mae securities.

Chapter 8. The Significance and Design of a National Mortgage Note Registry

The views expressed are those of the authors and do not necessarily represent those of the Federal Reserve Bank of New York or the Federal Reserve System.

1. The complex status of a servicer under the law arguably contributed to the wave of litigation. The authority of the servicer to take various actions is generally governed by contract; often a pooling and servicing agreement. These servicing agreements, at least in the private securitization market, are not available to borrowers, and so borrowers are left to wonder whether their servicers are accurately representing limitations in the scope of their authority (usually around modifications) or exceeding the scope of their authority when taking enforcement actions. With respect to the latter point, the law further complicates the issue when the mortgage loan is a negotiable instrument, because it is then possible for a servicer to be a "holder" of the mortgage note with the legal right to enforce and foreclose in its own name, even though another entity is entitled to the economic benefits of the mortgage loan. As discussed later on in the text, greater transparency as to servicer authority and the identity of the party with the real economic interest in a mortgage loan is one of the possible benefits for homeowners of a national mortgage registry.

2. See discussion below at note 34 on holder in due course status.

3. The mortgage note is the contract memorializing the obligation of the borrower to repay the loan. A separate document, the mortgage, is the document establishing that certain real property secures the loan. As discussed in greater detail in the text, although these are separate documents, the intent of the overall transaction is to vest in one entity both the right to enforce the note and the right to enforce the mortgage and to ensure that the rights are always transferred together. This is true regardless of whether a jurisdiction has a "lien theory" of mortgages (viewing the mortgage as merely a security interest) or a "conveyance theory" of mortgages (viewing the mortgage as conditionally conveying the subject property).

4. See, for example, Silver-Greenberg (2012), describing federal regulators' efforts to levy fines for robosigning, and White (2012), describing robosigning practices.

5. For example, because of the number of cases that challenged the right of MERS to foreclose a mortgage where it was identified as the mortgagee of record as nominee of the lender, MERS ultimately revised its rules to require that all such mortgages be assigned to the foreclosing party and such assignment be recorded in the land records. Also see Levitin (2013) for a discussion of other concerns resulting from the common

agent status of MERS and MERS's reliance on employees of servicers to act as agents of MERS, which introduces other questions about agency.

6. We have been involved in the drafting of a statute that would create such a registry, but it must be understood as a work in progress. The initial draft of our proposal has been circulated quite widely among government and mortgage industry participants but has not yet been introduced in any legislative forum. Although we believe it has merit and are optimistic that it may ultimately become law in some form, we also recognize that it will continue to evolve before that occurs.

7. Permanent Editorial Board, Uniform Commercial Code, 2011, *Application of the Uniform Commercial Code to Selected Issues Relating to Mortgage Notes.*

8. UCC § 3-104 defines a negotiable instrument (with certain exceptions) as an unconditional promise or order to pay a fixed amount of money, with or without interest or other charges described in the promise or order, if it fulfills the following conditions:

1. It is payable to bearer or to order at the time it is issued or first comes into possession of a holder.
2. It is payable on demand or at a definite time.
3. It does not state any other undertaking or instruction by the person promising or ordering payment to do any act in addition to the payment of money, but the promise or order may contain (a) an undertaking or power to give, maintain, or protect collateral to secure payment; (b) an authorization or power to the holder to confess judgment or realize on or dispose of collateral; or (c) a waiver of the benefit of any law intended for the advantage or protection of an obligor.

9. UCC § 3-301. There is one important exception to this rule, where the note has been lost, stolen, or destroyed, in which case there must exist adequate protection of the party against whom the note is being enforced before the court will permit enforcement.

10. This might be the case, for example, if the party in possession took the note (not yet indorsed to any party) as collateral for a loan and upon default of its counterparty had the right to enforce the note. In contrast, a note held in custody for another party is not transferred to the custodian for the purpose of giving the custodian rights to enforce the note.

11. UCC § 3-203. Indorsement is entirely unnecessary if the note was originally made to or has previously been indorsed to "bearer"; see *Bank of New York v. Raftogianis*, 10 A.3d 236, 240 (N.J.Super.Ch.Div. 2010). All of these matters are more fully developed in Whitman (2014).

12. Whitman (forthcoming). And although the paper with the inked signature may reflect best evidence of the terms of nonnegotiable notes, enforcement of the note does not rest on its existence.

13. Despite the important legal distinctions between negotiable and nonnegotiable instruments, it is often impossible to know in advance of litigation whether a note is negotiable. Several respected legal academics have argued for years that residential mortgage notes, even the Fannie Mae or Freddie Mac uniform note, are nonnegotiable. However, in recent years a handful of courts have issued rulings that support the view that the standard Fannie Mae-Freddie Mac one-to-four-family residential note is negotiable.

14. UCC § 9-203(b).

15. UCC § 9-330(d).

16. The use of custodians does not materially change the analysis. The mortgage note still needs to be physically moved to the custodian of the purchaser (with any required indorsement). The industry has seen a consolidation among entities providing custodial services in recent years, but multiple loan custodians remain. And even when the purchaser of a mortgage note uses the same custodian as the seller of the note, the note must be located within the custodian's records and physically moved (and perhaps indorsed) to files maintained by the custodian for the benefit of the purchaser.

17. This practice, having the contract memorializing the debt of the borrower to the lender (the note) be a separate document from the document reflecting the collateral securing the note (the mortgage or deed of trust), reflects the desire on the part of lenders to ensure that their mortgage notes qualify as "negotiable" (see definition in note 8 above). Negotiable notes are special because a person that purchases the note can obtain the special status of a holder in due course. If a person qualifies as a holder in due course, that person can look to enforce the negotiable note without being subject to most defenses that the obligor might have to paying. The concept of holder in due course generally comes into play when the loan originator (or some third party involved in the origination) behaved in a dishonest manner, and the borrower now in default wants to argue that he or she does not have to pay on the note because of the dishonest behavior. If the party enforcing the note is a holder in due course, the borrower will not be able to assert the dishonest behavior as a defense to payment in most cases. A holder in due course also takes free of the borrower's claim that she is entitled to a payment from the original obligee, thereby reducing the amount that the borrower owes. Another benefit of being a holder in due course is that it cuts off most third-party ownership claims to the note.

18. UCC § 9-203(g).

19. *Singleton v. Wells Fargo Home Mortgage*, 2012 WL 1657345 (U.S. Dist. Ct., W.D. Mo. 2012); *Dauenhauer v. Bank of New York Mellon*, 562 F. App'x 473 (6th Cir. 2014); *Reynolds v. Bank of Am., N.A.*, 2013 WL 1904090 (U.S. Dist. Ct., N.D. Tex. 2013); *U.S. Bank v. Howie*, 280 P.3d 225 (Kan. Ct. App. 2012).

20. There are two other main advantages. See Section IV of this chapter for a discussion.

21. The concept for MERS relied on three basic legal principles: (a) every state provides a mechanism for lenders to secure loans by taking an interest in real estate—most commonly, mortgages and deeds of trust; (b) every state designates certain places where mortgages or deeds of trust must be recorded to be valid against a bona fide purchaser; and (c) every state permits a person or entity to hold legal title in the public land records as nominee for another person or entity that is the true party in interest. Beyond these basic principles, MERS was to operate within local procedural requirements and rely on its members to comply with the law of the state where the underlying property was located. MERS's origin and legal structure are described in detail in Peterson (2011).

22. In theory a borrower can always discover who is entitled to enforce his or her mortgage note by demanding production of the original note, but in practice this is completely unrealistic.

23. Current law requires that a borrower be notified as to the party that services his or her loan. The effectiveness of such notices is not clear. In the course of developing our proposal, we have heard from several borrower representatives that the current set of notices is not working and that having a registry that identifies the servicer, the party on whose behalf the servicer is servicing, and the scope of the servicer's authority to modify loans is needed.

24. An exception to this exists with respect to electronic mortgage notes where the MERS eRegistry serves as the source for identifying who has "control." See discussion of eNotes in text. According to a MERS eRegistry brochure, more than 300,000 eNotes have been registered on the MERS eRegistry.

25. With one exception, the law as it exists today would not support this outcome. The exception relates to electronic notes that, if in paper form, would qualify as negotiable instruments under the Uniform Commercial Code (known under the law as a "transferable record") and then only if the obligor under the note agreed to treat the electronic note as a transferable record at the time the note was issued. Assuming the existence of a transferrable record, the law today accords legal significance to the records of any system that is used to evidence the obligee so long as the system "reliably establishes that person as the person to which the transferable record was issued or transferred." To the extent that such a system is proven to exist, its records identify the person with "control" of the transferrable record. A person with control of a transferrable record is generally treated as the holder of a negotiable instrument under Article 3 of the Uniform Commercial Code.

The current law addressing eNotes falls short of the vision for a National Registry in several important respects. First, it only captures notes that are originated in electronic form. As the comments to UETA note, "the possibility that a paper note might be converted to an electronic record and then intentionally destroyed, and the effect of such action, was not intended to be covered by [UETA]." This might have been an acceptable policy choice if either the market for transferrable records took hold or the costs of maintaining paper associated with traditional residential mortgage instruments were manageable, but neither of these realities has proven true. It has been over fifteen years since the law supporting transferable records was enacted, and yet the adoption rate for transferrable records remains low. And if the financial crisis taught us anything, it is that managing the paper related to residential mortgage notes can be costly. Second, the current law only captures eNotes that would have been negotiable instruments if in paper form and only if they are in a control system. This causes several problems. Most significantly, it is impossible to know at the time of the origination of an eNote whether one has rights related to a transferable record or rights to a payment intangible. This is because the rights will turn on a determination after the fact that (a) the note would have been negotiable had it been issued in paper form, (b) the obligor agreed to treat the note as a transferrable record, and (c) the system used to identify interests in the transferrable record is reliable. With respect to this last element, UETA and ESIGN provide a safe harbor that includes six separate requirements that would need to be proved if the nature of the system is challenged. We are not aware of any contested cases of foreclosure of a mortgage based on a transferable record.

26. See *Montgomery County., Pa. v. MERSCORP Inc.*, No. 14-4315, 2015 WL 460411 (3d Cir. 2015).

27. After circulating the first draft of our proposal, we received feedback across all stakeholder groups that suggested that there would be little objection to including such a requirement. It was noted that there may be a few situations where a lender would choose not to record its mortgage, such as loans made between family members. Such lenders are unlikely to sell such loans in the secondary mortgage market and therefore would not have as strong an interest to deposit the loan in the National Registry. Of course, if use of the National Registry is made mandatory, this might be more of an issue.

28. *Lang v. Butler*, 483 P.2d 994, 996 (Colo. App. 1971); *Citimortgage, Inc. v. Barabas*, 950 N.E.2d 12, 18 (Ind. Ct. App. 2011), vacated, 975 N.E.2d 805 (Ind. 2012); *Pinney v. Merchants' Nat'l Bank of Defiance*, 72 N.E. 884, 887–88 (Ohio 1904); *Fifth Third Bank v. NCS Mortg. Lending Co.*, 860 N.E.2d 785, 788–89 (Ohio Ct. App. 2006).

When the Mortgage Electronic Registration system (MERS) was established, it was assumed that litigants would have a corresponding obligation to give notice to MERS as the recorded holder of the mortgage and that MERS would then notify the actual holder. However, several courts refused to find such a duty to give notice to MERS, because it was "merely" a nominee for the actual holder. See *Mortg. Elec. Registration Sys., Inc. v. Sw. Homes of Ark.*, 301 S.W.3d 1, 5 (Ark. 2009); *Citimortgage, Inc. v. Barabas*, 950 N.E.2d 12, 18 (Ind. Ct. App. 2011), vacated, 975 N.E.2d 805 (Ind. 2012); *Landmark Nat'l Bank v. Kesler*, 216 P.3d 158, 169–170 (Kan. 2009).

29. *Ameribanc Sav. Banks v. Resolution Trust Corp.*, 858 F. Supp. 576, 583 (E.D. Va. 1994); In re Beaulac, 298 B.R. 31, 36 (Bankr. D. Mass. 2003) (trustee in bankruptcy

acting as bona fide purchaser); *Kan. City Mortg. Co. v. Crowell*, 239 So. 2d 130, 131 (Fla. Dist. Ct. App. 1970); *Federal Nat'l Mortg. Ass'n v. Kuipers*, 732 N.E.2d 723, 726–27 (Ill. App. Ct. 2000); *Brenner v. Neu*, 170 N.E.2d 897, 899 (Ill. App. Ct. 1960); *Henniges v. Johnson*, 84 N.W. 350, 353 (N.D. 1900); *Kalen v. Gelderman*, 278 N.W. 165, 170 (S.D. 1938); *Fannin Inv. & Dev. Co. v. Neuhaus*, 427 S.W.2d 82, 89 (Tex. Civ. App. 1968); *Marling v. Milwaukee Realty Co.*, 106 N.W. 844, 845 (Wis. 1906).

30. A large number of suits have been filed by local recorders against MERS, usually to recover damages for lost revenue, but nearly all have been dismissed. See, for example, *Christian County Clerk ex rel. Kem v. Mortgage Electronic Registration Systems, Inc.*, 515 Fed.Appx. 451 (6th Cir. 2013) (based on Kentucky law); *Fuller v. Mortgage Electronic Registration Systems, Inc.*, 888 F.Supp.2d 1257 (M.D.Fla. 2012); *Brown v. Mortgage Electronic Registration System, Inc.*, 903 F.Supp.2d 723 (W.D.Ark. 2012); *Jackson County ex rel. Nixon v. MERSCORP, Inc.*, 915 F.Supp.2d 1064 (W.D.Mo. 2013). Contra, see *Montgomery County, Pa. v. Merscorp. Inc.*, 16 F.Supp.3d 542 (E.D.Pa. 2014).

31. At a minimum, the paper note will have to be marked as deposited in the National Registry. Whether the paper should be stored for some period of time or destroyed, and which party is tasked with storing and/or destroying the paper, are policy questions that will have to be resolved. Our experience with similar issues that arose as paper check collection transitioned to electronics suggests that in the near term stakeholders will likely advocate for keeping the paper (even if the paper no longer has legal effect and despite the potential fraud risk discussed in the text), but longer term, as stakeholders gain comfort with the National Registry retaining the paper, will no longer be a concern.

32. Ordinarily, that is true. But see *Provident Bank v. Community Home Mortg. Corp.*, 498 F.Supp.2d 558 (E.D.N.Y. 2007), in which the loan originator had borrowers sign two identical original promissory notes and subsequently sold them to two different secondary market investors. The court treated them as a single note and found that the first secondary market purchaser to take possession had thereby perfected the transfer and hence prevailed.

33. This means either a prior or current indorsement in blank, or a chain of indorsements leading to the present registrant; see UCC §§ 3-204, 3-205.

34. See UCC § 3-301(i) (holder is person entitled to enforce); UCC § 1-201(21) ("holder" means the person in possession of a negotiable instrument that is payable either to bearer or to an identified person that is the person in possession).

35. UCC § 3-302.

36. UCC § 3-301(ii).

37. UCC § 2-302(a).

38. Once deposited, it would no longer be possible to provide possession of a mortgage note to a person without giving such person the rights to enforce the mortgage note. This may raise some issues that will have to be considered in drafting the law, but we anticipate that those issues will be able to be resolved.

39. Of course, if the thief were to transfer the mortgage note to a person without knowledge that the note was stolen, the transferee would be a holder.

40. UCC § 9-203(b).

41. UCC § 9-309(4).

42. UCC § 9-312(a).

43. UCC § 9-303(a).

44. UCC § 9-330(d).

45. This is so because UCC § 9-309(4), which provides for automatic perfection, applies only to *sales* of instruments and not security interests in instruments.

46. UCC § 9-330(d).

47. See 15 USC sec. 7021.

48. UETA sec. 16(d); 15 USC sec. 7021(d).

Chapter 9. Informed Securitization

1. Academics as well as policy makers focused on interest rate risk rather than credit risk as a source of systematic instability. See Wachter (forthcoming).

2. See Herring and Wachter (1999) for the role of optimists in setting real estate prices. Although publicly traded companies do provide a means to short sell real estate, they do so imperfectly because their valuations do not only reflect real estate prices. Other attempts at creating indices to short sell real estate have not succeeded in part due to the heterogeneity of real estate.

3. The fundamental value is the price that is equal to the discounted present value of the net income that can be generated.

4. See Wachter (2015) for a discussion of the comparative financing of the bubbles in the United States and Europe. Financial institutions increased their leverage in Europe through portfolio covered bonds.

5. The cooperative would coordinate a mutual loss pool acting as a reserve to cover mortgage default losses. Members would contribute to the mutual loss pool based on equity capital and volume of mortgages securitized.

REFERENCES

Acharya, Viral V., Matthew Richardson, Stijn Van Nieuwerburgh, and Lawrence J. White. 2011. *Guaranteed to Fail: Fannie Mae, Freddie Mac, and the Debacle of Mortgage Finance.* Princeton: Princeton University Press.

Adelino, Manuel, Antoinette Schoar, and Felipe Severino. 2015. "Changes in Buyer Composition and the Expansion of Credit During the Boom." MIT Sloan Working Paper. Cambridge, MA: MIT University Press.

Admati, Anat and Martin Hellwig. 2013. *The Bankers' New Clothes.* Princeton, NJ: Princeton University Press.

Adrian, Tobias and Adam Ashcraft. 2012. "Shadow Banking Regulation." Federal Reserve Bank of New York Staff Report no. 559, April.

Ambrose, Brent, Michael LaCour-Little, and Anthony Sanders. 2004. "The Effect of Conforming Loan Status on Mortgage Yield Spreads: A Loan-Level Analysis." *Real Estate Economics* 32 (4): 541–69.

Ambrose, B. W., A. Pennington-Cross, and A. M. Yezer. 2002. "Credit Rationing in the U.S. Mortgage Market: Evidence from Variation in FHA Market Shares." *Journal of Urban Economics* 51 (2): 272–94.

Ambrose, Brent and Arthur Warga. 2002. "Measuring Potential GSE Funding Advantages." *Journal of Real Estate Finance and Economics* 25: 129–50.

American Law Institute. 2001. *Principles of Corporate Governance: Analysis and Recommendations.* Philadelphia, PA: American Law Institute.

Anderson, Simon P., Andre de Palma, and Jacques-Francois Thisse. 1992. *Discrete Choice Theory of Product Differentiation.* Cambridge, MA: MIT University Press.

Apgar, W. C., A. Bendimerad, and R. S. Essene. 2007. *Mortgage Market Channels and Fair Lending: An Analysis of HMDA Data.* Joint Center for Housing Studies of Harvard University.

Aragon, Diego, Andrew Caplin, Sumit Chopra, John V. Leahy, Marco Scoffier, and Joseph Tracy. 2010. "Reassessing FHA Risk." NBER Working Paper no. 15802, March. Cambridge, MA: National Bureau of Economic Research.

Arrow, Kenneth J. and Robert C. Lind. 1970. "Uncertainty and the Evaluation of Public Investment." *American Economic Review* 60 (June): 364–78.

Ashcraft, Adam, Morten Bech, and W. Scott Frame 2010. "The Federal Home Loan Bank System: The Lender of Next-to-Last Resort." *Journal of Money, Credit, and Banking* 42: 551–83.

Ashcraft, Adam B. and Til Schuermann. 2008. "Understanding the Securitization of Subprime Mortgage Credit." *Foundations and Trends in Finance* 2 (3): 191–309.

Ashcraft, Adam B. and Til Schuermann. 2009. "The Seven Deadly Frictions of Subprime Mortgage Credit Securitization." *World Scientific Studies in International Economics* 10 (2009): 325–43.

Autry, Charles T. and Roland F. Hall. 2009. *The Law of Cooperatives*. Business Law Section. Chicago: ABA Publishing.

Baker, Malcolm and Jeffrey Wurgler. 2013. "Do Strict Capital Requirements Raise the Cost of Capital: Banking Regulation and the Low Risk Anomaly." NBER Working Paper no. 19018. Cambridge, MA: National Bureau of Economic Research.

Bakker, B., G. Dell'ariccia, L. Laeven, J. Vandenbussche, D. Igan, and H. Tong. 2012. "Policies for Macrofinancial Stability: How to Deal with Credit Booms." International Monetary Fund Staff Discussion Notes, 1-1.

Barakova, Irina, Paul Calem, and Susan Wachter. 2014. "Borrowing Constraints During the Housing Bubble." *Journal of Housing Economics* 24 (June): 4–20.

Basel Committee on Banking Supervision. 2008. "Range of Practices and Issues in Economic Capital Modeling." Consultative Document, August.

Bennett, Rosalind L., Mark D. Vaughan, and Timothy J. Yeager. 2005. "Should the FDIC Worry about the FHLB? The Impact of Federal Home Loan Bank Advances on the Bank Insurance Fund." FDIC Center for Financial Research Working Paper 2005-10.

Bernanke, B. S., M. Gertler, and S. Gilchrist. 1999. "The Financial Accelerator in a Quantitative Business Cycle Framework." *Handbook of Macroeconomics* 1: 1341–93.

Bessembinder, Hendrik, William Maxwell, and Kumar Venkataraman. 2013. "Trading Activity and Transaction Costs in Structured Credit Products." *Financial Analysts Journal* 69 (6): 55–67.

Bhutta, Neil and Daniel R. Ringo. 2014. "The 2013 Home Mortgage Disclosure Act Data." *Federal Reserve Bulletin* 100 (6): 1–32.

Bipartisan Policy Center Housing Commission. 2013a. "Housing America's Future: New Directions for National Policy." February 25. http://bipartisanpolicy.org/library/housing-americas-future-new-directions-national-policy/.

Bipartisan Policy Center Housing Commission. 2013b. "Modeling the Impact of Housing Finance Reform on Mortgage Rates." Andrew Davidson & Co., Inc. January.

Black Knight Financial Services. 2014. "LPS Applied Analytics Data." Retrieved April 2014 from http://www.bkfs.com/Data-and-Analytics.

Bocian, Debbie Gruenstein, Keith S. Ernst, and Wei Li. 2008. "Race, Ethnicity and Subprime Home Loan Pricing." *Journal of Economics and Business* 60 (1–2): 110–24.

Bocian, Debbie Gruenstein, Wei Li, and Keith S. Ernst. 2010. *Foreclosures by Race and Ethnicity: The Demographics of a Crisis*. Durham, NC: Center for Responsible Lending.

Bohn, James G. and Brian J. Hall. 1999. "The Moral Hazard of Insuring the Insurers." In *The Financing of Catastrophe Risk*, ed. K. Froot, 363–89. University of Chicago Press, Chicago.

Bond, Christopher S. ("Kit") et al. 2013. *America's Future: New Directions for National Policy*. Washington, D.C.: Bipartisan Policy Center.

Boyack, Andrea. 2011. "Laudable Goals and Unintended Consequences: The Role and Control of Fannie Mae and Freddie Mac." *American University Law Review* 60 (5): 1489.

Brancato, Carolyn Kay and Christian A. Plath. 2005. *Corporate Governance Handbook*. New York: Conference Board.

Brickman, David. 2013. "K-Deals: A Model for the Future of Mortgage Securitization." Freddie Mac, September 9. http://www.freddiemac.com/news/blog/david _brickman/20130906_mortgage_securitization.html.

Brunnermeier, Markus K. and Yuliy Sannikov. 2014. "A Macroeconomic Model with a Financial Sector." *American Economic Review* 104 (2): 379–421.

Business Roundtable. 2010. "Principles of Corporate Governance." White paper, April. http://businessroundtable.org/uploads/studies-reports/downloads/2010 _Principles_of_Corporate_Governance_1.pdf.

Campbell, John. 2013. "Mortgage Market Design." *Review of Finance* 17 (1): 1–33.

Campbell, John and Robert Shiller. 1988. "Stock Prices, Earnings, and Expected Dividends." *Journal of Finance* 63 (3): 661–76.

Campbell, Sean and Canlin Li, and Jay Im. 2014. "Measuring Agency MBS Market Liquidity with Transaction Data." FEDS Notes 2014-01-31. Board of Governors of the Federal Reserve System.

Canner, Glenn B., Stuart A. Gabriel, and J. Michael Woolley. 1991. "Race, Default Risk and Mortgage Lending: A Study of the FHA and Conventional Loan Markets." *Southern Economic Journal* 58 (1): 249–62.

Caplin, Andrew, Anna Cororaton, and Joseph Tracy. 2012. "Is the FHA Creating Sustainable Homeownership?" NBER Working Paper no. 18190, June. Cambridge, MA: National Bureau of Economic Research.

Case, K. E. and R.J. Shiller. 1989. "The Efficiency of the Market for Single-Family Homes." *American Economic Review* 79 (1): 125–37.

Castelli, Francesca, Damien Moore, Gabriel Ehrlich, and Jeffrey Perry. 2014. "Modeling the Budgetary Costs of FHA's Single Family Mortgage Insurance." Congressional Budget Office, 2014-05.

Center for American Progress. 2010. *A Responsible Market for Rental Housing Finance: Envisioning the Future of the U.S. Secondary Market for Multifamily Residential Rental Mortgages*. Washington, D.C.: Center for American Progress.

Center for American Progress, Mortgage Finance Working Group. 2011. "A Responsible Market for Housing Finance." January 27.

Chappatta, Brian. 2012. "Build America's First Deal Saves Schools $1.25 million." *Bloomberg News*, September 28.

Chen, Hui, Rui Cui, Zhiguo He, and Konstantin Milbradt. 2013. "Quantifying Liquidity and Default Risks of Corporate Bonds over the Business Cycle." University of Chicago Booth School of Business Working Paper no. 20638, October.

Coates, Ta-Nehisi. 2014. "The Case for Reparations." *Atlantic,* June. http://www
.theatlantic.com/magazine/archive/2014/06/the-case-for-reparations/361631/.

Cole, Rebel A. and Hamid Mehran. 1998. "The Effect of Changes in Ownership Structure on Performance: Evidence from the Thrift Industry." *Journal of Financial Economics* 50 (December): 291–317.

Collins, Brian. 2012. "FHFA: Spin Off Fannie and Freddie's Multifamily Units?" *National Mortgage News,* February 23. http://www.nationalmortgagenews.com
/dailybriefing/2010_543/spin-off-gse-multifamily-units-1029015-1.html.

Committee on Financial Services. 2013. "Committee Leaders Announce PATH Act
to End Taxpayer Bailout and Create Sustainable Housing Finance System." News
release, July 11. http://financialservices.house.gov/news/documentsingle.aspx
?documentid=342165.

Concentrance Consulting Group. 2005. "An Examination of Downpayment Gift Programs Administered by Non-Profit Organizations." U.S. Department of Housing
and Urban Development, C-OPC-22550/M0001.

Coughenour, Jay F. and Daniel N. Deli. 2002. "Liquidity Provision and the Organizational Form of NYSE Specialist Firms." *Journal of Finance* 57 (2): 841–69.

Damodaran, Aswath. n.d. "Return on Equity by Sector (U.S.)." Retrieved January 2016
from http://people.stern.nyu.edu/adamodar/New_Home_Page/datafile/roe.html.

Damodaran, Aswath, Kose John, and Crocker H. Liu. 1997. "The Determinants of
Organizational Form Changes: Evidence and Implications from Real Estate." *Journal of Financial Economics* 25 (10): 23–49.

Davidson, Adam, Alex Levin, and Susan Wachter. 2014. "Mortgage Default Option
Mispricing and Procyclicality." In *Homeownership Built to Last: Balancing Access,
Affordability, and Risk after the Housing Crisis,* ed. Eric S. Belsky, Christopher E.
Herbert, and Jennifer H. Molinsky, 290–316. Cambridge, MA: Brookings Institu-
tion and the Harvard University Joint Center for Housing Studies.

Davidson, Kate. 2015. "It's Official: First-Time Home Buyers Held Back in 2014." *Wall
Street Journal,* January 23.

Dechario, Toni, Patricia Mosser, Joseph Tracy, James Vickery, and Joshua Wright.
2010. "A Private Lender Cooperative Model for Residential Mortgage Finance."
Federal Reserve Bank of New York Staff Report no. 466, August. http://www
.newyorkfed.org/research/staff_reports/sr466.pdf.

Dechario, Toni, Patricia Mosser, Joseph Tracy, James Vickery, and Joshua Wright.
2011. "A Private Lender Cooperative Model for Residential Mortgage Finance." In
The American Mortgage System: Crisis and Reform, ed. Susan Wachter and Mar-
vin Smith, chap. 12. Philadelphia: University of Pennsylvania Press.

DeMarco, Edward J. 2010. "The Benefits of FHLB Membership." Remarks at the 2010
Federal Home Loan Banks Directors Conference, Washington D.C., April 28.

DeMarco, Edward J. 2011. "The Franchise Value of Federal Home Loan Banks." Remarks at
the 2011 Federal Home Loan Banks Directors Conference, Washington D.C., May 11.

DeMarco, Ed. 2013. "Housing Finance, Systemic Risk, and Returning Private Capital to the Mortgage Market." Remarks at the 49th Annual Conference on Bank Structure and Competition, Chicago, May 9.

DeMarzo, Peter. 2005. "The Pooling and Tranching of Securities: A Model of Informed Intermediation." *Review of Financial Studies* 18 (1): 1–35.

Demyanyk, Yuliya and Otto van Hemert. 2011. "Understanding the Subprime Mortgage Crisis." *Review of Financial Studies* 24 (6): 1848–80.

Ding, Lei, Roberto G. Quercia, W. Li, and Janneke Ratcliffe. 2011. "Risky Borrowers or Risky Mortgages Disaggregating Effects Using Propensity Score Models." *Journal of Real Estate Research* 33 (2): 245–77.

Duca, J. and D. C. Ling. 2015. "The Other (Commercial) Real Estate Boom and Bust: The Effects of Risk Premia and Regulatory Capital Arbitrage." Federal Reserve Bank of Dallas Working Paper no. 1504.

Duca, John V., John Muellbauer, and Anthony Murphy. 2011. "House Prices and Credit Constraints: Making Sense of the U.S. Experience." *Economic Journal* 121 (552): 533–51.

Duffie, Darrell, Ada Li, and Theo Lubke. 2010. "Policy Perspectives on OTC Derivatives Market Infrastructure." Federal Reserve Bank of New York Staff Report no. 424, January. http://www.newyorkfed.org/research/staff_reports/sr424.pdf.

Duhigg, Charles. 2008. "Tapping into Homes Can Be Pitfall for the Elderly." *New York Times,* March 2, Business section.

Ellie Mae. 2014. *Origination Insight Report.* Pleasanton, CA: Ellie Mae.

Elliot, Douglas J. 2010. "A Primer on Bank Capital." Brookings Institution Working Paper, January. Washington, D.C.: Brookings Institution Press. http://www.brookings.edu/~/media/research/files/papers/2010/1/29 capital elliott/0129_capital_primer_elliott.pdf.

Enterprise Community Partners. 2015. *Comparing the Four Housing Finance Reform Bills in Congress.* Washington, D.C.: Enterprise Community Partners. http://www.enterprisecommunity.com/resources/ResourceDetails?ID=0095590.

Esty, Benjamin C. 1997. "Organizational Form and Risk Taking in the Savings & Loan Industry." *Journal of Financial Economics* 44 (April): 25–55.

Fannie Mae. 2004. *Annual Report Pursuant to Section 13 or 15(d) of the Securities Exchange Act of 1934.* Washington, D.C.: Fannie Mae.

Fannie Mae. 2012a. *Analysis of the Viability of Fannie Mae's Multifamily Business Operating without a Government Guarantee.* Washington, D.C.: Fannie Mae.

Fannie Mae. 2012b. *An Overview of Fannie Mae Multifamily Mortgage Business.* Washington, D.C.: Fannie Mae.

Fannie Mae. 2015a. *Fannie Mae Multifamily Mortgage Business Information.* Washington, D.C.: Fannie Mae. https://www.fanniemae.com/content/fact_sheet/multifamily-business-information.pdf.

Fannie Mae. 2015b. "Over 25 Years of Multifamily Mortgage Financing Through Fannie Mae's Delegated Underwriting and Servicing (DUS) Program." http://www.fanniemae.com/resources/file/mbs/pdf/mbsenger_25yrs.pdf.

Federal Financial Institutions Examination Council. 2015. *Call Report*. TINY data. Retrieved January 2015 from https://cdr.ffiec.gov/public/.

Federal Home Loan Banks Office of Finance. 2014. "Federal Home Loan Banks: Combined Financial Report for the Year Ended December 31, 2013." March 28. http://www.fhlb-of.com/ofweb_userWeb/resources/13yrend.pdf.

Federal Housing Administration (FHA). 2008a. "Moratorium on Risk-Based Premiums for FHA Mortgage Insurance." Mortgagee Letter 2008–22, September.

Federal Housing Administration (FHA). 2008b. "Revised Downpayment and Maximum Mortgage Requirements." Mortgagee Letter 2008–23, September.

Federal Housing Administration (FHA). 2008c. "Revised Eligibility Requirements for FHA Roster Appraisers." Mortgagee Letter 2008–39, December.

Federal Housing Administration (FHA). 2009. "Appraiser Independence." Mortgagee Letter 2009–28, September.

Federal Housing Administration (FHA). 2010a. "Increase in Upfront Premiums for FHA Mortgage Insurance." Mortgagee Letter 2010-02, January.

Federal Housing Administration (FHA). 2010b. "Mortgagee Approval for Single Family Programs—Extended Procedures for Terminating Underwriting Authority." Mortgagee Letter 2010-03, January.

Federal Housing Administration (FHA). 2010c. "Changes to FHA Mortgage Insurance Premiums." Mortgagee Letter 2010–28, September.

Federal Housing Administration (FHA). 2010d. "Minimum Credit Scores and Loan-to-Value Ratios." Mortgagee Letter 2010–29, September.

Federal Housing Administration (FHA). 2010e. "Home Equity Conversion Mortgage Program—Introducing HECM Saver; Mortgage Insurance Premiums and Principal Limit Factor Changes for HECM Standard." Mortgagee Letter 2010–34, September.

Federal Housing Administration (FHA). 2011. "Annual Mortgage Insurance Premium Changes and Guidance on Case Numbers." Mortgagee Letter 2011-10, February.

Federal Housing Administration (FHA). 2012. "Single Family Mortgage Insurance: Annual and Up-Front Mortgage Insurance Premium—Changes." Mortgagee Letter 2012-04, March.

Federal Housing Administration (FHA). 2013a. "Revision of Federal Housing Administration (FHA) Policies Concerning Cancellation of the Annual Mortgage Insurance Premium (MIP) and Increase to the Annual MIP." Mortgagee Letter 2013-04, January.

Federal Housing Administration (FHA). 2013b. "Lender Insurance Program." Mortgagee Letter 2013-12, May.

Federal Housing Administration (FHA). 2013c. "Changes to the Home Equity Conversion Mortgage Program Requirements." Mortgagee Letter 2013–27, September.

Federal Housing Administration (FHA). 2013d. "Home Equity Conversion Mortgage (HECM) Financial Assessment and Property Charge Guide." Mortgagee Letter 2013–28, September.

Federal Housing Administration (FHA). 2014. "Home Equity Conversion Mortgage (HECM) Program: New Principal Limit Factors." Mortgagee Letter 2014-12, June.

Federal Housing Finance Agency (FHFA). 2011. "FHFA Announces Completion of RefCorp Obligation and Approves FHLB Plans to Build Capital." August 5. http://www.fhfa.gov/Media/PublicAffairs/Pages/FHFA-Announces-Completion-of-RefCorp-Obligation-and-Approves-FHLB-Plans-to-Build-Capital.aspx.

Federal Housing Finance Agency (FHFA). 2014a. 2015–2017 Enterprise Housing Goals, 79 Fed. Reg. 54,482, 54,493, and 54,494.

Federal Housing Finance Agency (FHFA). 2014b. Members of Federal Home Loan Banks, 79 Fed. Reg. 54,848–54,881. http://www.gpo.gov/fdsys/pkg/FR-2014-09-12/pdf/2014-21114.pdf.

Federal Housing Finance Agency (FHFA). 2015. *Fannie Mae and Freddie Mac Single-Family Guarantee Fees in 2014*. June 30. http://www.fhfa.gov/AboutUs/Reports/ReportDocuments/GFeeReport6302015.pdf.

Federal Reserve Bank of the United States. 2015a. "Mortgage Debt Outstanding." December. http://www.federalreserve.gov/econresdata/releases/mortoutstand/current.htm.

Federal Reserve Bank of the United States. 2015b. *Z.1 Financial Accounts of the United States: Fourth Quarter 2014*. Washington, D.C.: Federal Reserve Bank of the United States.

Federal Reserve Bank of the United States. 2015c. *Z.1 Financial Accounts of the United States: Historical Annual Tables 2005–2014*. Washington, D.C.: Federal Reserve Bank of the United States.

Feldman, Ron J. and Gary H. Stern. 2009. *Too Big to Fail: The Hazards of Bank Bailouts*. Washington, D.C.: Brookings Institution Press.

Financial Stability Oversight Council. 2011. *Study of the Effects of Size and Complexity of Financial Institutions on Capital Market Efficiency and Economic Growth*. Washington, D.C.: Financial Stability Oversight Council.

Flannery, Mark J. and W. Scott Frame. 2006. "The Federal Home Loan Bank System: The 'Other' GSE." *Economic Review* 91 (3rd Quarter): 33–54.

Foote, Bruce E. 2009. *Assistance in FHA-Insured Home Loans*. Vol. RS229340, Congressional Research Service.

Foote, Christopher L., Kristopher Gerardi, and Paul S. Willen. 2008. "Negative Equity and Foreclosure: Theory and Evidence." *Journal of Urban Economics* 64 (2): 234–45.

Frame, W. Scott. 2003. "Federal Home Loan Bank Mortgage Purchases: Implications for Mortgage Markets." *Economic Review*, Federal Reserve Bank of Atlanta, Third Quarter.

Frame, W. Scott, Andreas Fuster, Joseph Tracy, and James Vickery. 2015. "The Rescue of Fannie Mae and Freddie Mac." *Journal of Economic Perspectives* 29 (2): 25–52.

Frame, W. Scott, Diana Hancock, and Wayne Passmore. 2012. "Federal Home Bank Advances and Commercial Bank Portfolio Composition." *Journal of Money, Credit and Banking* 44 (4): 661–84.

Frame, Scott, Larry Wall, and Lawrence White. 2013. "The Devil's in the Tail: Residential Mortgage Finance and the U.S. Treasury." *Journal of Applied Finance* 23 (2): 61–83.

Frame, W. Scott and Lawrence J. White. 2004. "Regulating Housing GSEs: Thoughts on Institutional Structure and Authorities." *Federal Reserve Bank of Atlanta Economic Review* 89 (2): 87–102.

Freddie Mac. 2012. *Report to the Federal Housing Finance Agency: Housing Finance Reform in the Multifamily Mortgage Market.* McLean, VA: Freddie Mac.

Freddie Mac. 2014. "Multifamily Lenders." Freddie Mac. Retrieved February 7, 2015, from http://www.freddiemac.com/multifamily/sellerservicers/completelist.html.

Frederick, Donald A. 1997. "Coops 101: An Introduction to Cooperatives." Cooperative Information Report no. 55. United States: Department of Agriculture.

Friewald, Nils, Rainer Jankowitsch, and Marti G. Subrahmanyam. 2014. *Transparency and Liquidity in the Structured Product Market.* October.

Fullerton, David J. and C. Duncan MacRae. 1978. "FHA, Racial Discrimination and Urban Mortgages." *Real Estate Economics* 6 (4): 451–70.

Fuster, Andreas and James Vickery. 2014. "Securitization and the Fixed-Rate Mortgage." Federal Reserve Bank of New York Staff Report no. 594, June (original version issued January 2013). http://www.newyorkfed.org/research/staff_reports/sr594.pdf.

Gabriel, Stuart A. and Stuart S. Rosenthal. 1991. "Credit Rationing, Race, and the Mortgage Market." *Journal of Urban Economics* 29 (3): 371–79.

Geiger, Daniel. 2014. "CMBS Market Comes Charging Back to Life." *Crain's New York Business*, May 6. http://www.crainsnewyork.com/article/20140506/REAL_ESTATE/305049995/cmbs-market-comes-charging-back-to-life.

General Accounting Office (now Government Accountability Office). 1990. "Government-Sponsored Enterprises: The Government's Exposure to Risks." Report GGD-90-97, August 15. http://www.gao.gov/assets/150/149461.pdf.

Ginnie Mae. 2014. "Multifamily Program." Ginnie Mae, last modified November 13. http://www.ginniemae.gov/products_programs/programs/Pages/Multi_family Program.aspx.

Goodman, Laurie. 2014. "A Realistic Assessment of Housing Finance Reform." Washington, D.C.: Urban Institute, August. http://www.urban.org/sites/default/files/alfresco/publication-pdfs/413205-A-Realistic-Assessment-of-Housing-Finance-Reform.PDF.

Goodman, Laurie and Jun Zhu. 2014a. "The GSE Reform Debate: How Much Capital is Enough?" *Journal of Structured Finance*, 20 (1), Spring: 37–49.

Goodman, Laurie and Jun Zhu. 2014b. *GSE Reform: Diversification Is Critical in Sizing the Capital Requirement in the New Regime*. Washington, D.C.: Urban Institute.

Goodman, Laurie, Jun Zhu, and Taz George. 2015. "Four Million Mortgage Loans Missing from 2009 to 2013 Due to Tight Credit Standards." *Urban Institute*, April 2. http://www.urban.org/urban-wire/four-million-mortgage-loans-missing-2009-2013-due-tight-credit-standards.

Goodman, Laurie S. and Landon D. Parsons. 2012. "The Case for Alternative Credit Enhancement Structures in GSE Securitizations." *Journal of Structured Finance* 18 (1): 76–84.

Gorton, Gary and Guillermo Ordoñez. 2014. "Collateral Crises." *American Economic Review* 104 (2): 343–78.

Gould Ellen, Ingrid, John Napier Tye, and Mark Willis. 2010. *Improving U.S. Housing Finance through Reform of Fannie Mae and Freddie Mac: Assessing the Options*. New York, NY: Furman Center for Real Estate and Urban Policy.

Gould Ellen, Ingrid and Mark Willis. 2011. "Improving U.S. Housing Finance Through Reform of Fannie Mae and Freddie Mac: A Framework for Evaluating Alternatives." In *The American Mortgage System: Crisis & Reform*, ed. Susan M. Wachter and Martin Smith, chap. 13. Philadelphia: University of Pennsylvania Press.

Government Accountability Office. 2005. *Mortgage Financing: Additional Action Needed to Manage Risks of FHA-Insured Loans with Down Payment Assistance*. Washington, D.C.: Government Accountability Office.

Government Accountability Office. 2007. "Federal Housing Administration: Decline in the Agency's Market Share Was Associated with Product and Process Developments of Other Mortgage Market Participants." GAO-07-645. Washington, D.C.: Government Accountability Office.

Government Accountability Office. 2010. "The Cooperative Model as a Potential Component of Structural Reform: Options for Fannie Mae and Freddie Mac." GAO-11-33R. November 15.

Green, R., R. Mariano, A. Pavlov, and S. Wachter. 2009. "Misaligned Incentives and Mortgage Lending in Asia." In *Financial Sector Development in the Pacific Rim*, vol. 18 of *East Asia Seminar on Economics*, ed. Takatoshi Ito and Andrew K. Rose, 95–111. Chicago: University of Chicago Press.

Green, Richard K. and Ann B. Schnare. 2009. "The Rise and Fall of Fannie Mae and Freddie Mac: Lessons Learned and Options for Reform." Emperisis LLC Working Paper, November. http://www.usc.edu/schools/price/lusk/research/pdf/wp_2009-1001.pdf.

Green, Richard K. and Susan M. Wachter. 2005. "The American Mortgage in Historical and International Context." *Journal of Economic Perspectives* (19) 4: 93–114.

Griffith, John. 2013. "A Comparison of Plans to Reform Our Housing Finance System." Center For American Progress, July 19. https://www.americanprogress.org/issues/housing/news/2013/07/19/69881/a-comparison-of-plans-to-reform-our-housing-finance-system/.

Guggenmos, Steven, Jun Li, Harut Hovsepyan, Tom Shaffner, and Yu Guan. 2012. "Multifamily Property Valuations." Freddie Mac, April 12. http://www.freddiemac.com/multifamily/pdf/mf_property_valuations.pdf.

Gyourko, Joseph. 2011. "Is FHA the Next Housing Bailout? A Report Prepared for the American Enterprise Institute." Washington, D.C.: American Enterprise Institute.

Gyourko, Joseph, Peter Linneman, and Susan Wachter. 1999. "Analyzing the Relationships among Race, Wealth, and Home Ownership in America." *Journal of Housing Economics* 8 (2): 63–89.

Hancock, Diana and Wayne Passmore. Forthcoming. "How the Federal Reserve's Large-Scale Asset Purchases (LSAPs) Influence Mortgage-Backed Securities (MBS) Yields and U.S. Mortgage Rates." *Real Estate Economics.*

Hancock, Diana and Wayne Passmore. 2010. "An Analysis of Government Guarantees and the Functioning of Asset-Backed Securities Markets." Finance and Economics Discussion Series Paper 46. Washington: Federal Reserve Board.

Hancock, Diana and Wayne Passmore. 2011a. "Catastrophic Mortgage Insurance and the Reform of Fannie Mae and Freddie Mac." In *The Future of Housing Finance: Restructuring the U.S. Residential Mortgage Market*, ed. Martin Baily, 111–45. Washington, D.C.: Brookings Institution Press.

Hancock, Diana and Wayne Passmore. 2011b. "Did the Federal Reserve's MBS Purchase Program Lower Mortgage Rates?" *Journal of Monetary Economics* 58 (5): 498–514.

Hansmann, Henry. 1996. *Ownership of Enterprise.* Cambridge, MA: Harvard University Press.

Hansmann, Henry. 1999. "Cooperative Firms in Theory and Practice." *LTA [Liiketaloudellinen Aikakauskirja*, the Finnish Journal of Business Economics] 48 (4), April: 387–403.

Hanson, Samuel G., Anil K. Kashyap, and Jeremy C. Stein. 2011. "A Macroprudential Approach to Financial Regulation." *Journal of Economic Perspectives* 25 (1): 3–28.

Hanson, Samuel G., David S. Scharfstein, and Adi Sunderam. 2014. "Fiscal Risk and the Portfolio of Government Programs." Harvard Business School Working Paper. Cambridge, MA: Harvard University Press.

Harrington, Scott and Greg Niehaus. 2003. "Capital, Corporate Income Taxes, and Catastrophe Insurance." *Journal of Financial Intermediation* 12 (4), October: 365–89.

Haughwout, A., R.W. Peach, J. Sporn, and J. Tracy. 2012. "The supply side of the housing boom and bust of the 2000s." In *Housing and the financial crisis*, ed. Edward L. Glaeser and Todd Sinai, 69–104. Chicago: University of Chicago Press.

Haurin, Donald, Chao Ma, Stephanie Moulton, Maximilian Schmeiser, Jason Seligman, and Wei Shi. 2014. "Spatial Variation in Reverse Mortgages Usage: House Price Dynamics and Consumer Selection." *Journal of Real Estate Finance and Economics:* 1–26.

Henehan, Brian M. and Bruce L. Anderson. 2001. "Considering Cooperation: A Guide for New Cooperative Development." Cornell University College of Agriculture and Life Sciences Working Paper, February. Ithaca, NY: Cornell University Press.

Hermalin, Benjamin and Dwight Jaffee. 1996. "The Privatization of Fannie Mae and Freddie Mac: Implications for Mortgage Industry Structure." In *Studies on Privatizing Fannie Mae and Freddie Mac,* 225–302. Washington, D.C.: U.S. Department of Housing and Urban Development, Office of Policy Development and Research, U.S. General Accounting Office. U.S. Department of the Treasury. Congressional Budget Office.

Herring, R. J. and S. M. Wachter. 1999. "Real Estate Booms and Banking Busts: An International Perspective." *Wharton Real Estate Review* 4 (1), Spring 2000.

Herring, R. and S. Wachter. 2003. "Bubbles in real estate markets." In *Asset Price Bubbles: Implications for Monetary, Regulatory, and International Policies,* ed. George Kaufman. 217–30, Cambridge, MA: MIT Press.

Hirschman, Albert. 1970. *Exit, Voice and Loyalty: Responses to Decline in Firms, Organizations, and States.* Cambridge, MA: Harvard University Press.

Holmes, Andrew and Paul Horvitz. 1994. "Mortgage Redlining: Race, Risk, and Demand." *Journal of Finance* 49 (1): 81–99.

Holmstrom, Bengt. 1999. "Future of Cooperatives: A Corporate Perspective." *LTA* 4 (99), April: 404–17.

Hopkins, Cheyenne and Clea Benson. 2014. "Senate Bill Seeks to Wind Down Fannie Mae in Five Years." *Bloomberg News,* March 17. http://www.bloomberg.com/news/2014-03-16/senate-fannie-mae-wind-down-bill-leaves-investor-fate-to-courts.html.

Hunt, J. P., R. Stanton, and N. Wallace. 2012. "U.S. Residential-Mortgage Transfer Systems: A Data-Management Crisis." In *Handbook of Financial Risk,* vol. 4, *Data Risk,* ed. Margarita S. Brose. Cambridge, England: Cambridge University Press.

Immergluck, D. 2011. "From Minor to Major Player: The Geography of FHA Lending During the U.S. Mortgage Crisis." *Journal of Urban Affairs* 33 (1): 1–20.

Inside Mortgage Finance. 2004. *Mortgage Market Statistical Annual—2004 Yearbook.* Bethesda, MD: Inside Mortgage Finance Publications.

Inside Mortgage Finance. 2006. *Mortgage Market Statistical Annual—2006 Yearbook.* Bethesda, MD: Inside Mortgage Finance Publications.

Inside Mortgage Finance. 2008. *Mortgage Market Statistical Annual—2008 Yearbook.* Bethesda, MD: Inside Mortgage Finance Publications.

Inside Mortgage Finance. 2010. *Mortgage Market Statistical Annual—2010 Yearbook.* Bethesda, MD: Inside Mortgage Finance Publications.

Inside Mortgage Finance. 2012. *Mortgage Market Statistical Annual—2012 Yearbook.* Bethesda, MD: Inside Mortgage Finance Publications.

Inside Mortgage Finance. 2013. *Mortgage Market Statistical Annual—2013 Yearbook.* Bethesda, MD: Inside Mortgage Finance Publications.

Inside Mortgage Finance. 2014a. "Jumbo, Home-Equity Lending Show Signs of Strength in 2013, Nibble at Agency Hegemony." *Inside MBS & ABS* 2014 (9). Retrieved April 2014 from http://www.insidemortgagefinance.com/issues/imfpubs_imf/2014_9

/latest_data/Jumbo-Home-Equity-Lending-Show-Signs-of-Strength-in-2013-
    -1000026373-1.html.
Inside Mortgage Finance. 2014b. *Mortgage Market Statistical Annual—2014 Yearbook.*
    Bethesda, MD: Inside Mortgage Finance Publications.
Inside Mortgage Finance. 2014c. "Securitization Market Shivers in Late 2013 As MBS
    and ABS Production Drops Sharply." *Inside MBS & ABS* 2014 (1). Retrieved July
    2014 from http://www.insidemortgagefinance.com/issues/imfpubs_ima/2014_1
    /latest_data/Securitization-Market-Shivers-in-Late-2013-As-MBS-and-ABS
    -Production-Drops—1000025728-1.html.
Inside Mortgage Finance. 2015. *Mortgage Market Statistical Annual—2015 Yearbook.*
    Bethesda, MD: Inside Mortgage Finance Publications.
Integrated Financial Engineering, Inc. (IFE) 2010a. *Actuarial Review of the Federal
    Housing Administration Mutual Mortgage Insurance Fund Forward Loans for
    Fiscal Year 2010.* Washington, D.C.: U.S. Department of Housing and Urban
    Development.
Integrated Financial Engineering, Inc. (IFE) 2010b. *Actuarial Review of the Federal
    Housing Administration Mutual Mortgage Insurance Fund HECM Loans for Fiscal
    Year 2010.* Washington, D.C.: U.S. Department of Housing and Urban Development.
Integrated Financial Engineering, Inc. (IFE) 2012. *Actuarial Review of the Federal
    Housing Administration Mutual Mortgage Insurance Fund Forward Loans for
    Fiscal Year 2012.* Washington, D.C.: U.S. Department of Housing and Urban
    Development.
Integrated Financial Engineering, Inc. (IFE) 2014a. *Actuarial Review of the Federal
    Housing Administration Mutual Mortgage Insurance Fund Forward Loans for
    Fiscal Year 2014.* Washington, D.C.: U.S. Department of Housing and Urban
    Development.
Integrated Financial Engineering, Inc. (IFE) 2014b. *Actuarial Review of the Fed-
    eral Housing Administration Mutual Mortgage Insurance Fund HECM Loans for
    Fiscal Year 2014.* Washington, D.C.: U.S. Department of Housing and Urban
    Development.
Jaffee, Dwight. 2010a. "Reforming the U.S. Mortgage Market Through Private Market
    Incentives." University of California–Berkeley, Haas School of Business Working
    Paper, November. Berkeley, CA: University of California Press.
Jaffee, Dwight M. 2010b. "The Role of the GSEs and Housing Policy in the Financial
    Crisis." Washington, D.C.: Financial Crisis Inquiry Commission, February.
Jaffee, Dwight M. and John M. Quigley. 2007. "Housing Policy, Mortgage Policy, and
    the Federal Housing Administration." University of California–Berkeley Working
    Paper W07-004. Berkeley, CA: Institute of Business and Economic Research.
Jeanne, O. and A. Korinek. 2010. "Managing Credit Booms and Busts: A Pigouvian
    Taxation Approach." NBER Working Paper no. w16377. Cambridge, MA: National
    Bureau of Economic Research.

Jeske, Karsten, Dirk Kruger, and Kurt Mitman. 2013. "Housing, Mortgage Bailout Guarantees, and the Macro Economy." *Journal of Monetary Economics* 60: 917–35.

Joint Center for Housing Studies of Harvard University. 2011. *America's Rental Housing: Meeting Challenges, Building on Opportunities.* Cambridge, MA: Harvard University Press.

Joint Center for Housing Studies of Harvard University. 2013. *America's Rental Housing: Evolving Markets and Needs.* Cambridge, MA: Harvard University Press.

Joint Center for Housing Studies of Harvard University. 2014. *The State of the Nation's Housing.* Cambridge, MA: Harvard University Press.

Joint Committee on Taxation. 2014. *Estimates of Federal Tax Expenditures for Fiscal Years 2014–2018.* Washington, D.C.: Congress of the United States.

Jones, David and John Mingo. 1999. "Credit Risk Modeling and Internal Capital Allocation Processes: Implications for a Models-Based Regulatory Bank Capital Standard." *Journal of Economics and Business* 51 (2): 79–108.

Karikari, J. A., Voicu, I., and Fang, I. 2011. "FHA vs. Subprime Mortgage Originations: Is FHA the Answer to Subprime Lending?" *Journal of Real Estate Finance and Economics* 43 (4): 441–58.

Kashyap, Anil K., Raghuram G. Rajan, and Jeremy C. Stein. 2008. "Rethinking Capital Regulation." Proceedings of the Federal Reserve Bank of Kansas City Economic Policy Symposium, Jackson Hole, WY, August, 431–71.

Keys, Benjamin J., Tanmoy Mukherjee, Amit Seru, and Vikrant Vig. 2010. "Did Securitization Lead to Lax Screening? Evidence from Subprime Loans." *Quarterly Journal of Economics* 125 (1): 307–62.

Kinney, Mary. 2013. "The Fundamental Role of Multifamily Housing." *Mortgage Banking* 72 (10), January.

Kochhar, Rakesh and Richard Fry. 2014. "Wealth Inequality Has Widened Along Racial, Ethnic Lines Since End of Great Recession." Pew Research Center.

Krimminger, Michael and Mark A. Calabria. 2015. "The Conservatorships of Fannie Mae and Freddie Mac: Actions Violate HERA and Established Insolvency Principles." Cato Working Paper no. 26, February 9. http://www.cato.org/publications/working-paper/conservatorships-fannie-mae-freddie-mac-actions-violate-hera-established.

Kroszner, Randall. 2009. "The Community Reinvestment Act and the Recent Mortgage Crisis." In *Revisiting the CRA: Perspectives on the Future of the Community Reinvestment Act.* New York and San Francisco: Federal Reserve Bank.

Lai, R. N. and R. Van Order. 2014. "Securitization, Risk Taking and the Option to Change Strategy." *Real Estate Economics* 42 (2): 343–62.

Lamm-Tennant, Joan and Laura T. Starks. 2001. "Stock Versus Mutual Ownership Structures: The Risk Implications." *Journal of Business* 66 (January): 29–46.

Lea, Michael. 2010. *International Comparisons of Mortgage Product Offerings.* Research Institute for Housing America, September.

Lee, D., C. J. Mayer, and J. Tracy. 2012. "A New Look at Second Liens." NBER Working Paper no. w18269. Cambridge, MA: National Bureau of Economic Research.

Lee, Soon-Jae, David Mayer, and Clifford W. Smith. 1997. "Guaranty Funds and Risk-Taking: Evidence from the Insurance Industry." *Journal of Financial Economics* 44 (April): 3–24.

Levitin, Adam J. 2013. "The Paper Chase: Securitization, Foreclosure, and the Uncertainty of Mortgage Title." *Duke Law Journal* 63 (3): 637–734.

Levitin, Adam J., Andrey D. Pavlov, and Susan M. Wachter. 2012. "Will Private Risk-Capital Return? The Dodd-Frank Act and the Housing Market." *Yale Journal on Regulation* 29 (1): 155–80.

Levitin, A. J. and S. M. Wachter. 2012. "Explaining the Housing Bubble." *Georgetown Law Journal* 100 (4): 1177–1258.

Levitin, Adam J. and Susan M. Wachter. 2015. "Second Liens and the Leverage Option." *Vanderbilt Law Review* 68. University of Pennsylvania, Institute for Law & Economics Research Paper No. 15-13.

Linneman, Peter, Isaac F. Megbolugbe, Susan M. Wachter, and Man Cho. 1997. "Do Borrowing Constraints Change U.S. Homeownership Rates?" *Journal of Housing Economics* 6 (4): 318–33.

Linneman, Peter and Susan Wachter. 1989. "The Impacts of Borrowing Constraints on Homeownership." *Real Estate Economics* 17 (4): 389–402.

Lockhart, James B. 2011. "Underwater: Are We Drowning or Surfacing?" In "The Future of U.S. Housing Finance: Five Points of View," *Journal of Structured Finance* 17 (2): 36–80.

Lucas, Deborah. 2011. "The Budgetary Cost of Fannie Mae and Freddie Mac and Options for the Future Federal Role in the Secondary Mortgage Market." Testimony before the Committee on the Budget, U.S. House of Representatives, June 2. https://www.cbo.gov/sites/default/files/06-02-gses_testimony.pdf.

Lucas, Deborah and Robert McDonald. 2007. "Valuing Government Guarantees: Fannie and Freddie Revisited." In *Measuring and Managing Federal Financial Risk*, ed. Deborah Lucas. Chicago: University of Chicago Press.

Lucas, Deborah and David Torregrosa. 2004. *Updated Estimates of the Subsidies to the Housing GSEs*. Washington, D.C.: Congressional Budget Office.

McCoy, P. A., A. D. Pavlov, and S. M. Wachter. 2009. "Systemic Risk Through Securitization: The Result of Deregulation and Regulatory Failure." *Connecticut Law Review* 41: 493.

McCoy, Patricia A. 2008. "The Moral Hazard Implications of Deposit Insurance: Theory and Evidence." *Current Developments in Monetary and Financial Law* 5: 417–41.

McKenzie, Joseph A. 2002. "A Reconsideration of the Jumbo/Non-Jumbo Mortgage Rate Differential." *Journal of Real Estate Finance and Economics* 25 (2–3): 197–213.

Merrill Lynch. 2015. "BofA Merrill Lynch Index Yields." Retrieved January 2015 from https://research.stlouisfed.org/fred2/categories/32347.

Mester, Loretta J. 2010. "Scale Economies in Banking and Financial Regulatory Reform." *Region* 24 (September): 10–13.

Mian, Atif and Amir Sufi. 2009. "The Consequences of Mortgage Credit Expansion: Evidence from the U.S. Mortgage Default Crisis." *Quarterly Journal of Economics* 124 (4): 1449–96.

Mian, Atif and Amir Sufi. 2015. "Household Debt and Defaults from 2000–2010: Facts from Credit Bureau Data." Kreisman Working Papers Series in Housing Law and Policy no. 28. Chicago: University of Chicago Press.

Min, David. 2013. "How Government Guarantees Promote Housing Finance Stability." *Harvard Journal on Legislation* 50: 482.

Morgenson, Gretchen and Joshua Rosner. 2011. *Reckless Endangerment.* New York: Henry Holt.

Mortgage-Backed Securities Online (eMBS). 2015. "Fixed Rate Issuance by Agency." Retrieved March 10, 2015, from http://www.embs.com/secure/cgi-bin/asp/Aggr .asp?AggrName=Issuance&Lvl=AGY.

Moss, David A. 2004. *When All Else Fails: Government as the Ultimate Risk Manager.* Cambridge, MA: Harvard University Press.

Mosser, Patricia C., Joseph Tracy, and Joshua Wright. 2013. "The Capital Structure and Governance of a Mortgage Securitization Utility." Federal Reserve Bank of New York Staff Report no. 644, October.

Moulton, Stephanie, Donald R. Haurin, and Wei Shi. 2014. "An Analysis of Default Risk in the Home Equity Conversion Mortgage (HECM) Program." Social Science Research Network, July 20. http://ssrn.com/abstract=2468247.

Moulton, S. and R. Quercia. 2013. "Access and Sustainability for First Time Homebuyers: The Evolving Role of State Housing Finance Agencies." Cambridge, MA: Joint Center for Housing Studies, Harvard University.

Munnell, Alicia H., Natalia Orlova, and Anthony Webb. 2012. "How Important Is Asset Allocation to Financial Security in Retirement?" CRR WP 2012-13. Chesnut Hill, MA: Center for Retirement Research, Boston College.

Munnell, Alicia H., Matthew S. Rutledge, and Anthony Webb. 2014. "Are Retirees Falling Short? Reconciling the Conflicting Evidence." CRR WP 2014-16. Chestnut Hill, MA: Center for Retirement Research, Boston College.

Murphy, Michael E. 2012. "Fannie Mae and Freddie Mac: Legal Implication of a Successor Cooperative." *DePaul Business & Commercial Law Journal* 10 (Winter): 171–211.

Nakajima, Makoto and Irina A. Telyukova. 2013. "Reverse Mortgage Loans: A Quantitative Analysis." Federal Reserve Bank of Philadelphia Working Paper 13-27, June 4.

Nakamura, Leonard. 2010. "Durable Financial Regulation: Monitoring Instruments as a Counterpart to Regulating Financial Institutions." Federal Reserve Bank of Philadelphia Working Paper 10-22.

Narasimhan, Shekar. 2013. "Housing Finance Reform: Essential Elements of the Multifamily Housing Finance System." Statement before the Senate Committee on Banking, Housing and Urban Development, 113th Congress.

Nelson, Arthur C. 2009. "The New Urbanity: The Rise of a New America." *Annals of the American Academy of Political and Social Science* 626 (1): 192–208.

Nothaft, Frank E., James E. Pearce, and Stevan Stevanovic. 2002. "Debt Spreads between GSEs and Other Corporations." *Journal of Real Estate Finance and Economics* 25: 151–72.

Office of Investor Education and Advocacy. 2013. *Interest Rate Risk—When Interest Rates Go Up, Prices of Fixed-Rate Bonds Fall.* Washington, D.C.: Securities and Exchange Commission.

Office of Management and Budget (OMB). 2014. *Loan Guarantees: Subsidy Reestimates.* Washington, D.C.: Office of Management and Budget.

Packel, Israel. 1970. *The Organization and Operation of Cooperatives.* Philadelphia: Joint Committee on Continuing Legal Education of the American Law Institute and the American Bar Association.

Passmore, Wayne. 2005. "The GSE Implicit Subsidy and the Value of Government Ambiguity." *Real Estate Economics* 33 (3): 465–86.

Passmore, Wayne, Shane M. Sherlund, and Gillian Burgess. 2005. "The Effect of Housing Government-Sponsored Enterprises on Mortgage Rates." *Real Estate Economics* 33 (3): 427–63.

Pavlov, A. and S. Wachter. 2009a. "Mortgage Put Options and Real Estate Markets" *Journal of Real Estate Finance and Economics* 38 (1): 89–103.

Pavlov, Andrey and Susan M. Wachter. 2009b. "Systemic Risk and Market Institutions." *Yale Journal on Regulation* 26 (1): 445–55.

Pavlov, A., S. Wachter, and A. A. Zevelev. Forthcoming. "Transparency in the Mortgage Market." *Journal of Financial Services Research.*

Peterson, Christopher L. 2011. "Two Faces: Demystifying the Mortgage Electronic Registration System's Land Title Theory." *William & Mary Law Review* 53 (1): 111.

Pinto, Edward J. 2012. *How the FHA Hurts Working-Class Families and Communities.* Washington, D.C.: American Enterprise Institute.

Piskorski, Tomasz, Amit Seru, and Vikrant Vig. 2010. "Securitization and Distressed Loan Renegotiation: Evidence from the Subprime Mortgage Crisis." *Journal of Financial Economics* 97 (September): 369–97.

Price Waterhouse. 1990. *An Actuarial Review of the Federal Housing Administration's Mutual Mortgage Insurance Fund.* Washington, D.C.: U.S. Department of Housing and Urban Development.

Protess, Ben. 2010. "Thrift Banks' Long Decline." *N.Y. Times DealBook,* December 8. http://dealbook.nytimes.com/2010/12/08/thrifts-last-stand/.

Qi, Ming and Xiaolong Yang. 2009. "Loss Given Default of High Loan-to-Value Residential Mortgages." *Journal of Banking & Finance* 33 (May): 788–99.

Quercia, Roberto G., Lei Ding, and Carolina Reid. 2012. *Balancing Risk and Access: Underwriting Standards for Qualified Residential Mortgages*. Chapel Hill, NC: UNC Center for Community Capital.

Quercia, Roberto G., George W. McCarthy, and Susan M. Wachter. 2003. "The Impacts of Affordable Lending Efforts on Homeownership Rates." *Journal of Housing Economics* 12 (1): 29–59.

Quercia, Roberto G. and Michael A. Stegman. 1992. "Residential Mortgage Default: A Review of the Literature." *Journal of Housing Research* 3 (2): 341–79.

Rajan, Raghuram G. 2005. "Has Financial Development Made the World Riskier?" Proceedings of the Federal Reserve Bank of Kansas City Economic Policy Symposium, Jackson Hole, WY, August, 313–69.

Rajan, U., A. Seru, and V. Vig, 2010. "The Failure of Models That Predict Failure: Distance, Incentives and Defaults." *Chicago GSB Research Paper* (08–19).

Remy, Mitchell. 2014. *Fair-Value Estimates of the Cost of Selected Federal Credit Programs from 2015 to 2024*. Washington, D.C.: Congressional Budget Office.

Rodda, David T., Christopher Herbert, and Hin-Kin Lam. 2000. *Evaluation Report of FHA's Home Equity Conversion Mortgage Insurance Demonstration*. Washington, D.C.: U.S Department of Housing and Urban Development. DU100C000005978, Task Order no. 12.

Scharfstein, David and Adi Sunderam. 2011. "The Economics of Housing Finance Reform." In *The Future of Housing Finance: Restructuring the U.S. Residential Mortgage Market*, ed. Martin N. Baily, 146–98. Washington, D.C.: Brookings Institution Press.

Scharfstein, David and Adi Sunderam. 2014. "Market Power in Mortgage Lending and the Monetary Transmission Mechanism." Harvard Business School Working Paper. Cambridge, MA: Harvard University Press. (Formerly "Concentration in Mortgage Lending, Refinancing Activity, and Mortgage Rates." NBER Working Paper 19156, June 2013. Cambridge, MA: National Bureau of Economic Research.)

Securities Industry and Financial Markets Association (SIFMA). n.d. "U.S. Bond Market Issuance and Outstanding." Retrieved March 10, 2015, from http://www.sifma.org/research/statistics.aspx.

Segal, William and Edward J. Szymanoski. 1998. "Fannie Mae, Freddie Mac, and the Multifamily Mortgage Market." *Cityscape* 4 (1): 59–91.

Seidman, Ellen, Phillip Swagel, Sarah Wartell, and Mark Zandi. 2013. "A Pragmatic Plan for Housing Reform." Milken Institute, Moody's Analytics, and Urban Institute Working Paper, June 19.

Sherlund, Shane. 2008. "The Jumbo-Conforming Spread: A Semiparametric Approach." Finance and Economics Discussion Series 2008-01. Washington, D.C.: Federal Reserve Board.

Shiller, R. J. 2006. "Long-Term Perspectives on the Current Boom in Home Prices." *Economists' Voice* 3 (4): 1–11.

Shiller, R. J. 2012. "Finance and the Good Society." *Finance and Development-English Edition* 49 (1): 53.

Shiller, Robert. 2014. "Why Is Housing Finance Still Stuck in Such a Primitive Stage?" *American Economic Review* 104 (5): 73–76.

Shin, H. S. 2009. "Securitization and Financial Stability." *Economic Journal* 199 (536): 309–32.

Silver-Greenberg, Jessica. 2012. "As Foreclosure Problems Persist, Fed Seeks More Fines." *New York Times*, April 1, B1.

Smith, Scott and Jesse Weiher. 2012. "Countercyclical Capital Regime: A Proposed Design and Empirical Evaluation." FHFA Working Paper 12-2.

Song, Zhaogang and Haoxiang Zhu. 2014. "Mortgage Dollar Roll." MIT Sloan School of Management, April 5. Cambridge, MA: MIT University Press.

Sparshott, Jeffrey and Kris Hudson. 2015. "Sluggish Housing Starts Belie Builders' Confidence." *Wall Street Journal,* April 16, 2015. Retrieved April 25, 2015, from http://www.wsj.com/articles/housing-starts-up-2-in-march-1429187637.

Stearns, Richard C. n.d. *Racial Content of FHA Underwriting Practices, 1934–1962.* Baltimore, MD: Langsdale Library, University of Baltimore.

Svenstrup, M. 2002. *Mortgage Choice—The Danish Case.* Department of Finance, The Aarhus School of Business. November 29.

Swagel, Philip L. 2010. "Testimony before House Committee on Financial Services, on the Future of Housing Finance—A Review of Proposals to Address Market Structure and Transition." September 29. Washington, D.C.

Swanson, Jann. 2013. "FHA Fund Doesn't Need Treasury Draw After All; Groups Call for Fee Reduction." *Mortgage News Daily,* March 4, 2013. http://www.mortgagenewsdaily.com/03042014_hud_budget_fha.asp.

Szymanoski, Edward J., William Reeder, Padmasini Raman, and John Comeau. 2012. "The FHA Single Family Insurance Program: Performing a Needed Role in the Housing Finance Market." U.S. Department of Housing and Urban Development, Office of Policy Development and Research Worker Paper HF-019, December 31. https://www.huduser.gov/portal/publications/hsgfin/fha_singlefamily_dec2012.html.

Tarullo, Daniel. 2011. "Industrial Organization and Systemic Risk: An Agenda for Further Research." Speech, September 15. http://www.federalreserve.gov/newsevents/speech/tarullo20110915a.htm.

Terris, Harry and Marc Hochstein. 2010. "Eye on GSE Reform." *American Banker Association* 175 (December): 7.

Thomas, Jason. 2013. "Fannie, Freddie, and the Crisis." *National Affairs* 17 (Fall). http://www.nationalaffairs.com/publications/detail/fannie-freddie-and-the-crisis.

Thomas, Jason and Robert Van Order. 2010. "Housing Policy, Subprime Markets, and Fannie Mae and Freddie Mac: What We Know, What We Think We Know and What We Don't Know." George Washington University Working Paper, Novem-

ber. Washington, D.C.: George Washington University Press. http://research
.stlouisfed.org/conferences/gse/Van_Order.pdf.

TRACE. 2014. "Securitized Product Tables." Transaction Information. Retrieved
March 10, 2015, from http://www.finra.org/Industry/Compliance/Market
Transparency/TRACE/FactBook/index.htm.

U.S. Census Bureau. 2002. *American Housing Survey for the United States: 2001.* Washington, D.C.: U.S. Government Printing Office.

U.S. Census Bureau. 2015a. *Residential Vacancies and Homeownership in fhe Fourth
Quarter 2014.* January 29. http://www.census.gov/housing/hvs/files/qtr414
/currenthvspress.pdf.

U.S. Census Bureau. 2015b. "Selected Housing Characteristics 2012 American Community Survey 1-Year Estimates." Retrieved April 29, 2015, from http://factfinder2
.census.gov/faces/tableservices/jsf/pages/productview.xhtml?pid=ACS_12_1YR
_CP04&prodType=table.

U.S. Congressional Budget Office (CBO). 2001. *Federal Subsidies and the Housing GSEs.*
Washington, D.C.: U.S. Government Printing Office.

U.S. Congressional Budget Office (CBO). 2004. *Updated Estimates of the Subsidies to
the Housing GSEs.* Washington, D.C.: U.S. Congressional Budget Office.

U.S. Department of Housing and Urban Development. 2011. *Annual Report to Congress Fiscal Year 2011 Financial Status FHA Mutual Mortgage Insurance Fund.*
Washington, D.C.: U.S. Department of Housing and Urban Development.

U.S. Department of Housing and Urban Development. 2013. *Annual Report to Con-
gress Regarding the Financial Status of the FHA Mutual Mortgage Insurance Fund
Fiscal Year 2013.* Washington, D.C.: U.S. Department of Housing and Urban
Development.

U.S. Department of Housing and Urban Development. 2014. *Annual Report to Con-
gress Regarding the Financial Status of the FHA Mutual Mortgage Insurance Fund
Fiscal Year 2014.* Washington, D.C.: U.S. Department of Housing and Urban
Development.

U.S. Department of the Treasury. 2012. "Treasury Department Announces Further
Steps to Expedite Wind Down of Fannie Mae and Freddie Mac." August 17. http://
www.treasury.gov/press-center/press-releases/Pages/tg1684.aspx.

U.S. Department of the Treasury, Federal Reserve System, and Federal Deposit Insurance Corporation. 2012. "Regulatory Capital Rules: Standardized Approach for
Risk-weighted Assets; Market Discipline and Disclosure Requirements." June 18.
https://www.fdic.gov/news/board/2012/2012-06-12_notice_dis-d.pdf.

U.S. Department of the Treasury and U.S. Department of Housing and Urban Development. 2011. *Reforming America's Housing Finance Market: A Report to Congress.*
Washington, D.C.

U.S. House of Representatives. 2010. "Dodd-Frank Wall Street Reform and Consumer
Protection Act." Conference Report, June 29.

U.S. Securities and Exchange Commission. 2014. "Form 10-K: Federal Home Loan Mortgage Corporation." Washington, D.C.: Securities and Exchange Commission. http://www.freddiemac.com/investors/er/pdf/10k_021915.pdf.

Vandell, Kerry D. 1995. "FHA Restructuring Proposals: Alternatives and Implications." *Housing Policy Debate* 6 (2): 299.

Vickery, James and Joshua Wright. 2010. "TBA Trading and Liquidity in the Agency MBS Market." Federal Reserve Bank of New York Staff Report no. 468, August.

Vickery, James and Joshua Wright. 2013. "TBA Trading and Liquidity in the Agency MBS Market." *Economic Policy Review of the Federal Reserve Bank of New York.* May. http://www.newyorkfed.org/research/epr/2013/1212vick.pdf.

Wachter, Susan M. Forthcoming. "Credit Supply and Housing Prices in National and Local Markets." *Public Finance Review.*

Wachter, Susan. 2014. "The Market Structure of Securitisation and the US Housing Bubble." *National Institute Economic Review* 230 (1): R34–R44.

Wachter, Susan M. 2015. "The Housing and Credit Bubbles in the United States and Europe: A Comparison." *Journal of Money, Credit and Banking* 47 (1): 37–42.

Wallison, Peter J., Thomas H. Stanton, and Bert Ely. 2004. *Privatizing Fannie Mae, Freddie Mac and the Federal Home Loan Banks.* Washington, D.C.: American Enterprise Institute.

Weicher, John C. 1995. Comment on Kerry D. Vandell's "FHA Restructuring Proposals: Alternatives and Implications." *Housing Policy Debate* 6 (2): 417–37.

White, Alan M. 2012. "Losing the Paper—Mortgage Assignments, Note Transfers and Consumer Protection." *Loyola Consumer Law Review* 24 (4): 468–504.

White, Lawrence J. 2004. "Fannie Mae, Freddie Mac and Housing Finance: Why True Privatization Is Good Public Policy." Policy Analysis no. 528, October 7. Washington, D.C.: Cato Institute.

White, Tom and Charlie Wilkins. 2013. *Moving Toward a Viable Multifamily Debt Market with No Ongoing Federal Guarantee.* Washington, D.C.: American Enterprise Institute.

Whitman, Dale A. Forthcoming. "Transferring Nonnegotiable Mortgage Notes." *Florida A&M Law Journal.*

Whitman, Dale A. 2014. "What We Have Learned from the Mortgage Crisis About Transferring Mortgage Loans." *American Bar Association Real Property, Trust & Estate Law Journal* 49 (1): 1–70.

Wilson, Ellen and Robert R. Callis. 2013. "Who Could Afford to Buy a Home in 2009? Affordability of Buying a Home in the United States." Current Housing Reports, May. Washington, D.C.: U.S. Census Bureau.

Woodward, Susan and Robert Hall. 2009. "Lessons Learned and Options for Reform: What to Do About Fannie Mae and Freddie Mac?" Stanford University Working Paper. Stanford, CA: Stanford University Press. http://woodwardhall.wordpress .com/2009/01/28/what-to-do-about-fannie-mae-and-freddie-mac/.

Zandi, Mark and Cristian deRitis. 2010. "What If There Were no FHA?" Moody's Analytics: Economic & Consumer Credit Analytics, May. https://www.economy.com/mark-zandi/documents/2010-10-01-What-If-There-Were-No-FHA.pdf.

Zandi, Mark and Cris deRitis. 2011. "The Future of the Mortgage Finance System." Moody's Analytics: Economic & Consumer Credit Analytics, special report, February 7. http://www.economy.com/mark-zandi/documents/mortgage-finance-reform-020711.pdf.

Zandi, Mark and Cristian deRitis. 2013. "Evaluating Corker-Warner." Moody's Analytics: Economic & Consumer Credit Analytics, July. https://www.economy.com/mark-zandi/documents/2013-07-08-Evaluating-Corker-Warner.pdf.

Zandi, Mark and Cristian deRitis. 2015. "The Case for Lower FHA Premiums." Moody's Analytics: Economic & Consumer Credit Analytics, January. https://www.economy.com/getlocal?q=5cc421dd-4480-4961-b576-2594d0aab92e&app=eccafile.

Zanjani, George. 2007. "Regulation, Capital, and the Evolution of Organizational Form in US Life Insurance." *American Economic Review* 97 (3): 973–83.

CONTRIBUTORS

W. Scott Frame is a senior policy advisor at the Federal Reserve Bank of Atlanta. His major fields of study are financial institutions and real estate. Frame has been with the Federal Reserve Bank of Atlanta since 2001, although he spent two years as the Belk Distinguished Professor of Finance at the University of North Carolina at Charlotte. He was actively involved with the response to the financial crisis in various ways, including as a special advisor to the U.S. Treasury Department (2008) and as a consultant to the President's Council of Economic Advisers (2010). Frame has published widely in economics and finance journals. He received his doctorate in economics in 1996 and his master's degree in economics in 1993, both from the University of Georgia.

Meghan Grant is a research analyst on the Open Markets Desk of the Federal Reserve Bank of New York. She is a member of the mortgage markets team, where she conducts fundamental MBS research and designs tools used in the Fed's daily analytical and operational work. Prior to joining the MBS staff, she was an analyst on the Fed's Domestic Money Markets Desk, where she conducted the Fed's reverse repo operations and calculated the federal funds rate every morning.

John Griffith is a senior analyst and project manager at Enterprise Community Partners, Inc., where he focuses on housing market research and policy analysis related to mortgage finance and impact investing. Prior to joining Enterprise, he was an economic policy analyst at the Center for American Progress, where he published regular columns and reports on housing finance and federal credit programs. He previously worked as an analyst with the Social and Economic Policy Division of Abt Associates, researching federal homeless assistance, affordable housing, and community development programs. He has testified before Congress on foreclosure prevention, and his writing has been published widely.

Diana Hancock is a senior associate director in the Research and Statistics Division at the Federal Reserve Board. She oversees programs involved in monitoring, analyzing, and measuring aspects of the U.S. financial system. She has published articles that examine the impacts of capital adequacy regulations and monetary policy on commercial bank lending, investments, lending rates, liability mix, and profitability. Additional publications consider the effects of bank lending on regional activity, small business formation, and economic growth; the role of government-sponsored enterprises in U.S. housing finance; and the effects of the Federal Reserve's portfolio on mortgage markets. She holds a Ph.D. in economics from the University of British Columbia.

Stephanie Heller is presently a senior vice president and deputy general counsel in the Legal Group of the Federal Reserve Bank of New York. She provides legal support to the operations areas of the bank, including funds and securities transfer services, cash and currency distribution, and fiscal agency services. Heller is also responsible for providing legal support to the bank on technology and procurement matters. Heller earned her law degree from New York University School of Law in 1991. She is a member of the New York and Washington, D.C., bars and a member of the Permanent Editorial Board for the Uniform Commercial Code.

Akash Kanojia is a trader and policy analyst on the Open Markets Desk of the Federal Reserve Bank of New York. He serves on the Fed's mortgage staff, responsible for executing MBS operations, managing the Fed's MBS portfolio, and analyzing mortgage market fundamentals. He is a specialist on GSE reform and formerly covered municipal bond markets. Prior to joining the bank, he was a consultant at McKinsey & Company, specializing in financial institutions. He holds an M.P.P. from the Harvard Kennedy School, and a J.D. from the New York University School of Law. He is also a CFA charterholder and a member of the New York Bar.

Patricia C. Mosser is a senior research scholar at Columbia University's School of International and Public Affairs and the founding director of a new initiative on central banking, monetary policy, and prudential oversight. Previously, she was deputy director of the Office of Financial Research at the U.S. Department of Treasury, overseeing the Research and Analysis Center. Prior to the OFR, Mosser was a senior manager in the Markets Group at the Federal Reserve Bank of New York, where she was responsible for financial market analysis, monetary policy and foreign exchange operations, and analysis of financial stability and reform. Before that, she served as an economist in the New York Fed Research Department and was an assistant professor of economics at Columbia University. She has a Ph.D. in economics from MIT and an M.Sc. with distinction from the London School of Economics and Political Science.

Kevin A. Park is a graduate research assistant at the UNC Center for Community Capital and a doctoral candidate in the Department of City and Regional Planning at the University of North Carolina at Chapel Hill. His doctoral dissertation concerns the market competition and relative performance of FHA and private mortgage insurance. He holds a master's of public affairs from Brown University and a graduate certificate in geographic information sciences from the University of North Carolina. Prior to coming to North Carolina, he served as a research assistant at Harvard University's Joint Center for Housing Studies and a research fellow at the Rhode Island Economic Policy Council.

Wayne Passmore is a senior advisor in the Research and Statistics Division at the Board of Governors of the Federal Reserve System. He works on projects concerning housing finance, financial institutions, and macroprudential regulation. His current research focuses on systemic risk, securitization, shadow banking, government-sponsored enterprises, and the effects of the Federal Reserve's portfolio on mortgage markets. His published work has appeared in journals such as the *Journal of Banking and Finance*; *Journal of Monetary Economics*; *Journal of Money, Credit, and Banking*; *Journal of Real Estate Finance and Economics*; and *Real Estate Economics*. Before joining the Federal Reserve Board staff, Mr. Passmore was at the Federal Home Loan Bank of San Francisco. He began his career as an economist with the Federal Reserve Bank of New York. He received his Ph.D. in economics from the University of Michigan.

Roberto G. Quercia is Trudier Harris Distinguished Professor and Chair in the Department of City and Regional Planning at the University of North Carolina at Chapel Hill. He is director of the UNC Center for Community Capital, the leading center for research and policy analysis on the transformative power of financial capital on households and communities in the

United States. Quercia is a mortgage finance expert who has published numerous articles, primarily on the topics of low-income homeownership, affordable lending and the assessment of lending risks, and homeownership education and counseling.

David Scharfstein is the Edmund Cogswell Converse Professor of Finance and Banking at Harvard Business School. His current research focuses on financial intermediation and financial regulation, including research on housing finance, bank funding, money market funds, the growth of the financial sector, and government risk management. Scharfstein is a research associate of the National Bureau of Economic Research, a member of the Financial Advisory Roundtable of the Federal Reserve Bank of New York, and vice president of the American Finance Association. He is also chair of doctoral programs at Harvard Business School and chair of Harvard's Ph.D. in business economics. During 2009–2010, Scharfstein was senior advisor to the U.S. Treasury secretary, working on policy related to the financial crisis.

Phillip Swagel is a professor at the University of Maryland School of Public Policy, where he teaches courses on international economic policy. He is also a non-resident scholar at the Milken Institute and the American Enterprise Institute. Professor Swagel was assistant secretary for economic policy at the Treasury Department from December 2006 to January 2009. He was previously chief of staff at the Council of Economic Advisers and an economist at the Federal Reserve Board of Governors and the International Monetary Fund. Swagel received a Ph.D. in economics from Harvard University.

Joseph Tracy is an executive vice president and special advisor to the president at the Federal Reserve Bank of New York. Prior to his current position, he was director of research there. His primary research interests include housing and urban economics as well as unions and collective bargaining. Before joining the New York Fed, Mr. Tracy was an associate professor at Yale University and Columbia University. He holds a Ph.D. from the University of Chicago.

Susan M. Wachter is the Sussman Professor and professor of real estate and finance at The Wharton School of the University of Pennsylvania. Wachter is a former assistant secretary for policy development and research at the U.S. Department of Housing and Urban Development and chairperson of

Wharton's real estate department. She is the cofounder and current codirector of the Penn Institute for Urban Research (Penn IUR) and author of more than two hundred scholarly publications, including fifteen books. She frequently comments on national media and testifies to the U.S. Congress on housing policy.

Dale A. Whitman is James E. Campbell Missouri Endowed Professor Emeritus of Law at the University of Missouri School of Law. He is one of the nation's premier experts on property and mortgage law and is the author or coauthor of five books and numerous articles in the field. From 1991 to 1997 he served as co-reporter of the American Law Institute's Restatement (Third) of Property (Mortgages) with Professor Grant Nelson. From 1994 to 1997, he served on the executive committee of the Association of American Law Schools (AALS), and in 2002, he served as president of AALS. He was the reporter for the Uniform Non-Judicial Foreclosure Act, approved in 2002. His teaching fields include property, real estate finance, and land use planning.

Mark A. Willis is the senior policy fellow at New York University's Furman Center for Real Estate and Urban Policy. Prior to joining the Furman Center, the Ford Foundation invited him to be a visiting scholar following his nineteen-year career in community development banking at JPMorgan Chase, developing and overseeing the bank's efforts to strengthen low- and moderate-income communities. Before joining Chase, Willis held various positions in housing, economic development, and taxation with the City of New York. Prior to that, he headed the Regional Economics Staff at the Federal Reserve Bank of New York. He serves on the boards of a wide range of banking and community-oriented organizations and has written and lectured widely. He has a J.D. degree from Harvard Law School and a Ph.D. in urban economics and industrial organization from Yale University.

Joshua Wright is the chief economist at iCIMS, where he uses proprietary data from more than 4,500 organizations to analyze emerging trends in the U.S. labor market. Previously, he was a U.S. economist with Bloomberg L.P., analyzing U.S. monetary policy, housing, and labor markets. He also worked at the Federal Reserve Bank of New York, where he helped build the Federal Reserve's agency MBS portfolio of over $1 trillion, among other responses to the global financial crisis. As a researcher, he published on housing and mortgage markets and advised policy makers across the legislative and executive branches of government. A graduate of the Harvard Kennedy School and a CFA charterholder, his work has also appeared in the New York Fed's *Economic Policy Review,* the *Liberty Street Economics* blog, the *Bloomberg Economics Brief,* and the *New York Times.*

INDEX

Lightning Source UK Ltd.
Milton Keynes UK
UKOW05n0414100217

294080UK00013B/202/P